Just A Regular Guy

Lee;

I hope you enjoy the book,
thanks for reading it!

Charlie Morris

Just A Regular Guy

By
Charlie Morris

As Told To
Dean Siegman

iUniverse, Inc.
New York Lincoln Shanghai

Just A Regular Guy

iUniverse books may be ordered through booksellers or by contacting:

iUniverse
2021 Pine Lake Road, Suite 100
Lincoln, NE 68512
www.iuniverse.com
1-800-Authors (1-800-288-4677)

ISBN-13: 978-0-595-40453-7 (pbk)
ISBN-13: 978-0-595-84827-0 (ebk)
ISBN-10: 0-595-40453-7 (pbk)
ISBN-10: 0-595-84827-3 (ebk)

Printed in the United States of America

Contents

1

I really only wanted to be a regular guy, not someone's hero, but somewhere I got crossed up.

Nothing in my childhood suggested that I was destined for anything more than the ordinary life that my father and his father before him lived. I was a baby boomer, born on May 29, 1947, the first child of Charles Joseph Sr. and Helen Morris. My father served with the Navy in the South Pacific during World War II and, as it was with many war veterans, the first thing he did when he came home was to get married and have a child. We lived a plain vanilla existence in the blue-collar town of Cuyahoga Falls, Ohio, sometimes referred to as Caucasian Falls because of its all white population. Neighboring Akron, with its massive tire industry, provided a lot of jobs for guys like my father. He worked as a machinist as did his father. I had no reason to believe that my life would turn out to be any different than theirs.

Early on I had a good relationship with my father. He wasn't very athletic but he loved fishing and some of our happiest times were spent on local lakes. Even though my birthday usually fell on a school day he allowed me to play hooky and took me fishing as a birthday present. But my dad could get mean sometimes, too, and it always seemed that I would bear the brunt of his anger when anybody in our house did something wrong. He treated my two sisters like princesses, and my brother was nine years younger than me, so it was always me who got thrashed. But I could take it.

Like most boys of that era I loved to play outside and, living in a neighbor-hood with lots of kids, there was always some sort of game to get in. I was a pretty big kid, always kind of chubby. I don't know exactly how I got that way but I do know that if you would put it on a plate I'd eat it. My grandmother didn't help any. Whenever I would go visit her she would always have a whole cake or pie just for me. My heftiness wasn't due to inactivity, that's for sure. I would ride my bicycle everywhere, especially in the summer where my favorite destination was Water Works Park. I would spend my days swimming there with my friends. In the fall my weight made me popular as a lineman for our pickup football games. I always liked football. I wasn't very coordinated as a child but being on the line in a football game could hide my awkwardness. Not so in baseball and basketball where I was always the last one picked for a team. I wasn't very good at playing those sports. I remember one time I tried to catch a fly ball and it hit my nose instead of my glove. It was the only broken bone I suffered as a child.

It's funny how some events and people stand out from your childhood. For me one of those people was Billy Garrett. He was a boy from our neighborhood when I was about 12 years old. Billy was in an accident when he was quite young and it left him with a mental disability. He was about 18 when I knew him. The kids in the neighborhood would make fun of him because he talked funny, dressed oddly, and was still riding a bicycle when everyone else his age was driving cars. For some reason I still don't totally understand, I befriended Billy. I went out of my way to be nice to him. I even made him my helper on the paper route that I had at the time. There were times that I'd be a little short of money when some of my customers didn't pay their bill on time but I always made sure that I gave Billy his wages. Like I said, I don't know why I did it, but looking back I was always glad that I did. My relationship with Billy was my first lesson in understanding what it was like to have a disability.

Our family wasn't poverty stricken but we did have our share of money problems. As I was growing up our country went into a bit of a recession and jobs were sometimes hard to find. My mother wasn't exactly a financial wizard either and sometimes her budgeting methods would get us into trouble. She was the type that would bounce a $15 check and write a $25 check to cover it. When I was fourteen my dad was laid off from his job at Chrysler. During the summer I worked with him doing odd jobs. We would pour cement sidewalks, tar roofs, and paint houses and businesses. I didn't care much about being paid. One day my dad gave me the $6 I needed to buy a season pass to Water Works park and that was all I cared about. Eventually my dad found work at a small machine shop but was earning less money so he had to work a lot more hours to compensate. It still didn't keep my parents from having to file bankruptcy. We lost everything we had including our house. I even lost the old '49 Mercury that my dad and I were going to fix up together. My dad pleaded with the man from the bank to let me keep it but it ended up going to the scrap yard for $25. During that time I learned to hate eggs. It seemed that was all we ever ate because it was all we could afford. We had scrambled eggs for breakfast, egg salad sandwiches for lunch, and fried egg sandwiches for dinner. Sometimes my grandparents would help out and bring over a load of groceries for us. We made our way through these times but there was never any money to spare.

Money wasn't the only problem at the Morris household when I was a kid. Both of my parents had health issues. I was ten years old when my mother had her first heart attack. She collapsed right in our house. While my dad frantically tried to give her artificial respiration, I knelt beside my mother and rubbed her head. When the fire department came, my dad had to drag me away from her. I didn't want to leave her. As if that wasn't traumatic enough for a young boy, two years later my dad had his first heart attack. My dad didn't exactly have a healthy lifestyle. I was chubby but he was really overweight. At one time he was five feet ten inches tall and weighed 285 pounds. He smoked way too much and, at times, drank too much. After his heart attack the doctors put him on a special diet and he did lose some weight, but it wasn't long before he put it back on again. He never did quit smoking. Health problems continued to plague him throughout his life, eventually causing him to retire from working while he was still in his forties.

I started out liking school and I did pretty well in it, too. Sometime around the fourth grade though, I changed. I wasn't an evil child. Mostly it was just mischief like talking in class or getting into the occasional fight with a classmate, stuff like that. My first business venture did get me into a little more serious trouble. A friend of mine used to steal "True Men" magazines for the occasional pictures of naked women they had in it. He'd give the magazines to me and I'd sell them out of my school locker. Some teacher caught me and, for that, I got called into the principal's office. That principal was famous for having a special paddle made for him by one of the shop classes. It was concave and made to fit right between your butt and your leg. Rumor was that nobody, no matter how tough you were, ever left his office without crying. So, I'm in his office and he's yelling at me about how those damn screwing books I was selling was the reason young women got raped. I didn't know much about that but I didn't argue with him. He told me to bend over and he wound up with that paddle and blasted me. I thought I was going to go through the wall. This guy had a special method for spanking. He didn't give you three quick hits. He hit you once and then talked to you about why what you did was wrong and all the while the stinging in your butt was building up to a crescendo. Then he'd give you another blast and, after another interlude, a third smack. I had made up my mind before I went into his office that no matter what he did I wasn't going to cry. Nobody had ever made me cry before and I wasn't going to let him be the first. Between the second and third hits I could feel the tears stinging my eyes but I wasn't going to give him the satisfaction of knowing it. So during his between-the-hits lecture I turned around and yelled at him, "Hit me, dammit." Surprisingly, he started laughing. He said, "No, I think two's enough for you today. But if you ever get caught again you're going to get four." Let me tell you, I never got called into his office again.

My grades went down and I always got grounded by my parents because of it. I just didn't like school. You'd never see me carry any books home. It wasn't that I couldn't get better grades, I just didn't want to. I took those standardized intelligence tests and my teachers would call my parents in and tell them that I scored in the top 10% of all the kids in Ohio. But I was always in the bottom of my class with grades. I kept them up just high enough so that I was able to play sports. One class I always did well in was math. For some reason I always enjoyed it and in that class something clicked in my brain that made it easy for me to understand. My football coach was amazed. He used to tell me, "I just don't get it. Everything is easier than math. How come you get such rotten grades?" All I know is that I liked math and didn't like the other classes. I just didn't have any interest in them.

By the time I got to high school I stopped getting whippings for misbehaving, but I still wasn't a good student. I was always in some kind of trouble either by mouthing off to teachers or getting in a fight. Looking back I was kind of an arrogant kid. I played football for Falls High and I thought I was good enough that I didn't need to go to summer practices. I would just join the team when school started in the fall. I didn't look for trouble but somehow it was always able to find me and one day, in biology class, it found me in a big way. We had an older teacher and, because he was old, we used to pester him quite a bit. I was on his list of major troublemakers and was told that one more incident would get me thrown out of the class. That would mean no more football so I was on my best behavior for awhile. That day one of the teacher's favorite students, who sat directly behind me, tried to test the limits of my good behavior. He found some metal clips used for steel shelving in the classroom and while the teacher was writing something on the blackboard he shoved the cold metal pieces down my back. The shock of the cold metal hitting my back caused me to yell out. The teacher turned around and started reading me the riot act. I kept my mouth shut as I got the clips out of my shirt and held them in my hand. The more I thought about it the angrier I got and, as I got mad, I started jingling those clips in my hand. Finally, my anger got the best of me and while the teacher was still scolding me I turned around and clocked that kid. The teacher started screaming. He thought I killed the kid. He was laying on the floor and I threw the clips at him. I ended up in the principal's office and my parents had to come and get me. At that time we had just moved from Cuyahoga Falls to the next town over, Stow. I was allowed to remain at Falls High because I played football and had already attended Falls High for one year. But this episode changed the principal's mind about letting me stay. In fact, he suggested to my parents that I might be better served if I left

Falls High and transferred to Stow. He told them that I was falling into the wrong crowd and that a change of venue might be good for me. I also think that he didn't like students getting KO'd in the middle of biology class. That day was my last at Falls High School.

Stow was a smaller high school with fewer students. I didn't like the school right from the start. It was hard to get to know people, especially when you ended up transferring there in the middle of a school year. I ended up hanging out with the same kind of social misfits I had at Falls High. I tried playing football but there was an assistant coach who hated me for some reason. Maybe it was because I was working so I couldn't go to summer practices. I played for one season, but when he became the head coach the next year my high school football career was over.

I tried to attend the high school social events such as dances. At Falls High none of the guys would dance. We would all just hang out on the sidelines ogling all the cute girls. At Stow, however, all the guys danced. When I found this out, I had to get my little sisters to teach me how to dance. I ended up enjoying dancing and I was pretty good at it. I even had my share of short term romances in high school, none of them very serious, but I liked being around a pretty girl.

Learning to drive was a big thing with me. I didn't start off too well. I had my first car wreck long before I got my driver's license. One day I went with my dad to visit one of his old buddies. As my dad did with all of his old buddies they started drinking and, as the afternoon wore on, my dad got pretty snockered. I felt that he was in no condition to drive home so when it came time to go I told him that I would drive him home. He said, "Since when do you know how to drive." I lied and told him that mom let me drive all the time with her. He must've been pretty drunk because I convinced him and he gave me the keys. I was doing fine until I turned at one corner and there were some people standing in the road waiting to cross the street. I got distracted by them and I didn't watch where I was going. I plowed right into the back of a '57 Chevy. The Chevy was hardly damaged, but my dad's Oldsmobile had a severely crunched front fender. My dad didn't say much, but he never let me drive with him again until he was quite old and didn't drive anymore.

My father, being a Navy veteran who served in World War II, instilled in me the belief that a young man was supposed to serve his country with military service. He never talked much about his wartime experiences. Occasionally, when he'd have a little too much to drink, he might tell me about some of the good times he had while in the Navy. Sometimes he'd talk about his escapades with his buddy while they were stationed in Hawaii. He'd never talk about the bad experiences he had in the Pacific during the war. Only when I was older and he would get very drunk would he open up a little. I remember him telling me about how their ship was anchored off an island occupied by the Japanese. He said that the Japanese had so many dead on these islands, both their soldiers and prisoners of war, that they would have to dig big pits to put the bodies in and soak them in gasoline and burn them. He said that the stench of the burning flesh would come out to their ship in a smoky cloud. He never forgot that horrible smell and I knew by the way that he talked about it that it affected him. I never asked much about his combat experiences and he didn't talk much about them.

My first real life hero was John Kennedy. During the 1960 presidential debates I learned that Kennedy was a war hero and a Navy man to boot. Since my dad was a Navy man, and my plan was to eventually join the Navy, I immediately felt a bond with him. Actually, I was infatuated with him. He seemed to have everything; the looks, the charisma, the bravery, the character. It didn't hurt that we shared a birthday, both born on May 29, thirty years apart.

When I was 15 the Cuban Missle Crisis had a profound effect on me. Maybe it was because of my admiration of President Kennedy or the idea that the Russian invasion was close at hand that I felt the call to serve my country. I came home from school after hearing the news and, filled with patriotic zeal, announced to my dad that I wanted to quit school and join the Navy and stop those Russians in their tracks. I really expected that he would be proud of my decision and he would give me his blessing. After all, he had quit school to join the service when he was just a little older than me. But instead of a hug, he hauled off and hit me so hard it knocked me off my feet. I was flabbergasted. As he stood over me he said, "You goddamned kids don't know nothing about war." It wasn't until I was older that I would understand what he meant by those words.

It was about this time when my relationship with my father really started to deteriorate. I was always trying to act older than I was and he just wanted me to act my age and enjoy my youth. I never really had any thoughts of going to college after high school. I hated school and couldn't wait to get out. I was so fed up with school in my junior year that I even convinced my parents to sign a permission paper so that I could join the Navy. Fortunately, the Navy recruiter convinced me that it was in my best interest to finish high school before joining up.

America's involvement in Vietnam began when I was in high school. Like most people I didn't know much about the history of Vietnam or what brought about our country's involvement in their fight. President Kennedy told us that we needed to defend the Vietnamese people from communism and that's all I needed to know. When our country finally sent combat troops to Vietnam I watched the television news reports from the battles with interest. The main reason I paid attention to what was happening in Vietnam was that some of my older buddies were being sent there. I believed that young men should serve their country, but I also felt an obligation to my buddies to be with them as they fought for freedom. I actually felt that I was letting them down by not being there with them. I felt the need to be there, and the sooner I could be done with all of this school nonsense the sooner I could join them.

I had no idea at the beginning of my junior year that I would meet someone that would be with me for the rest of my life. It was in driver's education class that I met Fran. I noticed her right away. I was a screw-up in all my other classes but in driver's education I was okay so she didn't know what a bad student I really was. I started walking home with her and met her at some of the school dances. It didn't take too long before we were an item. She was a pretty, tiny little thing; the all-American girl type. She got good grades and had nice friends. Her parents weren't too happy when we started dating. Although I tried to be nice to them most of the time, they thought she could do better.

During my senior year at high school I found my dream job: working at a gas station. I really loved it. Mostly all I did was pump gas, though sometimes my boss would let me do some minor mechanical work. I was just happy to get out of school and go to work. I liked it so much, in fact, that I missed thirty days of school my senior year, most of those days spent at the gas station. That's the first place the truant officers would look for me when I showed up absent at school. I earned $1 an hour. My boss would let me borrow against my earnings and some weeks I would owe him more than what I made. Most of the money I made went to put gas in some junker car I'd be driving at the time. The rest was spent taking Fran out on dates. I never was able to save any money.

I still liked to eat and even the fact that I had a pretty little girlfriend didn't make me want to lose any weight. In fact, I put on over 40 pounds during my senior year. By the time I graduated I weighed 240 pounds. I suppose that's partly due to the fact that I wasn't playing football anymore and wasn't getting the physical exercise I once did. My eating habits didn't help either. I could eat a large pizza all by myself as a late night snack. I would buy a pound of baloney and a loaf of bread for lunch. One time, just for something to do, a buddy and me went to the A&W drive-in and I told our car hop to bring me one of everything on the menu. She brought it out on three loaded trays. I ate it all, too.

The big news during my high school days were the civil rights movement and the race riots going on in some of the larger cities in our country. Growing up in an all-white neighborhood, I was never exposed to any race issues. In our segregated world, race wasn't an issue at all. My first real exposure to African-American life wasn't until I was 18 years old. I was working at the gas station and occasionally some of my buddies. who were already in the service, would stop by to hang out for a while. One time, one of my friends stayed a bit too long and he missed his bus back to Camp Lejune in North Carolina. His mother was worried that he would be in big trouble if he didn't report back to camp on time so she asked me if I would drive him back using their brand new car. I had never been out of the state of Ohio so I jumped at the chance even if it meant an all-night drive there and an all day return trip to Ohio. So off we went and, after driving through the night, I deposited him at his camp before his deadline. I didn't see much scenery on the way down as it was dark through most of the trip but I began my trip back in daylight so I could take in the scenery I missed on the way down. Back then there wasn't much of an interstate highway system, especially in North Carolina. Most of the roads were two lanes and so it was in the morning that I got behind a school bus on one of these roads. I was shocked at the condition of the houses I passed by. Most of them were held up on concrete blocks. They didn't have doors, just blankets hung in a doorway. I didn't live in a wealthy community, that's for sure, but I had never seen such poverty. Every time that school bus would stop in front of one of these houses bunches of little black children would come pouring out of them. There were so many kids that I could see they were sitting four or five to a seat on the bus. I thought to myself, "How can people live like this in the United States?" I saw black farmers plowing their fields behind mules, not tractors. And this was 1965. When I came back from that trip my whole attitude towards the civil rights movement changed. I felt I understood that there were problems here in America and that changes needed to be made to fix those problems.

Even though I did horribly academically, I ended up graduating from high school on time. My grade point average was 1.70, which was barely enough to get by. Out of 360 graduating students at our school I was 355th. I have to admit that Fran helped me a lot so I could graduate with her. I know she wrote six book reports for me so I could pass English. My mother couldn't believe the school was going to let me graduate. She sat in the gym during graduation exercises just knowing my name would never be called. Afterwards she told her friends the only reason they let me graduate was they didn't want me to come back. I was over-joyed to be finally done with school. Grades didn't matter in what I had planned for my future. I never really liked school but as time went on I grew to hate it. I was just happy to have my diploma and to be able to get on with my life free from drudgery of schoolwork. My relationship with Fran was still going strong.

We were even making future plans together. But our plans together would have to wait until I fulfilled my own personal plan, which was to join the Navy.

2

By the time I graduated I was already 18 and had registered for the draft after my birthday in May. It was no big deal. At that time they weren't drafting anyone until they were 19, so registering for the draft was just a formality, sort of like applying for a social security card. When I registered I wasn't even thinking of any possible draft deferment because, as far as I was concerned, I wasn't going to be drafted anyway. I was going to enlist. So, after graduation I took a couple of weeks off and then marched down to the Navy recruiting office in Akron to sign up. I took my written test and signed my papers enlisting for a four year stint. I was still a little overweight. I weighed 242 at the time which was a little over their maximum allowance for my height. It was no problem though, as my recruiter added an inch to my height and assured me that basic training would take care of the rest. He arranged for me to go to the induction center in Cleveland the next day where I would take my physical test. I was pretty excited and proud that I finally joined the Navy so I stayed up most of the night talking with Fran, my sisters, and my friends. The next morning my dad drove me to the bus station in Stow where I would get the bus to Cleveland. While I was waiting for the bus I got a little hungry so I ate a couple of cream sticks and a big carton of chocolate milk. It was about an hour's ride to downtown Cleveland and as soon as I arrived at the induction center I began the physical exam. It didn't last very long. One of the first things I did was take a urine test. Shortly after I gave them my sample, a Navy doctor came out and told me that my glucose level was too high to pass the physical. He told me that I needed to go to my personal physician and arrange for a glucose tolerance test and that I would need my doctor's approval before I could be inducted in the Navy. Dejected, I got back on the bus home and had to ashamedly tell my family and friends that my induction was going to be delayed a bit. The next day I made an appointment with my parent's doctor who, at the time, was an osteopath. I didn't care. I just wanted my approval papers signed so I could get in the Navy. He sent me to the Green Cross center to take the glucose tolerance test. It was pretty involved. I had to drink some horrible tasting liquid and then they took a blood sample. They repeated this process several times. In the end, when the doctor got the results, it showed that I wasn't diabetic and that I had no problem at all. He said that the combination of being excited, staying up

10

all night, and, most of all, the cream sticks and chocolate milk, was the reason my glucose level was elevated at the time I took my physical. He signed the approval form and the next day I got back on the bus to the Cleveland induction center. I gave my doctor's approval form to the Navy doctor. I remember that he was a big, overweight, and very mean and nasty man. He took one look at the form and threw it back at me. He said, "This is no good. I told you to go to a doctor, not an osteopath." Back then osteopaths were considered second rate and weren't widely accepted by the established medical community. I could feel my notorious temper boiling over. I told him, "Look, you told me to get a glucose tolerance test and that's what I did. And I paid for it with my own money, too. Now you're telling me it's no good?" He looked at me and said, "I don't care. I'm not letting you in until you get the test done by a proper doctor." Then I really exploded. I told him, "Screw you. I'm not paying for any more doctors. I'll just go home and wait to be drafted. Forget the Navy." And, being the stubborn person that I was, that's exactly what I did. I didn't even try again even though it would have been an easy matter for me to get the approval from a M.D.. I was going to show them that I was not a person to be messed with, even if it meant abandoning my life-long dream of being in the Navy. I took the bus back home and, the next day, I was back working at the gas station.

Since my plan "A" didn't work out, it was time for me to develop a plan "B". All my family and friends told me I couldn't pump gas for the rest of my life so I got a job in a small factory where my dad worked. I knew right away that I didn't like it and, after a couple of days, I quit and went back to work at the gas station. It was the only thing I really liked to do. I liked being around cars and working on them. I realized, however, that I needed to find something more substantial, especially if I wanted to have any future plans with Fran. When I was 17, I worked during the summer for an electrician as his helper and I really liked the work. I got so good at it I could wire a house all by myself. I thought that being an electrician might be a good career for me, so I decided to try to get into their apprentice program. I went to their union hall in Akron to apply, but was told that the man I needed to talk with wasn't available. I was a little perturbed as I had taken a day off from my job at the gas station to apply. I tried again the following week and was told the same thing. Being as hard headed as I was, I gave up trying. I wasn't going to jump through hoops for anyone. Later, I found out that this was just a method they used to find out how much you really wanted the job. They were looking for perseverance. I heard that after your fourth visit you got to submit your application. Perseverance was not my strong suit at that time.

It wasn't easy for an 18 year-old male to find a good job back then. Most employers didn't want to make an investment in training someone who easily could be drafted in a year or so. Most civil service jobs, such as working for a city or being a police or fireman, gave preferential treatment to returning veterans, so it was nearly impossible for an 18 year old to get any employment there. At that time most American 18 year-old males either went to college, enlisted in the armed forces, or volunteered for the draft. Unless, of course, they had an iron clad draft deferment. Then they could do most anything they wanted to. Employers were more inclined to hire you if you had a good deferment.

As my employment plans stalled, so also did my plans with Fran. Ever since our senior year in high school I had been pestering her about getting married. In our original plan I was going to go into the Navy and we were going to wait until I was out before we got married. But then, since I wasn't going in the Navy, my pleading intensified. Her standard reply to my proposals was, "No. Not yet." As I did with everything else I had to deal with, I got tired of being rejected and I finally told her, "When you're ready to get married, you ask me." During those early years together we had our share of minor arguments and short breakups, but somehow we were able to get through them with our relationship still pretty much intact.

During the early part of winter in 1966, while I was still working at the gas station, I developed a pretty bad case of pneumonia. I didn't need to be hospitalized, but I required several weeks of rest at home. During that time Fran would visit me every day. I guess she started to feel sorry for me because one day she said, "You remember how you told me that when I was ready to get married that I should ask you?" I said, "So, are you asking me?" She said, "Yes" and, with that, we got engaged. Our marriage plans, however, hinged on what would happen to me in May when I turned 19 and would be eligible for the draft. If I got drafted, we would wait until my service was over before getting married. If I wasn't drafted, we would get married in June. It wasn't the greatest marriage plans ever conceived, but I was happy with it.

As I had during my senior year in high school, I continued to gain weight. Since I was not going to have the Navy career I wanted, there was no need for me to watch my weight and I put on pound after pound. Nobody seemed to mind. Fran never bothered me about it. Even though she was such a tiny little thing, she never mentioned that she thought I was becoming overweight. But I was, and, by the time my 19th birthday rolled around, I was rolling around 270 pounds.

Right on schedule Uncle Sam sent me an invitation to come down to my draft board and take a physical a month before my 19th birthday in 1966. Dutifully, I went to downtown Cleveland to take the first step towards my mandatory military service. The draft physical was an all day affair. It's funny, but it seems that when you're put into a strange situation with a bunch of guys it's easy to strike up quick friendships. That's the way it was down at the draft board that day. It was a bunch of young men trying to find some levity in a potential life-altering situation. I always found it easy to make new friends and, since I was such a cocky smart-ass, I became a sort of ringleader for a small group of us going through the physical that day. Halfway through the day we were given a lunch break and were marched off to the back room of a local restaurant. There were probably about fifty of us. The first thing I noticed about the restaurant was that the waitresses were gathering pieces of uneaten bread from other tables and putting the bread in baskets and then putting them on our tables. Then they brought in our food, which was absolutely horrible. I don't remember what it was but I knew I wasn't going to eat it. I got up from my table and said to my little group of newfound friends, "I ain't eating this crap. Come on, let's go get some real food." They followed me out and I led them to the cafeteria at the Federal Building where we had a nice lunch together. When we were done I marched them back to the draft board to complete our physicals. We were a little bit late getting back, which angered the sergeant in charge. Since I appeared to be the instigator, I was particularly out of favor with him. He was really upset at the end of the day when he had to tell me that I failed the physical. The reason: I was too overweight. This sergeant was so angry he told me, "If you would've passed the physical I wouldn't have let you go home. I would've thrown you in the army today." But, instead, I was going home. And I was going there with a 1Y deferment, which meant that I was qualified for military service only in time of war or national emergency. Since our involvement in Vietnam was not an official "war", I wasn't going to be drafted. I was told by my draft board that this deferment was only temporary, and that I had to report to a specified doctor every six months to have my weight checked. I didn't have a problem with that, but I also didn't have any plans to go on any diets just so that I could get drafted. I was willing to go into the Army and serve my country if they wanted me, but they were going to have to take me as I was.

The first thing I did when I got home from the draft board was to go over to see Fran. "Guess what?" I said. "We're getting married next month." I have no idea why she didn't try to back out of her commitment. Here she was, a pretty and intelligent young girl, agreeing to marry a fat, hot-tempered, gas station attendant that wasn't even good enough to get drafted. Go figure. Fortunately for me, Fran must have been able to see beyond my shabbiness to a better person I could become. That or it was blind love. At any rate we proceeded with our wedding plans for June. We had to do most of the work ourselves as her parents weren't too keen on the idea of us getting married and my parents were in no financial position to help us out. We made arrangements with my minister to get married in my church in Stow. We rented a little apartment that came furnished, which was a good thing because neither of us had any of our own furniture and no money to even buy some second hand things. I was pretty excited. My future was looking bright.

Like I said, Fran's parents weren't too enthused about us getting married so young. Her mother told me that they wouldn't interfere with our plans under one condition. She wasn't going to let her daughter marry a guy who worked in a gas station. I must have been really in love because I agreed to let Fran's uncle arrange an interview for me at a company in Akron that made pneumatic valves. In my typical fashion, I almost ruined my chances for the job when I was late for my interview. I had to wait for a guy to relieve me at the gas station before I could go for the interview. He showed up a little late. I hurriedly changed into some new pants and shirt that I bought just for the occasion. Since I was running late I decided to take a shortcut and jump over a small drainage ditch in the back of the gas station to get to my car. I didn't quite make it and I slipped and fell into the mud. I showed up for the interview late, wearing a pair of torn and muddy pants. Fortunately, they were understanding, (or Fran's uncle had a lot more pull there than I thought) and I got the job.

My job title was assembly man, putting together valves on the assembly line. I didn't like the job. In fact, I hated the monotony of the menial tasks I had to perform. I liked the extra money, though. Right off, I was making $2 an hour, which was 50 cents an hour more than I made at the gas station. After my four-week probationary period I was able to join the union and I was making $3 an hour, double what I was making at the gas station. But the best part of the job for me, were the people I worked with. I got along great with everyone and enjoyed talking with them at breaks and lunchtime. It made the drudgery of the job more tolerable.

Our wedding day came up quickly. On June 4, 1966, at a little church in Stow that at one time was a public aquarium, Fran and I made our vows. It wasn't a big affair. My cousin Denny, who got married the year before, was my best man. Fran's sister was her maid of honor. It was a very warm day and the church wasn't air-conditioned. I was terribly overweight, and was made even more uncomfortable by the suit I was wearing. It looked like something right out of the 1950's; a nice, heavy, wool material. For some reason the jacket fit well but the pants were much too large. That was odd considering my girth at that time. Before the ceremony began, my cousin, noticing how uncomfortable I appeared, told me that it wasn't too late to jump in his convertible and make a quick get-away. I don't remember much about the ceremony, or what our minister said as we stood in front of the altar. All I remember is sweating profusely and having the feeling that my pants were constantly falling down. But as uncomfortable as I was that day, I was the happiest guy on the face of the earth. I was getting married to my high school sweetheart, my one true love. Life was going to be great.

We didn't have much of a formal wedding reception. After the service we just went over to my parent's house and while the women were upstairs opening wedding gifts, the men congregated downstairs drinking beer and smoking. It wasn't anything fancy. We didn't have a hired band or a catered dinner, but we were happy with our wedding day.

We didn't have a honeymoon, either. We got married on a Saturday and we were both back to work on Monday. We didn't have any money to go anywhere. Besides, we were anxious to get on with married life. Later that summer we spent a weekend camping on Lake Erie. We've always considered that as our little honeymoon.

Our first apartment together was a converted upstairs of a two-story house in Cuyahoga Falls. It had one bedroom, and it must have been a kid's room at one time because it had built-in bunk beds. This didn't create much of a problem for a newly married couple. We would just hop in to the lower bunk and snuggle up together. I imagine it was a little less comfortable for Fran having to share a single bed with a nearly 300 pound partner. She never complained though. The whole apartment was furnished and we paid $89 a month in rent. Any extra money we had left at the end of the month went towards some new furniture we had on lay-away at a local furniture store.

We both enjoyed ourselves during our early-married life. We were both 19 and mostly carefree. We weren't rich by any stretch of the imagination but we always had enough to get by. We also had enough to have some good times together whenever we felt like it. Some days we would just look at each other and say "I'm in the mood for some Cedar Point fries" and we would jump in the car and take off for a weekend at the amusement park on Lake Erie. Back then, there wasn't any such thing as a credit card. Whatever we wanted to buy we saved for until we could pay cash for it. We didn't have any bills aside from our meager rent. We also didn't have any immediate plans to have children. There would be plenty of time for that later. For the time being we were happy just being together.

I always tended to do things spontaneously and one day, soon after we were married, I passed by a pet shop and saw a cute little terrier puppy in the window. I felt a little dog was just what we needed in our little apartment, so I went in and bought it and brought it home. Looking back, it probably wasn't the smartest decision I ever made. I probably should go back and pay some money to our first landlord for all the damage that little dog did. With both of us working all day the dog was left alone in the apartment. As puppies are known to do, this one chewed on furniture, peed on rugs, and generally wreaked havoc while we were gone for the day. We'd have newspapers all over the floor to try and housebreak her, but she never quite got the concept. The papers only created another problem. In the early morning as I would leave for work it was difficult for me to avoid stepping in a pee-soaked newspaper. Invariably I would step in one in my stocking feet and then I'd have to retreat to the bedroom for new socks. One morning I was so proud of myself for dodging all of the soaked newspapers. Before I put my dirty work boots on I kissed Fran goodbye at the door. While I was kissing her I felt something warm on my leg and looked down to see my little dog squatting over my socked foot. I was a little more tolerant back then of minor irritations and was able to laugh about it.

My favorite television show at the time was "The American Sportsman". I really aspired to be one of the great hunters and fishermen that were on that show. I particularly liked the pheasant hunting they showed on the program, and fell in love with the German Shorthair pointers they used in the hunts. Even though I had never seen this type of dog, except on that television show, I knew I had to have one. About six months after we were married we moved out of our little apartment (thankfully, before the little dog completely destroyed it). We moved to a small rental house in Stow. There was another young couple that lived in the other rental house on the property and the young man had a brother who bred German Shorthairs. As luck would have it, he just happened to have a female that he hadn't been able to sell. I jumped at the opportunity and we now owned two dogs. I didn't care. I knew it wouldn't be long before there was an episode of "American Sportsman" featuring Curt Gowdy pheasant hunting in Ohio with Charlie Morris and his prize winning hunting dog.

In the meantime, every spare moment I had was spent with my cousin Denny hunting or fishing. He lived in an apartment above a garage on a farm in Kent. There was a lot of open land there where I could work with my German Shorthair, and he would work with his two Labrador retrievers. I just loved anything to do with the outdoors. Sometimes we'd go out fishing in the evening and just stay out all night in the boat. We didn't need to catch anything. The peace and solitude was enough for me. I also joined a shooting club and would shoot trap two nights a week. Fran was really tolerant of all my outdoor activities so, for me, married life was just great.

I really enjoyed that German Shorthair. I named her Gretel and she was my faithful buddy. Every weekend we would go out into the fields and spend the morning together. Even when it wasn't hunting season, I would go out without a gun and just watch her flush out birds. She really liked me, too. She wasn't allowed in our little house, so I kept her on a chain that was connected to a cable between two trees. This gave her a little freedom of movement while also keeping her securely in the yard. If I came in late at night, and she would hear me, she would make a ruckus until I would go out and talk to her for awhile. One night, Fran and I went to the drive in movie and, during the show, a pretty strong thunderstorm came through. Gretel was deathly afraid of thunder, but I wasn't too worried as she had her doghouse for shelter from the storm. We got home late and as we pulled into the driveway Fran reminded me to be quiet so as not to arouse Gretel. We got into the house without disturbing her and went to bed. The next morning I got up and looked out the window and saw Gretel lying motionless on the ground. I ran outside and called to her, but there was no response. She was dead. Apparently the storm got her so riled up that she broke her neck trying to get free of her tether. I felt terrible. My parents thought I was nuts because I literally went into mourning for several weeks. After all these years I still feel bad about what happened to that dog.

It didn't take long for me to realize that factory work wasn't a good long-term career solution for me. I was working long hours, sometimes up to 80 hours a week, just so that we could save up a little money. Even though I didn't like factory work, when I had the chance to work for Massey Ferguson at their factory in Cuyahoga Falls I jumped at the opportunity. The money was much better. I was making almost as much in 40 hours as what I used to make working 80.

I still didn't have any concrete plans for my future. At this time, I thought that I would never have to consider going into the service again. I figured that since they didn't want me, I didn't want them either. I thought my draft deferment was ironclad. I wasn't doing anything to put weight on. but I wasn't doing anything to take it off either. It was pretty easy for me to maintain my bulk and, thus, stay out of the draft. I had some big ideas about working hard for a while, saving some money, and then going to college to become an accountant. The memory of how much I hated school was fading quickly. Working in a factory everyday was changing my mind about the value of education.

One of the activities I enjoyed that wasn't impaired by my increased weight was bowling. I enjoyed it as a child, but it was just for fun then. After we got married, Fran and I joined a bowling league and I started taking it more seriously. I was terrible when I started out, but eventually got better at it the more I bowled. I even got the "most improved bowler" award at the end of the year. I watched the Pro Bowlers Tour on television and then would try to imitate some of the bowling styles of the professional bowlers. I read instruction books by Dick Weber and others. I was obsessed with becoming a good bowler. I even had visions of one day becoming good enough to get on the pro tour. When I was working the second shift at the factory, I would leave the house a couple hours early and bowl a couple of games before work. I thought that if I practiced hard enough I could make myself into a great bowler. Although I never got beyond being a recreational bowler, it was one of the first things I ever did with discipline and dedication.

I got into another sport where being overweight is not a great handicap: Softball. I organized a team at our shop and got the union to sponsor us and buy us uniforms. I was elected manager of the team. I also played catcher providing a wide backstop for our pitcher. As manager I would schedule practices and games. I also decided who played and who sat on the bench. It wasn't an easy job, especially when some of our better players didn't see the necessity for practice. I tried to be fair, and I believed that the guys that put in the work should be the ones who played, even if there were players of higher ability sitting on the bench. This proved to be an unpopular position, and I didn't make it through the first season before my managerial duties were taken away.

That wasn't the end of my administrative baseball career though. One day my cousin Denny called me up. He told me that he had signed us up to be coaches in the Kent Baseball Little League. Now Denny wasn't much of an athlete. He grew up a farmboy, and didn't have much interest in sports other than hunting and fishing. I couldn't help wondering what possessed him to get us both involved in Little League Baseball. Well, it turned out that Denny, being the good hearted guy he was, felt sorry for a team that wasn't going to be allowed in the league because they didn't have a coach. When I went to the first practice and met the team I understood why they couldn't find a coach. Our team was made up of a group of boys from Kent's only black neighborhood. So there we were, a farm boy from rural Ohio and a fat guy from Caucasian Falls, trying to coach a bunch of black kids in baseball. Up to that point I never had any real contact with black people, but, being young and naïve, I didn't see any problem. After all, they were just a bunch of kids who wanted to play ball. What could be hard about that?

The first problem came when Denny asked the team at the first practice who wanted to pitch. All 26 kids on the team raised their hands. I could see that I needed to teach Denny how to be more judicial, so I asked the kids, "Who pitched last year?" That narrowed it down to four kids, and we moved on from there. I told the rest of the kids to go to the outfield and catch some fly balls I would hit to them. I guess the kids were only motivated to pitch, because when they got to the outfield they all sat down in the grass. I found out that practicing under the warm afternoon sun was not a high priority for them. I explained, rather succinctly, my theory that those who worked hard in practice would be the ones who played in the games. That seemed to give them the motivation they needed to stand up in the outfield. They still complained about it though.

The next problem was finding a sponsor so that we could buy some team uniforms. No local business seemed interested in having their company's name on the backs of a bunch of black kids. We eventually found someone who agreed to buy 18 shirts. There were 26 kids practicing so that meant we had to cut 8 kids from the team. That wasn't a pleasant task. To ease the pain Denny and I put our own money together and bought 26 baseball caps. We told the eight kids that we cut that they could keep the hats and still practice with the team. They did and they rode their bikes to all the games, too. When we got our final roster we had 14 black kids and 4 white kids.

The next problem was something I never would have imagined. We had four pitchers, two black and two white. Whenever I would replace a black pitcher with a white pitcher automatically a white catcher would replace the black catcher. When I replaced the white pitcher with a black on the same would happen with a black catcher. I let it go on for a couple of days, but finally I had enough. I called a team meeting before practice and I laid down some of Charlie's law. I told them that there wasn't going to be any more black and white on our team. I said that I would decide who pitched and who caught and it didn't matter what color either of them was. We were a team, and our skin color had nothing to do with anything we did as a team. I told them that if anyone had a problem with this policy that they should leave now. No one left. We never had any more problems like that for the rest of the season. I realized that the kids didn't mean anything with their racial separation. It's just the way they were taught and how they perceived things were done. I didn't see it that way, and they ended up accepting my view.

During the season there was a small black kid who came to me during practice one day and told me that he wanted to pitch. I had seen this kid throwing during practices and knew that he had no control. He threw the ball hard but it went all over the place. I told him that if he wanted to be a pitcher that he would have to practice everyday on his own and learn how to control his throwing. He complained that he didn't have anybody he could throw to. I said that if he really wanted to pitch that he'd find somebody.

We also had a white kid on our team whose parents were college professors who just returned to the United States from an assignment in Japan. This boy had played on Japanese Little League teams and he was one of our best players. One day, the little black kid who wanted to pitch showed up at this white kid's house and pleaded with him to catch while he worked on his pitching. The white kid agreed and every day they would play catch together at his house before practice. In the process they also became good friends.

Later, at one of our games, the mother of the white kid came up to me and thanked me for arranging for her son to have someone to play catch with. She told me that when her and her husband accepted the positions at Kent State that they had to arrange for their housing in Kent from Japan. They rented a house, sight unseen, not knowing that it was in a black neighborhood. They didn't have any problem with the neighborhood, but they found out that their son couldn't find any playmates. They thought they were going to have to move and then the little black kid showed up wanting to play with their son. She was happy that her son now had a friend in the neighborhood. I told the mother that I really didn't arrange anything, that the kids did it all on their own. It was a good lesson for me to learn that blacks and whites could get along and cooperate with one another if we would just let go of our prejudices.

3

In 1968 some things happened that brought about a change in attitude with me. This change in attitude ended up changing my entire life. I went down for my regular draft weigh-in in May. When I got on the scale it showed I was almost 300 pounds. The nurse who was weighing me looked at the scale and said, "Whew, Uncle Sam sure don't want you, fat boy." I felt humiliated. I knew I was overweight, but no one had ever ridiculed me about it before. I didn't take too kindly to being called "fat boy", that's for sure. Some time later I was sitting on our sofa in our little house reading the newspaper. Suddenly, I heard a loud crack and the sofa collapsed beneath me. I was beginning to realize that my weight was becoming a problem. Then, during a phone conversation with my mom, I mentioned to her that Fran and I weren't going out too much anymore. It seemed that we weren't getting together with our friends as much as when we first got married. My mom told me that the reason we weren't getting invited over to friend's houses was that because I was so heavy they were afraid that I was going to damage their furniture. My weight was now a social problem too. Then I started looking at my beautiful, trim, petite wife and started thinking how embarrassed she must be to have such a tub of lard for a husband. It got to the point where if we went shopping I would always walk four or five steps behind her so that people wouldn't think we were a couple. I was ashamed of my appearance and I decided to do something about it.

My first attempts at dieting were half-hearted at best. I looked for diets that didn't require too much sacrifice and, when they failed to work, I would move on to another one. I remember one that a dietician gave my father after he had his heart attack. It involved eating broiled cube steak and salad. Now, I'm sure that there was a quantity limit in this diet, but I didn't listen for that part. All I heard was broiled cube steak and salad and I thought that I could adjust to that pretty easily. So, I started eating cube steaks and salads for dinner. Not just one cube steak though. I'd usually go through five or six at a sitting. And not just a little dinner salad either. I'd fill a large mixing bowl with a head of lettuce and pour a whole bottle of dressing over it. I didn't have any trouble sticking with that diet, but I didn't lose much weight on it either.

I went from one extreme to another. One time I overheard my mother and sister talking about a diet. They were both pretty heavy themselves and were always talking about the latest diet from the "Ladies Home Journal" or something. This time they were talking about a diet that involved eating oranges. I heard them say, "an orange for breakfast and an orange for lunch" but I missed hearing what you were supposed to eat for dinner. I assumed it was another orange, so I started on my orange diet eating nothing but oranges, three meals a day. Well, this diet worked. In two weeks I lost 25 pounds. The only trouble was that by the third week I started feeling a little woozy most of the time. One night, I was at my bowling league and I got ready to roll my first frame. I mustered up all my strength and sent the ball down the alley. It went slowly for a few feet, then dribbled into the gutter. I thought I was dying. I went to the pay phone and called my mom. I said, "Remember that diet you and Cheryl were talking about, the one where you eat oranges three meals a day?" She said, "You dummy. You eat an orange for breakfast and lunch, and then eat whatever you want for dinner." I immediately got off the phone and ran over to the snack bar for a cheeseburger and fries. I felt a lot better after I had something in my stomach. That was the end of the orange diet for me though.

The one good thing that the orange diet did was to get me down to a weight where I started looking and feeling better. If nothing else it strengthened my resolve to continue to lose weight. I decided that I didn't need a specialty diet or a set of instructions to follow. I figured that all it required was a little common sense and a little discipline. Instead of being concerned with what I ate I focused on how much I was eating. Now, instead of eating an entire large pizza, I would eat only one or two slices. Instead of eating a whole pot of spaghetti, I would measure a one-cup portion and have two meatballs with it. I accompanied my self-designed diet with a little physical exercise, too. I had some weights gathering dust in the attic. I brought them down and started doing a little weight training everyday. I started seeing results, and gradually kept losing weight. By the time the year 1969 came around I was down to 250 pounds. I was feeling pretty good about myself. There was only one problem. I figured that Uncle Sam was going to feel better about me, too.

My idea of going to college never materialized. I don't know if I lacked the initiative, or if I was just getting too set in the everyday life of trying to earn a living, but an accounting degree never got beyond the "talking about it" stage. I still wasn't satisfied with my factory job and, with my new, trimmer physique, I decided to try to become a police officer in Stow. I studied diligently for the written test, which was the first step in the application process. I did well on it, but not well enough to compete with the returning veterans whose armed service records accounted for bonus points added to their test scores. I was back in the factory. By this time my weight was down to 240 and I realized that my draft status was probably going to change to 1A. In April of 1969 I called my draft board to find out when my next draft review was going to be. They told me it would be in May. I had about a month to make some critical decisions about my future.

When I graduated from high school in 1965, America's involvement in Vietnam had just begun, and the general attitude in the country was that we needed to fight communism wherever it threatened to invade a foreign land. By 1969 that attitude had changed drastically. The Vietnam war was unpopular, and young people rose up in protest over the draft and our country's involvement in what was perceived as an unjust and unwinnable war. I didn't have much of an opinion about Vietnam, and I didn't have any animosity towards those young men who refused to be drafted. I did have the strong, ingrained belief that to serve my country was my duty, and I wasn't going to do anything to avoid being drafted. That didn't mean that I wanted to be drafted, or that I wasn't going to try to have some say so as to how I would serve.

I sat down with Fran and we discussed our options. At that same time, my friend Ron was also becoming eligible for the draft. He had been deferred for four years while serving an apprenticeship in the machine tool trade with Chrysler. His apprenticeship was over and so was his draft deferment. He was talking about enlisting in the Army for three years so that he could sign up to be a machinist. Fran and I figured that a three-year enlistment with a choice of jobs was better than a two year draft induction with no choice. I was still stubborn about considering trying the Navy again. I still felt the sting of rejection from my experience with them four years earlier. Besides, the Navy only offered a four-year enlistment. So in May of 1969 Ron and I, with our wives blessing, set off for the Army recruiting center.

The first thing we did at the recruiting center was to take a barrage of aptitude tests to find out if we were qualified for the jobs we selected. Ron, of course, signed up to be a machinist. I signed up for aviation electronics. I still had fond memories of when I worked the one summer with the electrician and I thought that electronics might provide me the same sort of satisfaction. We both got very high scores on all our tests. We moved on to our physicals, which we also passed with flying colors. I never bothered to mention the trouble I had with the Navy physical and my blood test, and nothing abnormal showed up in the blood test I took here. Having passed all our tests we returned to the recruiter to get our job guarantees and sign our enlistment papers. Ron got his guarantee as a machinist, but my guarantee was for avionics, not aviation electronics. Avionics, I found out, was a six-week course that basically taught you to be a door gunner in a helicopter. The electronics classes were all filled up and this was the closest thing that the Army could offer me. I told the recruiter that it was a crappy job. He said that if I signed up for avionics that they would do their best to get me into electronics the first time an opening came up. I told him, "You guys will tell me anything to get me to sign up, but I ain't signing nothing." I got up and walked out leaving Ron to enlist in the Army on his own.

As was my norm, I got angry and spiteful, so I walked down the block and marched into the Navy recruiting office and said, "What can you guys do for me?" The recruiter talked to me for a while and it didn't take long to convince me that the Navy was the branch of service where I belonged. My old dream of becoming a Navy man was once again close to becoming a reality. All I had to do was to convince Fran.

As it turned out, it didn't require much of a hard sell. All I was doing, really, was going back to my original plan I had when I graduated from high school. The only difference was that I was 22 years old and had been married for three years already. To me that was no big deal, and I think Fran sensed the frustration I was having with my job situation and felt like that this might be my only chance to change it. We even talked about the possibility that I might be stationed at some base, somewhere nice and warm near the ocean, where she might be able to come and live with me. The next day, with Fran's blessing, I signed the papers to enlist in the Navy.

One of the points I used to sell Fran on the Navy was the Vietnam factor. Although the subject of Vietnam never came up in my discussions with the Navy recruiter, I just imagined that the worst that could happen to me is that I would be on a ship somewhere in the ocean off the coast of Vietnam. What could possibly happen to me? The Navy would keep me our of harm's way, unlike the Army where I would likely be thrown into some combat area sooner or later. I told Fran that the extra year I would have to serve in the Navy would be worth it just for that reason.

Really, I didn't give much thought to Vietnam when I enlisted in the Navy. Some of my friends who went into the service after high school were now returning from their tours of duty in Vietnam. They included my friend Billy, the friend I drove to his Marine base in North Carolina when I was 18 years old. He was shot in the leg while serving in Vietnam. It took a while to evacuate him and he ended up almost losing the leg. When he came home his leg was shriveled up and misshapen. He had trouble walking and was in pain most of the time. He didn't say much about what he experienced in Vietnam. None of the returning veterans did. I learned that it was not a topic for discussion. I could tell by the look in their eyes that it wasn't a good experience. I wasn't worried though. I was going in the Navy where I would be far away from the battlegrounds of Vietnam.

I felt very good about enlisting. Actually, it was a great relief. I always had underlying guilt feelings that, while most of my friends already did, or were doing, their service to the country, I didn't have to because I was too fat. I felt that people were talking behind my back asking, "Why doesn't he have to go in the service and my son does?" I felt that I was letting my friends and my country down, and I was glad that I finally had the opportunity to make amends.

4

It didn't take me long to get ready for my induction. Basically, I left everything up to Fran. I left her with a rented house she wasn't going to be able to afford on her own. She made plans with Ron's wife to move in with her while Ron and I went off to the service. I also left Fran with an old beagle dog that my uncle gave me to help me get over my grief over the loss of Gretel. That old beagle smelled so bad we wouldn't bring it inside, and it howled so loud outside that the neighbors complained. I figured that the old dog wasn't going to last long with Fran after I left, and I was right. Fran always said that it was the landlord that made her get rid of it. I was never completely convinced that was the truth, but, nonetheless, that dog was gone before I came home on my first leave.

I gave my notice at work, which, at the time, was still Massey Ferguson. They had a pretty good deal for employees that went into the service. They guaranteed us a job when we came back and also counted our time in the military as seniority along with all the incremental pay raises that went with it. I was assured that when I got done with my Navy duty in four years that I would have a job making pretty good money.

I didn't have an elaborate sendoff. The night before I left I said goodbye to my family. I didn't get any "I'm proud of you, son" speech from my dad. He really didn't say much at all about my enlistment. By that time I pretty much gave up on the idea of trying to please my father. I didn't know whether I did or I didn't, but at this point in my life it really didn't matter much either way.

I didn't know how emotional I would get saying goodbye to Fran, and I didn't want any scenes down at the Navy Induction Center in Cleveland, so we said our farewells at our house. It just so happened that we lived around the corner from the Greyhound station. So, on the day I was to report to the Navy, I kissed Fran, picked up my duffel bag, and got on the bus to Cleveland. I was off on the greatest adventure of my life.

I got down to the induction center and was immediately placed in a group of guys, none of which I had ever seen before. It didn't take long for us to bond together, though. After several hours of filling out forms and taking more physicals, we were sent on the Rapid Transit railroad to the Cleveland Airport where we would get on a plane to Chicago. I remember one rowdy guy in our group that went through our Rapid Transit car grabbing all the pretty young girl's butts. He said he figured he wasn't going to be able to do it for a while and wanted to get it out of his system. He did it to one young girl who was standing near me in the crowded car. She turned and gave me a nasty look as I blurted out, "It wasn't me, ma'am. I'm a married man."

We got to the airport and boarded the plane to Chicago. Now, you have to remember, I had been out of the state of Ohio only once in my entire life, and I had never been on a plane. For me taking a jet to Chicago was a pretty exciting way to begin my Navy career. My love of cars, especially hot rods, made me imagine I was riding in a top fuel dragster as we roared down the runway. It was only a one hour flight to Chicago, but I enjoyed every minute of it. That flight began my love of flying. So far, Navy life was just great.

When we arrived in Chicago I began to learn how sometimes things in the military work very slowly and inefficiently. It was already late at night by the time we arrived and we were all anxious to get some sleep after a long and exciting day. But the bus that was to take us to the Great Lakes Naval Center wasn't there, so we sat on our bags by the curb and waited. Finally, the bus showed up and, after an hour's ride, we arrived at the center.

Back in the late 1800's the Navy decided that it would be best if enlisted sailors would be trained before they got sent to the fleet so they built the first Naval Training Center in Maryland. In the early 1900's the Navy noticed that most of their recruits were coming from the Midwest. A group of Navy officers did a study and they decided it would be a good idea to build another training center in the Midwest and chose an area north of Chicago and south of Milwaukee on the shores of Lake Michigan. The Great Lakes Naval Training Station opened in 1911 and is the largest training facility in the Navy. It has over 1100 buildings on 1628 acres. There are over 50 miles of roadway within the grounds. It's a pretty impressive place, especially for a guy from Cuyahoga Falls, Ohio.

By the time we arrived at Great Lakes it was very late. Too late, it was decided, for us to be assigned to our quarters. We were told that instead of sleeping we were going to be made into "instant sailors".. We were pretty tired, but also were filled with adrenaline over what lay before us, so it was no big deal for us to be up for two straight days. We were placed in lines, given uniforms and sea bags, and spent the day filling out forms and getting poked and prodded and injected by a multitude of doctors and dentists. We were put into companies and assigned to a barrack. By the time we got into our beds it was 11:00 p.m. I remember that night that I had the greatest sleep I ever had. When they came and rousted us out of bed the next morning at 5:00 a.m. I was refreshed and ready to get on with whatever the Navy was going to do to me that day.

The Company Commander in our barracks was an old salt named Soboliewski. We just called him Ski. He only had a couple of months to go before retirement and was spending it at Great Lakes. He was an easy guy to get along with mainly because he was seldom around. We never knew where he went, but it didn't matter. Since I was one of the oldest guys in our company, he assigned me as squad leader. That didn't mean I had any authority, but it got me out of some of the nastier jobs that got assigned to new recruits.

Just like when I got to the Cleveland induction center and was put together with a bunch of strangers, here at Great Lakes I was with another group of guys I had never met before. They were from all over the country, with differing backgrounds and nationalities. There was one kid from a pretty affluent family who enlisted just to spite his parents. From the time he arrived at Great Lakes all he thought about was how to escape from the Navy. He made a couple of attempts, got caught, and was assigned a job as an office assistant. He was able to steal some maps of the grounds and tried his final escape. He eventually was caught on some railroad tracks and was released from the Navy. There also was a couple of Puerto Rican cousins who joined under the "buddy" system which allowed them to go through their entire enlistment together. During one of the tests that they gave us, one of the boys just went nuts while he was sitting at his desk. All of a sudden he started yelling and screaming and they had to drag him out of the room. He was released from his enlistment, too. His cousin was mad because he had to go through his entire four-year enlistment by himself and it wasn't his idea to join up in the first place. I was getting a real education about different people and different ways of life.

The first few days at Great Lakes we were given a battery of tests to determine what type of job we would be best suited for. Unlike the guaranteed enlistment of the Army, there were no guarantees of what you might end up doing in the Navy after you enlisted. I had no trouble with the tests. Like I always had, I scored high on them. So high, in fact, that I was offered some pretty prestigious jobs. I was even sent to a presentation about the Naval Academy in Annapolis. Due to my age and my marital status I wasn't even eligible for the Academy, but Ski told me to go anyway. I was impressed with the presentation and, after, I wondered what might have been if I had applied myself a little better at school. I was also offered the opportunity of going to Nuclear School. The problem with this was that it meant you had to extend your enlistment to 6 years and I didn't want to be in the Navy for that long. I turned down two offers of Officer's Candidate School for the same reason. All I wanted was to get into some sort of electronics training and, based on my test scores, I was pretty sure I would be able to.

It's funny. I spent much of my life wishing, hoping, and dreaming of getting in the Navy and as soon as I'm in, all I thought about was getting out. After the first few days, when the excitement of being in the Navy wore off, I found myself wondering if I had made the right choice. I admit that being away from Fran and home for the first time in my life had a lot to do with it. Still, I was already questioning whether the Navy was the best career move I could have made. Those feelings were mostly quelled every morning when we were called to muster. When I would hear the Star Spangled Banner, and would see our flag raised, I almost had to fight back tears. I was filled with pride. I was finally serving my country.

A typical day at Great Lakes began at 5:00 a.m. when we got up and immediately made up our bunks according to Navy standards. We dressed, made sure our footlockers were in order, then went outside for muster. After muster we went to the mess hall for breakfast. New recruits had to run everywhere they went. The only time you stopped was when you passed a company commander. There, you had to stop in front of him, salute, and shout out, "By your leave, sir." The company commander would then say, "Carry on" and you would continue running on your way. I got a kick out of one company commander who, the first time I came up to him, in a deep, gruff voice told me, "Carry on, Warthog." After that, I would go out of my way just to come up to him and have him say that.

They had what they called "Service Week" at Great Lakes, where everyone was assigned a particular job for the week. Most guys in my squad got assigned to KP, which meant they had to report to the mess hall at 3:00 a.m. and they worked straight through until 6:00 p.m. It wasn't a pleasant task. Fortunately, I developed the knack for folding clothes perfectly and, during these service weeks, that was the job Ski assigned me to. It was a lot easier and took a lot less time than KP. I would walk by the mess hall in the afternoon on my way to the recreation hall and would get dirty looks from the guys inside doing their KP duty. I was pretty good at washing clothes, too. There were no washing machines in our barracks. Everything was scrubbed by hand. Since I had extra time on my hands, and the guys doing KP were exhausted by the time they got to the barracks at night, I offered to wash their clothes for them. At fifty cents a load, I had a pretty nice little cottage industry going.

The job I really hated was guard duty, and I did everything I could to avoid it. It was usually doled out as a punishment for some minor infraction of regulations so I made sure I was up to snuff in everything I did. One time I made a minor mistake. My hair was getting a little shaggy so I had one of the guys in my squad trim up my neck with a razor. He squared it up neatly and I thought that I was looking like the proper Navy recruit. I didn't realize that Navy regulations call for the hair to be tapered at the back, not blocked off. As I was headed to the mess hall I stopped in front of a company commander. Instead of saying "Carry on", he looked me over and said, "That don't look like a regulation haircut, boy. You're on guard duty."

So, I was stuck on guard duty in the middle of July. It was hot and muggy and my job was to stand at attention, perfectly still, for hours at a time. There were lots of mosquitoes near Lake Michigan, but you weren't even allowed to swat at them as they bit you. You had to wear the white uniform with the Dixie cup hat and the neckerchief tie around your neck. The neckerchief had to be tied in a perfect square knot because the first thing the duty officer would do to you when you reported for inspection was to grab the ends of that neckerchief and pull hard on them. If you didn't have the square knot tied correctly, you would choke. We had a guy in our barracks who was very good at tying these neckerchiefs, so we would all have him tie ours before we would report for duty. I was in a hurry to report for my guard duty, so I ran into my barracks and had him quickly tie up my neckerchief. I put it over my neck and ran over to report. The duty officer that day just happened to be the same officer that called me "Warthog". He was a big and mean guy and the first thing he did was grab the ends of my neckerchief. Unfortunately, in his haste to tie it, my buddy from the barracks tied a slip knot instead of a square knot, and it immediately tightened up around my neck. The officer didn't let go until I was pretty red in the face from choking. One of the guys from the barracks saw what happened and ran back to the barracks and told my buddy that he better hide because old Charlie was going to be plenty mad when he got off guard duty. For the rest of my stay at Great Lakes I was careful to avoid doing anything that would cause me to have guard duty again.

One of the benefits for me of the intense physical activity that was a big part of basic training was that I lost weight. I reported to Great Lakes weighing 240 pounds. After nine weeks I was down to 206 pounds. My body was looking great. Unfortunately, it was covered up by an increasingly baggy uniform. My clothes never fit. I tried to get new uniforms, but was told that I was allowed only the size I was assigned to wear. Still, I was feeling a lot better about my physical self.

After a few weeks at Great Lakes we had to fill out forms that were commonly called "Dream Sheets". We used these forms to apply for the job we wanted to perform while in the Navy. Whatever job you applied for was grouped with two other jobs, usually less desirable ones. If the job you applied for was full up, you were automatically assigned to one of the other two jobs in that job group. My dream job, the one I really wanted, was Aviation Electronics. It was grouped with two other jobs, Aviation Ordinance, and Aviation Parachute Rigging, neither of which sounded too appealing to me. I was confident, however, that because of the high scores I got on my aptitude tests I was going to get my dream job. Little did I know that my scores would have nothing to do with it. Like a lot of things in the military, it was all the luck of the draw.

Seven weeks into boot camp we got our first liberty. We were given 12 hours off of the base. Where Great Lakes was located, it was equidistant from Milwaukee or Chicago. The guys in the barracks split up into two groups. One went to the State Fair in Milwaukee, and the other to the big city of Chicago. Most of my buddies went to Chicago, so I went with them. We got on a train that took us right to downtown. So, there we were, a bunch of young guys who had been sequestered on a Navy base for seven weeks without seeing any women. The first thing the guys wanted to do was to go see an "X" rated movie. It wasn't exactly what I had in mind but I went along with them. It was horrible. We went to some seedy theater in a bad neighborhood where there were a bunch of dirty, old men watching a bunch of naked women on a movie screen. I didn't last long before I got up and left. Several of my buddies joined me and we started walking the streets looking for a place to eat. We quickly found out that being in uniform didn't exactly cause businesses to roll out the welcome mat for us. This is in 1969, when the anti-war sentiment in this country was at its peak and, instead of being respected, military personnel were looked down upon. We finally found a little deli where we felt almost welcomed, so we went in. It just so happened that while we were in there eating, a peace march was going on in the street outside. I never had seen one before, so I got up to have a look. My buddies told me to ignore them; that they were always looking for men in uniform to start trouble with. I didn't want any trouble so I just watched from out the front window. The marchers were carrying signs that said, "Hell No, We Won't Go" and "Get Out Of Vietnam Now". I thought it was pretty interesting. Then I saw something that really stayed with me. There was a man on the street. He was about 40 years old or so. Maybe he was a proud World War II veteran, or maybe he had a son that was serving in Vietnam. I don't know. For whatever reason, he went up to one of the protesters, grabbed the sign out of his hands, and threw it on the ground. Before you knew it, a bunch of the other marchers came over and started beating on the man, hitting him over the head with their signs and generally roughing him up pretty bad. I thought to myself, "Here's a bunch of people supposedly marching for peace and non-violence, who don't want to serve our country, but are ready to beat the crap out of someone who disagrees with them." I didn't have a whole lot of respect for peace marchers after that.

We left the deli and just started walking the streets again looking for something to do. After a while, some guy came up to us and told us that it wasn't a good neighborhood for us to be hanging around, and advised us to get out of it. By this time I had enough of my liberty in Chicago. One of the guys suggested going to the USO club, and we all decided to go there and kill the time before our train back to the base left. We found the USO and it turned out that they held dances on the weekends for the servicemen on leave. There were some girls there, and I don't mean to sound disrespectful or anything, but none of them were very pretty. I was there just biding my time, drinking Cokes and eating cookies, when a girl, who was almost as big as I was, came up to me and asked me if I wanted to dance. I blurted out, "I'm married. I can't dance with you." I couldn't wait to get back to the base that night. It was just an awful day. We didn't really have any fun. But the worst part for me was how people treated us. As proud as I felt being in uniform, I realized that for most people it didn't mean anything at all. It seemed that the war in Vietnam had changed their attitudes.

Not much was said in our barracks about Vietnam. We didn't really know how much the Navy was involved in the war. We were pretty naïve and didn't realize that the Navy had a large inland force in Vietnam. To us, being in the Navy meant sailing on a large ship in a blue ocean somewhere. It wasn't until I picked up a magazine one day in our barracks's lounge and saw an article about the Riverines that I began to understand that the Navy was very involved in the fighting in Vietnam. The Riverines were part of what was called the "Brown Water Navy". It consisted of a fleet of smaller boats that patrolled the rivers and deltas of Vietnam. After reading the article I wasn't alarmed but rather thought that it was pretty neat that the Navy, my Navy, was also fighting the war in the trenches. I still never thought I would go to Vietnam and I believed that I would never be near the fighting. After all, I was going into Aviation Electronics.

Towards the end of our basic training the day came when we were notified of what schools we were assigned to. That was not a happy day for me. I was informed I would be going to Aviation Ordnance school, not Aviation Electronics as I had expected. Now, instead of learning electronics, I would be learning how to load bombs and weapons into aircraft. I was pretty upset. I stormed over to the officers and complained. I said, "How can I score so high on all my tests and then you give me this job? I got a wife. The only reason I joined the Navy was to learn a trade so that when I got out I could go home and get a decent job. Now my only hope is that United Air Lines will start hauling bombs!"

I wasn't the only unhappy guy in our barracks. There was a lot of griping that day. It was another learning experience for us about how the military sometimes doesn't use logic in making decisions. We had one guy, Gagliardi, who joined the Navy after completing two years of pre-med in college. He wanted to become a Corpsman to continue his medical training so when he got out he could finish his medical degree. He was assigned Yeoman school, which basically taught you how to be an office clerk. Then there was Whitey, a towhead from Kentucky, who had absolutely no idea what he wanted to be. The Navy assigned him to Corpsman school. It just didn't make any sense.

The next day we were still grumbling about our assignments when Ski called us to muster. He said that there was a blood shortage and that he needed some volunteers to donate blood. He asked that all who wanted to volunteer should take a step forward. Only two guys did. Ski told them to step back. Then he said, "Listen men. In that hospital over there, some of your brothers-in-arms are laying wounded from the war in Vietnam. They gave their blood for you and your country. They need your help now and I know that you won't let them down. Now, once again, everyone willing to give blood take a step forward." Our entire barracks did. We might not have been happy with the Navy on that day, but we weren't going to abandon the needs of our fellow servicemen. It was our first opportunity to do something meaningful.

So, off we marched to the hospital to give blood. I had never given blood before so I didn't know what to expect. When the nurse pricked my finger to get a sample, at first nothing came out. She grabbed my finger and squeezed it, and all of a sudden blood started spurting out. Whitey was behind me and when he saw all the blood, he fainted. He just didn't fall on the floor. On the way down he crashed into a cart that held bottles of blue dye. When the bottles hit the floor they shattered and splashed the blue dye all over our white uniforms. We all had a good laugh over that one. I said, "That would be great. Out on the battlefield a wounded man calls for a corpsman, and Whitey shows up, sees the guy bleeding, and passes out."

Despite the bad reputation that boot camp has, I enjoyed most of it. In fact, I probably could have spent all four years of my enlistment there and I would've been happy. I liked the camaraderie. One of the things I enjoyed doing during basic training was when we marched around the base there was a tunnel that went underneath the main road. It was a tradition that when you marched through the tunnel you sang "Anchors Aweigh". I always sang it the loudest out of anyone in our squad. During boot camp there were various competitions between divisions. There were competitions in academics, military drill, cleanliness, and athletics. The competitions all counted towards winning the honor flag for that category. At the Pass-In-Review march, during graduation, each division was led in by the honor flags they won. You could learn a lot about the makeup of a division by the honor flags they carried. Our division wasn't much good at anything but athletics, and we ended up winning that honor flag. I was proud to be the anchor of the tug-of-war team, and I believe my bulk was a major factor in our victories there.

Graduation from boot camp was near and I was still pretty disgruntled about my school assignment. I even went so far as to volunteer for the Riverines. I said, "Send me to Vietnam. It's got to be better than being a bomb humper." But I was told it was too late to make any changes so I resigned myself to my fate.

I was really happy that Fran was able to come to the graduation exercises. We had a chance to spend a little time together as we were given a liberty right before graduation. She came with her friend Faith, who I set up with my buddy Gagliardi. We had a nice time just walking the beaches of Lake Michigan and going out to eat at restaurants off the base. I was pretty proud of the way I looked. I had lost weight and put on muscle and felt really good in my dress whites during the Pass-In-Review. Fran got a kick out of when I was addressed by the Commandant as "Seamen Recruit Morris". Mostly, I was proud of what I had accomplished. I got through my first part of my Navy enlistment and, even though I wasn't getting the school that I really wanted, I still felt that I could make something good out of my Navy career.

5

After graduation from basic training, the Navy gave me a two-week leave before I had to report to Jacksonville, Florida, for my first school. I went home with Fran. At the same time, my buddy Ron was done with his Army basic training and was home, too. Ron's wife had moved in with Fran in our little rented house while Ron was in boot camp, but now was going to go with him to his first assignment. Fran couldn't afford the place on her own so we decided that while I went to school in Jacksonville, she would move back in with her parents. So, for much of the two weeks I had off, we were selling our furniture and making preparations for her move.

After my leave was over I flew to Jacksonville, then took a bus to the Naval Air Station. It was my first time in Florida and I remember the distinct smell as soon as I stepped off the plane. It was the beginning of September so it was still pretty warm down there. I didn't mind though. I liked it there from the moment I arrived at the base. I was one of the first arrivals for the school, which wasn't going to start for two weeks. During that time I was given menial duties to occupy my time. I spent a lot of time cleaning barracks and grooming the grounds. I still had lots of free time to explore the base. There were three swimming pools, a gymnasium, fitness rooms with weights, boats to rent for fishing on the St. Johns River, good chow halls, and even an enlisted man's club. Everything I needed and wanted was right there. It was a very large base and I was fascinated by the huge planes that took off and landed from there. When school started we were allowed to go into town, but we found, once again, that the townspeople weren't too fond of men in uniform, so I was content to spend my free time on the base.

The first day of class, the officers who were teaching us asked if any of us had any leadership experience. I raised my hand and told him I was a squad leader in boot camp. Since no one else raised their hands, he assigned me as class leader. I took my job pretty serious. There were about thirty guys in the class. Every morning my job was to muster the guys from the barracks and march them in formation to the school. I'd lead them in cadence songs as we marched. Eventually they joined in with me. There were also Marines that trained on the base and whenever we would pass by a group of them I'd have my guys shout out,

"Marines suck" in unison. Of course the Marines returned the greeting with their own rendition. Being a class leader had benefits, too. I didn't have to pull any watches or guard duty. I'd have to put guys on work details to clean the class-room every day. I'd always assign myself to Fridays because I knew the guys were anxious to get their weekends started. The Petty Officers didn't think I should do this. They thought a leader should always assign duties, but I considered myself just one of the guys so I didn't mind doing what they had to do too.

I only had one incident of a discipline problem when I was class leader. A young kid in the class decided that since we were of equal rank that he shouldn't have to take orders from me. One day, in front of the whole class, he told me so. He started yelling and screaming at me and got right into my face doing so. I just calmly said, "You're absolutely right." Then I sucker punched him knocking him to the ground. He got up hollering that he was going to report me, and that I was going to get thrown out of the Navy. He said that there was a whole class full of witnesses to back him up. Everyone in the class looked at each other and said, "I didn't see anything. Did you see anything?" I never had another problem with that kid.

We got paid every two weeks in the Navy. When I was at Jacksonville I got $29 every two weeks. From that I had to save enough money so that I could get home for Christmas and still have enough to buy some presents, too. My only extravagance I allowed myself while I was at Jacksonville was every Friday night the enlisted man's club had a t-bone steak dinner we could get for $2. Even though I had lost weight I still enjoyed eating, and I always looked forward to those Friday nights.

In class I was the number one student. As much as I hated high school, I really enjoyed the Navy school. We had classes in basic math through trigonometry. I had electronics classes and classes in weapons. We learned about rockets and mis-siles and jets. Even though it wasn't the school I wanted, I applied myself and did my best. I also discovered that I actually enjoyed learning.

Our barracks formed a football team, of which I was a member. We had enough guys that we had an offensive team and a defensive team. I was back at my old position on the defensive line. We played tackle football even though we had no protective equipment like helmets or shoulder pads. I liked the rough and tumble games. We played the Marines and beat them up pretty badly. We even played the team from the Aviation Electronics school, the one I wanted to get in. I took special pleasure in beating them. Eventually we got so good that nobody would play us any more. It was fun while it lasted though.

I was treated with respect by the teachers of our classes. They were always praising me for my grades and the way I performed my class leader duties. On Fridays, the teachers liked to leave early so sometimes they'd leave me in charge of the class. They'd give me the teacher's manual and I'd go over the material with the class, preparing them for upcoming tests. It was my first exposure to teaching and I liked it. I felt that the class looked up to me, and that was a good feeling. It made me feel important.

As much as I was enjoying being at Jacksonville, I still missed Fran. We talked about her possibly coming down and moving into one of the off base apartments. They cost $40 a month. One day one of the married guys in the class invited me over to see what his apartment looked like. While I was sitting in their tiny living room, I watched as a bunch of big cockroaches paraded across the floor and up the wall. That night I wrote Fran that I changed my mind. She should just stay where she was.

During one of the classes in Munitions, we were shown movies of Navy helicopters that provided support for the river patrol boats in Vietnam. I was infatuated with the noise and the flying; the door gunners peering over their machine guns out of a helicopter flying low over some jungle river. I had no idea that the Navy had this kind of involvement in Vietnam. I said, "This is for me." I found out that there was only one group that was doing this: the Seawolves.

The diverse topography of Vietnam caused the Navy to have to use different tactics and equipment to fight the war. The vast network of rivers and deltas required the development of the Patrol Boat River (PBR), which were actually converted pleasure craft. The only way to support the PBRs was with helicopters. In the beginning of the fighting in Vietnam the Army provided this helicopter support, but the Navy wasn't satisfied so they developed their own helicopter force using mostly castoff equipment from the army. They called this helicopter support group the Seawolves.

Towards the end of the 16 weeks of school at Jacksonville we filled out another "dream sheet". This one was more for where we wanted to go. I was surprised by many of the guys who put in for bases close to their homes. I didn't understand it. I joined the Navy to travel, to see things, and to learn. I was still excited about getting to exotic places like Chicago and Jacksonville. I didn't discuss any of my potential choices with Fran. I put in for the Seawolves. One of our Gunny Sergeants, who had done a tour in Vietnam and got a bullet in his butt for his efforts, found out what I was going to do. He came to me and said, "Morris, are you stupid or what? Aren't you married? Don't you want to have children?" I was not going to be dissuaded. In fact, my enthusiasm got some of my buddies to apply for the Seawolves, too. They thought that we would never get in; that the Seawolves were much too selective about who got in. It was really odd for me to want a job that would require me to fly in a helicopter. I obviously had never been in one. On top of that, I had a terrible fear of heights. Nonetheless, the Seawolves was my first choice on this dream sheet. My second choice was to get on an aircraft carrier. The new carrier, the John F. Kennedy, had just been launched and was on a world cruise. I envisioned myself as a launcher giving hand signals to a jet pilot and then crouching low as he zoomed by me and off into the wild blue yonder. My third choice was to get on a LST (Landing Ship Tank), a relatively new vessel in the fleet. It looked like a small aircraft carrier, but it was for helicopters, not planes.

Right before graduation from Jacksonville, we got our orders. All of us got in the Seawolves. I was thrilled, but my buddies weren't. They really thought we had no chance of getting in and only put in for it because I pestered them to. I guess the prospect of being on a gunship in Vietnam wasn't as thrilling for them as it was for me.

6

Getting in with the Seawolves meant more schools, three more to be exact. I wanted to arrange my school schedule so that I could spend as much time as I could at home in between traveling to the schools. Our final destination was California where we would wait for our orders to go to Vietnam. My plan was not to sign up for Door Gunner's school, which was in Alabama, until I got to California. Then I could stop off in Ohio on the way to and from Alabama. I was assigned the most difficult school first, so after Jacksonville, I went to Little Creek, Virginia, for Survival School.

It was February, 1970, when I got to Virginia. The first five weeks of the course had us in the classroom in the morning and doing physical training in the afternoon. The classroom part was pretty interesting and was taught by guys, mostly Marines, who had already served tours in Vietnam. We were taught about Vietnam, the people, the insurgents, and how to identify them. We were taught counter-insurgency tactics. We learned how to set up a perimeter and how to defend it with claymoor mines. We also learned how to use all the weapons that were deployed in Vietnam. For the first few weeks of physical training we were taught by Navy personnel. They were pretty hard on us, but they explained their intense methods by telling us that after two weeks the Marines would take over and they wanted us to be prepared for them. I did pretty well with most of the physical training. The one thing I had trouble with was getting myself over the eight-foot wall. I was still a pretty big boy, and the wall was a difficult challenge for me. I always needed a little assistance from someone to make it over. I was determined to be able to do it on my own so every night after dinner I would go out and practice it by myself. I never got really good at it, but I got so I didn't have to depend on anyone's help to get over that wall anymore.

The Navy used to march us in sort of a quick step wherever we went. When the Marines got a hold of us we did double time wherever we went. Double time to them was like a full run to me. We used to have to do it carrying all sorts of weapons and ammunition. There was one Marine Lieutenant that I remember from that school. He was a "mustanger", meaning he was an officer that came out of the enlisted ranks. This caused him to be highly respected by enlisted men and officers alike. But the thing that impressed me most was his chiseled appearing physique and how disciplined he was towards physical exercise. Everyday I would see him running, and he always carried weights with him while he ran. He impressed me so much that I took up running myself, something I would continue throughout most of my life.

In the sixth week of the school we were wakened early in the morning one day and told that we were going on a survival exercise for one week. We were told to pack our backpacks with no more than two chocolate bars and two packs of gum. No other food could be taken. We were bussed way out into the boonies and for the next five days we were given "on the job" training in survival techniques. We were divided into squads of ten men each. Each squad was given a live chicken and six potatoes, which was supposed to be enough food to get us through the week. My love of the outdoors and the things I learned hunting and fishing made me well adapted to this type of exercise. Since I was the only one who knew how to kill a live chicken, I was in charge of cooking. I figured that a cooked chicken would probably only last a day or two dividing it among six guys. But I thought that if we made chicken soup everyday, we would have the nourishment we required. So that's what I did. I found some tubers among the plants growing in the woods there and added them, along with a potato, each day to the soup. We never ate the chicken meat. By the fifth day the soup was getting pretty thin but at least we didn't starve. I never even had to dig in to my chocolate bars.

During the week we were taught orienteering, how to make our way using a map and compass. Everyday we had to find our way to another camp using the methods we were taught. Up to that point I was actually enjoying the survival exercise.

On the fifth night we were told to go to a place using our map and compass. It was the first time we had to do it in the dark, and it was much more difficult, especially considering how pitch dark it got in those woods at night. We had to wear goggles so that we wouldn't poke our eyes out on the many small branches that blocked our way. I ended up walking into a tree and the goggles made a cut on the bridge of my nose. It bled pretty good and looked worse than it actually was. When we finally arrived at the designated place it was midnight. We were told that the next morning our position would be attacked and that we should dig ourselves in. During the night we dug shallow trenches and then tried to disguise them by covering them with branches and leaves. The next morning we could hear our attackers coming in large trucks. I helped the other guys get in to their trenches and covered them up. I was the last to get in, partly because I was a little claustrophobic and wanted to spend as little time as I could in the narrow trench. It was pretty scary when the attackers arrived at our position. They did a lot of yelling and set off percussion grenades. The noise was frightening, but they were trying to duplicate what it would be like being attacked by the Viet Cong. I was shaking in my little trench. One of the grenades went off close to me, and the next thing I knew I felt a heavy foot standing on my groin area. I moaned, and then felt the barrel of an AK-47 on my nose. A big guy dressed all in black yelled at me, "Get up you American pig." Now, we were not allowed to resist capture or retaliate in any way. In fact, we had to sign a paper before the exercise began stating that we wouldn't. We were supposed to do all we could to avoid being captured but, if we were, we had to submit ourselves to our captors. I had now been awake for over 24 hours and had been under tremendous physical and emotional strain. After the excitement of the attack I completely forgot what I was allowed to do when I got captured. My captor asked me, "What's your name, pig?" I remained silent and, after a few seconds, he hauled off and hit me so hard I fell to the ground. I jumped back up and again he asked me my name. I just looked at him and he hit me again. This went on about four more times. He must have been getting tired of hitting me because he finally grabbed me and in a low voice said, "What did they teach you in class to say if you got captured?" All of a sudden it came back to me: Name, Rank, and Serial Number. He asked me again and I responded correctly. I must have had a little grin on my face when I said it because he got angry again and told me to take off all my clothes. It was still March and it was cold outside and I had to strip down to my underwear. Then he marched me to a stream and told me to get down in the stream and do push-ups at his command. The water was icy cold. I don't know whether he was trying to torture me, or if he just thought I needed a little reviving after being smacked around so much. After about twenty push-ups, he gave me back my clothes and marched me back to the road where I was assembled with the rest of my captured squad. Then our captors left and we had to find our way to the next coordinate, where we would face another attack. This went on all day and all night. We'd get to a place, dig in, get attacked, get captured, get slapped around, and then be sent on our way to the next spot.

After 24 hours straight of this, we came to a big open field with no enemy in sight. We thought, "We made it without being captured again. Thank God, we're done at last." Then our attackers came out of nowhere, charging up to us in jeeps and trucks throwing percussion grenades. They took us prisoner once more. Only this time we were all tied together with rope and marched off to a prisoner of war camp. It was meant to replicate a North Vietnamese prison and was made up of a bunch of makeshift huts. There were dirt holes we had to get in and small boxes that we were locked in. I got put in a box and, once I was in, I didn't think it was too bad. It was a little cramped when they locked the top, but there was a little air hole I found so I could at least breathe. Then the lid opened and they put another guy in the box with me. This time when they locked the top it was very tight, especially for a guy with claustrophobia. The guy that was in there with me started whining, but I told him to shut up. After a while I was let out and sent to be interrogated. I stood in front of a guy who started asking all kinds of questions. Although we had been taught not to divulge any information other than name, rank, and serial number, after being awake for nearly two full days, and the stress of being beaten and going without food, caused me to forget what we had been taught. I answered their questions. It wasn't as if I was surrendering or giving up. I didn't think I was giving out any critical information. Actually, I thought the exercise was over since they were writing on pads of paper with the survival school logo on it. I didn't realize that they were just tricking me to show me how easy it was to let your guard down. While I was being interrogated I could hear my buddies getting beat up in the adjoining rooms. I could hear them being thrown against the walls and occasionally would hear them screaming in pain, which I later found out was caused when their captors would squeeze their private parts. My interrogator watched my face as I heard these sounds and he told me that what I was hearing was what was going to happen to me next unless I cooperated. After getting beaten up many times in the past two days, I wasn't anxious to get another beating. It was all part of the psychological warfare though. I never did get another beating. We were then put in little makeshift hooches and told that we were going to be detained. We all were hoping that the survival exercise was nearly complete and we would be back at the base before nightfall, eating dinner at the chow hall. We were pretty disheartened at the prospect of spending another night in captivity. Just before dark they ordered us out of our hooches and we assembled by a flagpole. They raised the American flag and told us that we had all done a good job. I don't think any of us had a dry eye when that flag went up. Right then I realized just how serious a situation it was to serve in Vietnam. I knew one thing: I never wanted to be taken as a prisoner in Vietnam.

As bad as it was in that school for us enlisted men, the Navy officers who went through it had it even worse. There was one Commander who went through the school with us. He was on his way to a river boat base in Vietnam. After the school was over we all met for a steak dinner. He showed up but didn't eat with us. He was still visibly shaking from his ordeal at the school. He had bruises all up and down his arms. He told us he was very proud of the way we conducted ourselves. I heard later that he had to be sent home for a couple of weeks to recover from the survivor school before he went to Vietnam.

I was a little discouraged after the survival class. I was disappointed in myself that I had let my guard down while I was being interrogated. I was annoyed that I allowed myself to be tricked. Although everyone in my squad did the same thing, I felt like I let my guys down by answering the questions I was asked. The survival class had another profound effect on me. For the first time I started thinking about death. Actually, I became obsessed with it. I firmly believed that I was going to die in Vietnam. It was odd. I never considered that I might be wounded or crippled. There was only life or death, and my gut was telling me that I wasn't coming back from Vietnam alive.

I took a couple of days off before my next school in Maryland and went home to see Fran. It was there that I had another new experience. I started having nightmares. I never had any trouble sleeping before, but that first night I woke up in the middle of the night in a cold sweat. I don't remember what the nightmare was about, but I do know it scared me. When Fran asked me what was the matter, I brushed it off with the excuse that I wasn't used to sleeping in her parent's house, as that was where Fran was living at the time. I never told her about the foreboding of death that I was having. I figured she had enough to worry about already.

The school in Maryland was for Helicopter Armament, and was taught by the Army. In fact, it was conducted on an Army base. There were only six of us Navy guys at the school. I wanted to make sure no one would mistake me for an Army guy while I was on base, so I got a magic marker and wrote "Navy" on my sweatshirts. After the tension and strain of survival school, Helicopter Armament was like a vacation. We got to learn about, and use, all kinds of weapons. Being a hunter and skeet shooter, I enjoyed firing at targets and liked to show off my expertise. I breezed through this school with no problems. The only thing I didn't like about it was the Army food. One day they tried to feed me mutton and I told them, in no uncertain terms, what they could do with it. Other than that, the school was fine and after four weeks of it I was on my way to California.

On the way to California I stopped for a couple of days at home with Fran. Even though my California assignment was supposed to be my last stop before Vietnam, we didn't have any tearful goodbyes. I figured I'd be back home before Vietnam, since my plan was to sign up for Door Gunner school once I got to California. The Navy would then send me back east to Ft. Rucker, Alabama and then send me back to California after the school. I thought that those two trips would provide me with ample time to spend at home before I went overseas.

I was stationed at the Naval Air Station at Imperial Beach, about 20 miles south of San Diego. We were right on the Mexican border. We could even see the bull ring at Tijuana from our base. Normally, the Navy would keep you in California thirty days before sending you to Vietnam. They would keep you occupied during those thirty days with a variety of training, drills, and work duty. While I was there I had swimming classes, instruction in hand to hand combat using judo and karate techniques, and also some classes in small arms. I arrived at the base the last week of April 1970. I really liked it there and was just going to bide my time for a week or so before turning in my request for Door Gunner School.

I had been so busy with my schools the previous six months that I didn't have the time nor the inclination to keep up with what was happening in our country. I had no idea how much the protesting against the war had escalated. I knew that the war was unpopular, especially among college students, but I didn't know how defiant the students were becoming on college campuses. I found that out the first week in May when, at Kent State University, National Guard troops opened fire on protesting students, killing four of them. Before we even knew what had happened, we were notified that the base had been closed down. No Navy personnel were allowed to leave the base. The Navy was afraid that there would be reprisals towards anyone in uniform. So, for one week, I was sequestered on base watching the television for news on the shootings.

I was shocked. Obviously I had a vested interest in the story as I was from the Kent area. But I just couldn't believe that some of our men in uniform would actually shoot at unarmed college students. I didn't understand how they could. I knew that some of the protesters I had seen could be pretty annoying and aggressive. And I believed that some of them deserved a good thumping for their behavior. But to use live ammunition on them was unconscionable, as far as I was concerned. If the National Guard was so anxious to shoot at something, then send them over to Vietnam where the enemy is using bullets too. I'll stay here and deal with the taunts and occasional thrown rocks from college students. I was pretty disturbed about it, and in the days immediately following the shootings I was even more disturbed by the attitudes of some of our government officials regarding the incident. It was almost as if they were commending the National Guard for doing a good job in putting down the protest. Later in my life I would get a different perspective of the tragedy when one of my friends, who was in the National Guard at that time, was put on trial for his involvement in the shootings.

The Kent State shootings, coupled with my continuing thoughts of impending death, caused me to rethink my attitude towards what I was about to do in Vietnam. Being impulsive and stubborn, I withdrew my request for Door Gunner School and told the Navy that I would go to Vietnam if they sent me, but I would not carry, or fire, any weapons while I was there. The Navy had no problem with that, but it meant that I wouldn't be returning home before being sent over to Vietnam, and that was only a couple of weeks away.

As the time grew near for my orders to Vietnam, I found my mood getting more and more somber. Some of the training at the base helped take my mind off it for short periods of time. I got pretty interested in the judo and karate, and got to be pretty good at it, too. For some reason they always seemed to pair up a smaller guy with a larger guy. Although I had no interest in beating up a guy that was smaller than me, some of the bigger guys took advantage of the situation and really pounded their training opponents. One time one of the big guys in our unit really knocked one of my buddies around and after that I was always looking for the opportunity to get into a judo match with him, just to give him a taste of his own medicine. Towards the end of our training we had a tournament and I positioned myself to be able to have this guy as my opponent. Only trouble was I really didn't know him that well and we wore helmets that covered half our heads making us somewhat indistinguishable. As it turned out I gave my opponent quite a thrashing but it wasn't the guy I intended it for. I felt pretty bad about that. So did the guy I beat up.

Sometimes we would head off to Tijuana during our liberties. It was the first time I was ever out of the country. We were warned to stay on the main roads and not to venture off into the more seedier sections of town. I wasn't particularly fond of Tijuana and made sure I was always out of there before dark. I had to go there, though. I felt it was part of being a sailor to visit different port of calls and to sample the local culture.

The way the Navy worked it they gave out orders for Vietnam on Wednesdays and you shipped out on Saturday. In the two days between, you had to fly from San Diego up to San Francisco, where you would leave from Travis Air Force Base. I didn't think that they would ship anyone out on Memorial Day weekend, but I was wrong. I got my orders on the Wednesday preceding the holiday. About six of my buddies also got their orders, so on Thursday we all headed up to San Francisco. One of the guys had a cousin who lived there and she offered to drive us around the area on Friday. She took us up into the mountains and showed us some of the vineyards and wineries. But the thing that I remember most is Stanford University. That was one of the hotbeds of war protest activity and I was amazed at all the anti-war signs and graffiti that seemed to cover the entire campus. Oddly enough I found myself more and more feeling like I was on their side.

The most difficult part of leaving for Vietnam for me was not being able to say a proper good-bye to Fran. After I changed my plans about Door Gunner School, there wasn't any time for her to come to California, or for me to go back home. Fran refused to fly anywhere, so, when I got my orders, there was no way she could make it to San Francisco on a train in two days. So we just said good-bye over the phone. I still had my premonitions about my ultimate demise in Vietnam, but I never shared them with her. I was anxious to get on with this new part of my Navy life.

We were a pretty somber group that day before our flight to Vietnam. Everyone was pretty quiet and I found myself forced into the role of cheerleader. I told the guys that it probably was going to be great over there. We'd be on a nice base and have lots of free time. I even bragged that I had my duffel bag filled with weights so that I could really get myself in shape while I was over there. I can't remember much about what we did that day. I know we drank a lot of Schlitz beer in the tall cans. By the evening, as we boarded our plane, we all had a pretty good buzz going. I was pretty exhausted from trying to keep everyone's spirits up and it wasn't long after I got on the plane that I passed out. I was on my way to Vietnam.

7

The plane we flew to Vietnam in was a Continental Airlines commercial jet. It had stewardesses and everything. About the only noticeable difference between this plane and a regular commercial jet was that there were no first class seats. There were no tourists on this flight either. It was completely filled with military personnel from all branches of service. The state I was in when I boarded the plane prevents me from remembering a whole lot about what the flight was like. About all I do remember is that it was a very long flight. Twenty-six hours long to be exact.

I was sufficiently sobered up by the time we landed at Bien Hoa Air Base, which was about 19 miles northeast of Saigon. My first impression of Vietnam came as soon as I went out of the door of the plane. The heat almost knocked me right off my feet. It was the hottest place I've ever been. They said that Vietnam only had two seasons, a hot season and a rainy season, and I arrived in the hot season. As I walked down the stairs from the plane, I looked around at the activity going on at the base. Everywhere I looked there were guys wearing jungle fatigues carrying weapons of every kind. Right off the bat I knew that this was no training exercise. This was the real thing.

We were loaded into a bus and taken to downtown Saigon where we were quartered at the Annapolis Hotel. Aside from the name, there was nothing about this place that was like any hotel I was ever in. It probably was a hotel before the American government took it over and converted it to military barracks. I stayed in a room with the six guys I came over with. We slept in bunk beds just like we had at our bases in the States. We were kept in Saigon for three days of indoctrination. We were told that we would experience some culture shock, so we had classes that taught us some of the customs and ways of life of the Vietnamese people. One of the things they told us was that it was customary for two male friends to hold hands while they walked together. Back home this would mean only one thing, but in Vietnam it was quite normal. It still was hard to get used to. The most important thing we were taught was that our purpose in being in Vietnam was to be helpers to the Vietnamese people. We were not supposed to be their saviors.

On our first day in Saigon we were told that we would be going on a tour of the city and that we should bring our cameras. I was pretty excited about seeing the sights and brought two cameras with me. I had visions of a nice air-conditioned tour bus, like the ones back home, and was pretty disappointed when we were shuttled on an old gray military bus. As if that wasn't bad enough, all the windows were covered with metal grating, not exactly the view you wanted if you were trying to take pictures. It didn't take long to realize why the grating was there. All along the tour route people were throwing things at the bus. Old fruits and vegetables, bottles and cans, rocks, anything they could get their hands on, would bounce off the grating as we rolled along. I realized that the Vietnamese people hated us being there as much as we hated being there. These were the people we were supposed to be helping. We were never allowed off the bus. Not that any of us had the desire to get off. The city did have some beautiful buildings done in the French architectural style, but they were all covered in barbed wire. I took a few pictures through the windshield of the bus, but I had seen enough to know that I didn't want to spend any more time in Saigon than was absolutely necessary.

I was amazed at the number of people on the streets of Saigon. Many of them were farm families who were displaced from their land when the American forces came through. I noticed that some were very ingenious when it came to finding temporary shelter in the city. It seemed that all they needed was a few square feet of area and they would put up a cardboard shelter. What was unique was that they would cover the sides and tops of the cardboard with crushed beer and pop cans. They made sure that they used the same brand of beer or pop for the entire house. They were pretty unique dwellings, and there were communities of them all over the city.

People were begging everywhere. Those who weren't begging were trying to rob you. One of their schemes was that a guy on a motor scooter would come by a soldier or sailor and with a razor blade slice open their pants pocket that held their wallets. Another guy following in another scooter would grab the fallen wallet and disappear into the mass of humanity on the streets. One of my friends, Winters, had this happen to him, only the guy with the razor wasn't so adept and not only cut his pants, but his leg also. Winters not only lost his wallet, but a bit of his blood too.

Based on what I initially saw in Saigon, and what we were told to watch out for, I decided not to leave the friendly confines of the Annapolis Hotel during the three days I was in Saigon. The chow hall was three blocks away, so that meant I had to live on pop and candy bars, but I figured it was worth the sacrifice to avoid having to go out into the decrepit streets. I remember laying in my bunk that first night thinking, "What did I get myself into?"

After three days in Saigon, I was more than ready to get to my assigned base at Binh Thuy. A bus took us back to the air base at Bien Hoa, where we boarded a small Navy cargo plane, which flew us to Can Tho. Can Tho was home to a large military complex, which included an Army air base, an Air Force base, and the Binh Thuy Naval base. Can Tho was the second largest city in South Vietnam, and was strategically located on the Bassac River, a major waterway. It was in the heart of the Mekong Delta, which is at the southern end of Vietnam. We flew into the Army base and, as I got off the plane, I was amazed at seeing the long lines of Army helicopters, mostly Cobra gunships, that were on the airstrip. The Army base was dirty and brown and the temperature was just as hot as it was in Saigon. I got on a bus and was taken on a short ride down the road to Binh Thuy. On one side of the road at Binh Thuy was the Bassac River, which is where the Navy's River Patrol Force was headquartered. On the other side of the road, next to a concrete factory, was a 1500 foot air strip, some hangars, aircraft repair shops, green wooden barracks, and a chow hall. It was home to the Black Ponies, a squadron of fixed wing aircraft that was the Navy's only combat air support unit in Vietnam. It was also the home base of the Seawolves, and was to be my home during my tour of Vietnam.

The first thing we did when we arrived at Binh Thuy was to turn in all of our American money. It was exchanged for what was called "funny money", military script, which we could exchange for Vietnamese piasters whenever we went into town. We were then shown to our barracks, which were large two story buildings that had half wooden walls and half screen. As soon as we entered the barracks we were greeted with shouts of, "My replacement's here." The Seawolves were very friendly towards new guys and were always willing to help us get used to our new surroundings. They were unlike the Army who treated newbies with disdain. The guys in the barracks had arranged their lockers to form walls to give their bunks a little privacy. They called these arrangements "cubes" and the guys we were replacing offered us their cubes as a welcome to Vietnam gift. I got a top bunk on the second floor. I heard that the barracks had the biggest rats in Vietnam and I wanted to be as far away as possible from them. I later found out it was true what they said about the rats. They were as big as dogs and were everywhere you went. We weren't allowed to shoot them because the sound of gunfire would put the whole base on alert. So you learned to live with them. I didn't like it though.

It seemed like everyone in the barracks had a stereo, and the sound of rock and roll and country music was everywhere. One of the favorite songs in the barracks was Country Joe and the Fish's "Fixin' to Die Rag".

Yeah, come on all of you, big strong men,
Uncle Sam needs your help again.
He's got himself in a terrible jam
Way down yonder in Vietnam
So put down your books and pick up a gun,
We're gonna have a whole lotta fun.
And it's one, two, three,
What are we fighting for?
Don't ask me, I don't give a damn,
Next stop is Vietnam;
And it's five, six, seven,
Open up the pearly gates,
Well there ain't no time to wonder why,
Whoopee! we're all gonna die.

The guys were amazed that I already knew all the words to the song.

After we got settled in to our barracks we were given a walking tour around the base to show us where everything was located. The Navy base was much smaller than its Army and Air Force counterparts. There were nine detachments of Seawolves spread out in the Mekong Delta, of which Bin Thuy was the home base. Most of the gunships here were in for repair from the detachments. Unlike the lineup of helicopters at the Army base, each helicopter at Bin Thuy was parked in a spot surrounded by a three-sided concrete wall about three feet high. The runway was constructed out of corrugated metal. Although the Navy didn't have a PX, we could walk to one end of our base and use the one at the Army base. At another end of the base was the Army's Delta Dustoff unit. They were the helicopter ambulances used for casualty evacuation from the battlefields. I always got a somber feeling whenever I would see those choppers take off and land. There was an Army hospital there, too.

We were introduced to all of the officers. They were all very nice to us. I could tell immediately that this was a tight knit group. We were given our Seawolf patches and our black berets which identified us as part of the Navy's "River Patrol Task Force 116". After the brief indoctrination we were put right to work.

It didn't take long for me to get settled in to life at Binh Thuy. I was assigned to the ordnance shop. It was located in the back of one of the hangars. I worked on machine guns, rocket launchers, and other weapons systems. Outside of work and other duties, I spent a lot of time working out. I found out quickly that Vietnam was not a great place to run. Your main concern over there was how to stay cool and running wasn't a good way to do it. After a couple of tries, I gave up running for the duration of my time in Vietnam. I did work out with my weights, though, and continued building a body I could be proud of. I didn't smoke and didn't drink much. Occasionally I would drink a beer, but even though they were American brands, they tasted real funny. The rumor was that they put formaldehyde in the beer. It didn't matter. I was just trying to keep myself physically fit. I listened to the Armed Forces Radio station we had there. They played the same music we heard back home and it was comforting to hear an American voice over the radio. We also had an Armed Forces television station, but they mostly showed reruns of old American shows.

It didn't take long, either, for me to experience something I never felt before: homesickness. Back in the States I had been away from home for a full year and never had any problems. But one week after arriving in Vietnam I was feeling pretty bad. It had already been over a month since I saw Fran and the realization that it would be twelve more months before I would see her again was a little difficult to take. Although life on our base wasn't bad, we all hated being in Vietnam. All the guys knew exactly how many days it was until their tour was over. I started keeping track of mine too. It was a place where we didn't want to be and we weren't wanted.

One day, after I had been there about two weeks, I was working in the ordnance shop when two Navy officers came in. I could see that they were both pilots. They came up to me and asked if they could talk to me. I noticed that they had my personnel file with them. We went and sat down at a table in a little room at the back of the hangar. They said they had looked at my file and were very impressed with my test scores and my Navy record thus far. They said they were looking for a few men with leadership capabilities to become crewmen on a group of helicopters that were called the Sealords. They asked me if I was interested. I told them that the only reason I was working in the ordnance shop was because I refused to be a door gunner, and that even though I wasn't particularly thrilled about my job, my attitude towards manning a weapon hadn't changed. They smiled and said that was fine. The Sealord helicopters were called slicks, birds without any weaponry. I was still skeptical. Up to that point I had never given any thought to being on a helicopter crew. I had never even flown in one. They told me to come with them and they would give me a test ride to see how I liked it. So, before I knew it, I was strapped into the back seat of a chopper. They had arranged for me to go with a pilot who was taking a helicopter on a maintenance hop just to check it out and make sure everything was functioning properly. When he saw that he had a rookie passenger in his bird he decided to have a little fun. He took off and started making the tightest turns he possibly could. Of course when a helicopter turns it also tilts and you get the feeling that you're going to fall out. They always flew with the doors open so I got the full effect on every turn. I was grabbing on to anything I could, even though my seat strap was keeping me securely in the helicopter. The pilot and the co-pilot were both enjoying themselves and laughed every time they saw the look of terror in my face. This was more scary than any thrill ride at Cedar Point. It also was much more exciting, and before we landed I was hooked on helicopter flight. I wanted to be a Sealord.

The Sealord's main mission was to serve as a sort of pick up and delivery service to and from the Seawolf detachments in the field. They would deliver mail and supplies and also shuttle high ranking officers to wherever they wanted to go. There was even a special interior for the helicopter that was installed whenever an Admiral would ride with the Sealords. It all sounded good to me. With the Sealords I would get to fly but I wouldn't ever have to shoot a gun. I felt like I could have my cake and eat it too.

Immediately I left the ordnance shop and started in on my Sealord training. I didn't go to any formal schools though. It was all on the job training and it would take several weeks working in the line shack learning all about helicopter maintenance and pre-flight checks before I would actually get to go up in one again.

Getting into the Sealords really changed my attitude about being in Vietnam. It gave me a sense of purpose towards being there. I was excited about the prospect of flying everyday. The terrible homesickness gradually left, and I found myself counting the days until I would fly again instead of the days till I would be able to leave Vietnam. That all changed in a couple of weeks.

I was just about ready to be assigned to my own helicopter when I got called in from the line shack to see my Executive Officer. He told me that they had just received word that my father had suffered another major heart attack and was not expected to live. My family had requested that I be allowed to return home. He told me that I could receive a two-week emergency leave and asked me what I wanted to do. I thought for a moment, then said, "I guess I better go home."

My travel arrangements were hastily made, and before I knew it I was back on a plane to Saigon, and then on a jet back to the United States. I didn't even have time to get a dress uniform, and I had to travel in my olive drab work clothes. When I got to the States I ran into some Navy officer who took exception to the fact that I was traveling in my Vietnam field uniform. He wasn't going to let me finish my travel until I was properly dressed. He let me go after he was told of my extenuating circumstances.

It took 36 hours to get to Cleveland, and I thought that there was no way my father would still be alive. Fran picked me up at the Cleveland airport and told me that my father had made a dramatic recovery. He was in stable condition. He was so stable, in fact, that we had time for me to go and take a much needed shower before we went to the hospital to visit him. After a couple of days of visiting my father I realized he was in no imminent danger and Fran and I decided to take a couple days and get away all by ourselves. We went to Cedar Point and we really enjoyed just being together. We made up for the missed opportunity of saying good-bye before I left for Vietnam. I had the chance to tell her all the things that were going on over there.

Later that week, my father's doctors told us that it was doubtful that my father would ever be able to work again. They suggested that I might be eligible for a hardship discharge from the Navy so that I could remain home and help take care of my father. This led to some pretty intense discussions between Fran and me about what I should do. Although I was excited about my new position with the Sealords, my brief visit home had caused my original feelings towards Vietnam to return. I had no desire to go back to that horrid place. My premonitions about something bad happening to me there also returned. I was all for getting the discharge and staying home. But Fran had a different point of view. She didn't think I should give up my Navy career so easily. She didn't want us to be obligated to taking care of my parents for the rest of their lives. Most of all, she didn't want me to quit on something that I had committed to, even if it meant going back to a place where I didn't want to go. She wanted me to finish what I started and was pretty adamant about it, too. In the end, she won out and I agreed to go back to Vietnam, even if I was sure I was going to die there.

In the time left of my two week leave at home I relieved my feelings of dread by bragging to everybody about how when I got back to Vietnam the Navy was going to give me my own helicopter. By the time I had to leave home and I boarded my plane in Cleveland, I was resigned to my fate of eleven more months in Vietnam and I was going to make the best of it.

8

I returned to Vietnam not as a FNG (f****** new guy) but as a veteran. My surroundings at Bien Thuy were old hat. I was an accepted member of the Seawolves and the Sealords. I felt good being with my buddies again, and the feelings of homesickness quickly diminished. I was anxious to finish my training and to start flying. I even skipped my final school, the one that would have given me my wings to pin on my uniform. I didn't care about any wing pins. I just wanted to be up in a helicopter. I was assigned to be a crewman under another crew chief to finish my training before I was given my own bird. I was very excited about my job, and I was very proud of what I was doing, too. Nothing I had ever done in the past compared to what I was doing. Nothing ever gave me more satisfaction. For the first time in my life I had a real purpose. I was amazed that the Navy entrusted me with the care of a $500,000 piece of equipment. I had real responsibilities. I was responsible for the pilots. I was responsible for the passengers. I was responsible for delivering mail and supplies. I was responsible for picking up guys from the detachments so they could go home. With these responsibilities also came the respect of my peers. The pilots, though much higher in rank, treated me as a friend and an equal. We all relied on one another, and did our jobs accordingly.

I flew every chance I got, and I logged a lot of hours in the air. We were supposed to fill out forms after every time we flew so that we could be eligible for flight commendations. I didn't care about ribbons and medals, and I didn't fill out too many of the forms. Sometimes the pilots would fill them out for me. I was just overjoyed to be flying.

Life around Binh Thuy was fairly quiet, but every now and then you were reminded that you were in Vietnam, and there was a war going on. Often we heard the sounds of nearby mortar attacks. Our base was pretty safe from attacks, and only occasionally would the base be on alert. Some of the older guys said it was due to the fact that our neighbor, the owners of the concrete factory, paid off the Viet Cong not to attack the area. Every once in a while, late at night, we could see the "Cyclops" circling our base. The Cyclops was a gunship equipped with powerful lights that could illuminate a small area like it was daylight. As they would circle they would draw fire from the Viet Cong. They would follow the tracer bullets and then they would hover over an area, shining their bright light at the tracer's source. Next thing you knew, you would hear the sound of machine gun fire and a steady red glowing stream would pour out of the gunship. After a minute the lights would go off, and the chopper would be on its way again. Although this was a thrilling site to see from our base, it was also sobering to realize how close the enemy was to us.

The nearest village to the base at Binh Thuy was Binh Si Moi. It was known as a liberty town and wasn't much more than a few ramshackle buildings that housed makeshift bars that capitalized on soldiers and sailors with lots of piasters and no place else to spend them. New guys weren't allowed off the base until they had been in country for a while. Eventually a seasoned veteran would take the new guys to town and teach them the ropes. Just like in Saigon, there were lots of thieves and you didn't want to be caught all alone in the village. Mostly the guys went there to drink and to sit and talk to the pretty little Vietnamese women. As soon as they saw servicemen, they would go up to them and say, "Buy me a tea, G.I." That was all that was required for their attention, but at 300 piasters a cup, they made pretty good money. I suppose they made money other ways too, but being a happily married man, I wasn't interested in conversing with them, or anything else. At first I didn't spend a lot of time in Binh Si Moi, as I wasn't much of a drinker. I spent most of my free time working out and keeping myself in shape.

When I did go to town, I would try to engage any of the locals that spoke English in conversation. I wanted to find out how they felt about the war, and us being there. Most of them considered it "the United States war". I came to Vietnam with the idealistic view that the Vietnamese people would be embracing us as we fought to get them their freedom. What I found out was that most Vietnamese didn't care about freedom. They didn't even know what it meant. They were just simple rice farmers who got displaced from their land while we fought a war that they didn't want. It wasn't just the Viet Cong that hated us. The South Vietnamese people hated us too. They wanted us to get out of Vietnam so that they could return to their homes and get back to their simple, peaceful lives.

I loved my job, though. If I could have done it in a country at peace, I would have felt I was in heaven. My passion was flying. We flew all over the Mekong Delta, which encompassed most of southern Vietnam. Sometimes our missions would take us near the Cambodian border to the east. When you saw it from the air, away from the fighting and poverty, Vietnam was a beautiful place. We flew into some dangerous areas, too. Although we were not a gunship, I had to keep a few survival weapons on board in case we crashed or had to make an emergency landing. We had three rifles, some ammunition, and a grenade launcher on board. Part of my pre-flight check was to make sure these items were where they were supposed to be, and that they were operational. I hoped that I never would have to use them, remembering my short experience at survival school.

Fran wrote me nearly every day and I tried to write her as often, too. As I started flying more, I didn't have the time to write as much. I also couldn't tell her what I was doing, or where I was flying, as the missions became more dangerous. My mom would write me, and my dad would write me when I didn't write my mom enough. After a while the letters just left me with an empty feeling. Home was so far away, it was better not to think about it.

After three months, I was one of the "old guys" at our base. I was made a crew chief and was given my own helicopter, which was mine alone to take care of. The helicopters the Seawolves had were Bell UH-1B armed helicopters, which were hand-me-downs from the Army. Until Vietnam, the Navy didn't have any helicopter gunships. Since they were Army surplus, they had already seen a lot of service before the Navy got them. Most of them needed a lot of rejuvenation before they were ready to be used in Seawolf missions. My bird was a Bell UH-1L which was a little different than the gunships that the Seawolves flew. Besides being unarmed, my ship was bigger than the UH-1Bs. It was equipped with a winch and a hook so it could pick up and fly with large cargo attached to it. Although we weren't allowed to personalize our helicopters, like naming them after our wives and sweethearts like they did in World War II, I still took a lot of pride in my bird and did my best to keep it spotlessly clean. The engines ran on jet fuel, which would leave a trail of black soot and cover the tail sections of the chopper. I found some white hand soap that not only removed the black soot, but also left the tail section looking quite shiny clean. Aside from cleaning the bird, I had to do regular maintenance checks. I took my job very seriously. I never heard any complaints from any of the pilots that flew my bird about its mechanical condition. One time we went out on a mission to pick up an Army crew that had crashed their helicopter. When we landed at the pick up spot I jumped out of my helicopter and did my normal routine after every time we landed anywhere. I checked all of the stabilizers for any damage, and examined the bird for anything that might cause a problem. The Army pilots saw me and were amazed. They said, "If we had crewmen like you, we wouldn't have crashed." I took a lot of pride in my work, and it was gratifying to have it noticed by others.

I loved the work, but it wasn't easy. A twelve-hour day would seem like a cake walk. Most of the time we were working 16–18 hour days. We would take off at 6:00 A.M. and wouldn't get back to the base until 10:00 P.M.. Some days we just delivered mail, and some days we would be shuttling Admirals and Commodores around. Sometimes, if one of our buddies needed some flight time, we'd take them along on our missions. Four hours of flight time a month meant an extra $50 in pay. Most of our missions were uneventful, but sometimes we'd fly over a hot area and could see firefights taking place on the ground. Occasionally someone would try to shoot at us from the ground, but we could see the tracer bullets fall way short of their target. We flew much too high for rifles to hit us.

Some days were more exciting and rewarding than others. Since my helicopter was equipped with a winch and hook, it was used in a lot of training flights for pilots. I hated those training flights. All we would do was fly around the base picking things up and putting them back down. I wanted to get out into the country and do something worthwhile. One day, I was assigned a training flight, and as I was getting ready I noticed that there were eight bags of mail sitting on the loading dock that was supposed to be delivered to a little base near the Cambodian border. I went to the officer of the day and said, "Let me take that mail." He said, "No. You've got pilot training. Leave that mail alone." I was angry. As I did my pre-flight check I noticed that a small rubber bushing had worn off of the cargo hook. It didn't really make much difference in the way it worked, but I saw it as an opportunity to get off of pilot training for a day. I called to the officer of the day and pointed out the minor defect. I told him, "I can't train anybody today with the hook in this condition." He sighed at me and said, "Alright, what do you want to do?" I said, "Give me those bags of mail." It was easy for me to get the pilots to buy into this impromptu mission. We loaded the bags and flew out to a little river boat base. Basically, it was nothing more than a dock in the middle of a rice paddy. There was a small landing platform that was built on stilts in the water. There was also a small barracks, also built on stilts. There was nothing else around there. I never saw anything that was so isolated. The guys that were stationed at this base had literally nowhere to go. There was no town, no club, no nothing. They only got mail about once every three weeks, and we were circling over them about to make the delivery. The pilot called to the base to get clearance to land. We could tell that the guy who answered the radio was high. In a gruff voice he said, "What the hell you want to come here for?" The pilot told him we had mail to deliver. The guy answered, "You better not be lying, or you'll never leave this base alive." So much for warm welcomes. Fortunately, the rest of the guys on the base were overjoyed to see us. By the time we landed they were all out of the barracks and cheering us as we threw the mailbags out of the chopper. They were so excited about getting mail that they started handing it out right there on the landing pad. They were so grateful that we came, they insisted on making a special meal for us. Somehow the Navy had given them some little lobsters as part of their provisions, so they made the pilots a nice lobster dinner. I didn't eat lobster, so they made me an elegant dinner out of hot dogs. I really enjoyed spending a little time with them, and felt that this mail mission was one of the most worthwhile things I could have done. There was something I noticed there, though, that made me feel bad. One of the guys there got only one piece of mail, and it was a bill from a jewelry store for some ring he bought for his girlfriend. There was no letter from the girlfriend; just the bill from the jewelry store. I could just imagine how bad this guy felt, that after three weeks of being isolated in a rice paddy in some foreign country in the middle of a war, and all he got from home was a bill. It made me realize how forgotten some of the guys became in Vietnam.

Most of the missions I went on were pretty routine. We delivered mail and supplies and took high ranking officers to meetings. Sometimes these meetings would take place in the middle of nowhere, with just a concrete landing pad. The pilots and the officers would leave for the meeting and I was told to stay with the helicopter until they returned. Sometimes they'd be gone for several hours. After the first few times, I got wise. I cut off my Navy dungarees, and after they'd leave, I'd take off my flight suit and I'd sunbathe on the landing pads wearing only my newly made shorts. I never minded those missions after that.

About that time I started falling into another routine. I started drinking pretty heavily. I don't know exactly why I did it, whether it was because all my buddies did it, whether it was because it was the only thing we had to do in our free time, or whether it was to ease the homesickness pain. Whatever the reason, I drank a lot. At the time I was making about $300 a month and I wasn't saving any of it, or sending any home. I was drinking it all away. It was easy to do because most everybody there did it. My job had me on duty for 24 hours, then off duty for 24 hours. Those off duty hours gave me plenty of time to drink. As a crew chief, I wasn't supposed to drink any alcohol for 12 hours preceding a mission. Pilots were supposed to refrain for 24 hours before. Nobody did though. Part of my pre-flight check was to make sure we had lots of canteens on board filled with water. The water was necessary to help with the hangovers that invariably everyone on board always had. I guess I knew I was a long way from home, and that nobody was looking over my shoulder.

Eventually, our missions got to be more and more dangerous. It wasn't because of what we were doing, but because of where we were flying. The Navy started classifying these more dangerous flights as Special Missions 1 and 2. They also decided that to go on these special missions I would need to have guns installed in my helicopter. I whined and complained but, basically, I was told that if I wanted to continue flying I would have to learn to be a door gunner. If I didn't want to be a door gunner I could always go back to the ordnance shop. One of my buddies told me, "Charlie, they're going to get us killed." He quit flying and went back to ordnance. I guess my love for flying was greater than my non-violent beliefs, because I reluctantly agreed to learn to be a door gunner.

Now you would think with my background with hunting and skeet shooting I would have no problem shooting at a target with a machine gun. You would think I'd even enjoy it. But at first, I was absolutely terrible as a door gunner. They would take me up in my helicopter and throw wooden pallets into the river as targets and I would blast away, never even coming close to hitting them. One time they even dropped a 55 gallon drum figuring that I couldn't miss that. I used up a whole box of ammunition, and nearly melted the barrel of the gun, and never hit it. I think a big part of my failure to hit anything was that I was doing it half-heartedly. I didn't really want to be shooting a gun out of a moving helicopter, and I didn't care whether I hit anything or not. The only reason I was doing it was so I could continue to fly.

Finally, they brought in their best teacher, Bill Rutledge. They told me that if I still couldn't hit anything after he was through with me, that it would be the end of my flying career. Bill was very patient with me, and taught me how to track a target. He showed me how to watch for my tracer bullets, and then to just let that tracer line move right over the target. All of a sudden it was easy. I passed my door gunner qualifying test, and I was back in business.

They put a fixed gun mount in my helicopter, and we started doing special missions. On one of my first special missions we were sent to a riverboat detachment to pick up the bodies of some Vietnamese sailors. They died when the riverboat they were crewmen on was mined by the Viet Cong in the middle of the night while they were all sleeping. Seven of them died. As if that wasn't bad enough, because of when it happened, and where it happened, it took a week before their bodies were recovered. They finally floated up from the river bottom, and were put in body bags. When we arrived at the detachment Reb, my crewman, and I loaded the seven body bags onto my bird. There wasn't much room for cargo to begin with, and seven body bags made it a pretty tight fit. We ended up having to sit on the body bags. As soon as I sat down, I could feel the water-logged body in the bag squish. I immediately jumped up and told Reb, "I can't do this." I jumped off my helicopter, and jumped onto another that had landed next to us, and I flew back to the base with them. I should have got in trouble over that, but I guess the Navy was pretty understanding, considering the circumstances.

Out of all the special missions I went on, I remember the ones where we picked up bodies the most. It caused me to understand the grim realities of that war, which was that young men were dying. It never became a routine to pick up a body. I never became hardened to the point where my heart didn't ache every time I picked up one of those black plastic body bags. I was especially moved when it was one of our own that I had to pick up. Gradually, I began to feel different when I had to man the door gun. Whereas before, I couldn't even conceive the idea of shooting anybody, I found myself beginning not to care. I didn't care about the Vietnamese, but I cared about my buddies. If I had to shoot someone to keep them from killing one of my friends, so be it.

One memory of a special mission is very poignant. We flew to Det 6, which was at Song Ong Doc. It was a riverboat base, and the personnel there were quartered in what looked like plywood barges. The Viet Cong had mortared and rocketed the base, and we had to bring in extra body bags as there were a lot of casualties. As I went to pick up one of dead sailors, the commanding officer told me that the young man had been burned so bad that he melted right into his metal cot frame. I picked up the body bag and started to take it back to my helicopter. The CO said to me, "You know, he used to be as big as you are." That really hit me hard. Up until then all the body bags had been nondescript. They were pretty much all the same, and I never related to them. Now I had a point of reference. The body bag I was carrying contained the remains of someone who was just like me. It brought into stark reality what was really going on in Vietnam. I loaded the body into the helicopter, and we were about to take off when the pilot turned around to me and asked, "What's that horrible smell?" I explained that we had a body that had been burned up real bad. The pilot said, "I'm sorry, but we can't take him." I had to take him out and put him on the dock. As we flew away, I stared at that solitary body bag sitting on the dock.

Two days later we had to fly back to Song Ong Doc to pick up a Commodore who was assessing the damage done to the base. As he walked towards my helicopter, he passed by the body bag that was still lying on the dock. He asked me if I knew who was in the bag. I told him, "It's one of our own, Sir." He said, "Well, we can't leave him here. We're taking him with us." I was glad because I knew that the pilot would have to follow the Commodore's orders. So I loaded him up into the helicopter again. The Commodore got in, and as soon as he sat down he got a sick look on his face. He looked at me and said, "I'm sorry, son. We can't take him." Once again, as we took off, I stared at the lone body bag sitting on the dock. A sense of overwhelming sadness came over me. It was bad enough that a young man had to die in the middle of nowhere while serving his country, but now we couldn't even get his charred remains back to his grieving family. I felt helpless. I found out that an Army medevac chopper eventually picked him up. The bad feelings I had over that incident stayed with me for a long time.

However troubling that incident was, it didn't stop me from going on special missions. In fact, I started requesting every special mission that was offered, and, being the senior man in our group, I usually got what I requested. I was flying a lot. When I was flying it was easy to forget the pain, heartache, and misery that was below me. Then came the monsoons. I've never seen so much rain, so continuous. It was always raining. It rained so hard that I saw entire islands disappear. The constant rain also caused a lot of sickness among the Seawolf crewmen. Whenever we landed, the crewman was the first person out of the helicopter. He would direct the pilots to the parking place, and then tie down the rotors. We would always be soaking wet. Then we would take off again, and we'd fly at high altitudes where it got very cold. We'd be in the chopper shivering in our soaked clothes. A lot of guys caught colds, and because of the effect on the eardrums we weren't allowed to fly. Since I was able to avoid catching colds, I ended up flying everyday to take up the slack created by the sick crewmen.

It was during this time of flying everyday that I noticed two small sores on my right arm. I couldn't figure out how I got them, or where they came from. Gradually, there were red lines that extended from the sores up my arm to my shoulder. Then the red lines started going down my back and my arm started to hurt a lot. I went to see our corpsman and he took one look at me and told me I had blood poisoning. He gave me a shot of penicillin, and some antibiotic pills, and told me I shouldn't fly for two weeks. I went and told my CO the bad news. He said, "We might be able to find someone to fly for you tomorrow, but we're going to need to get the daily maintenance done on the bird today." So I went out and started working on my helicopter. Well, apparently the corpsman reported my condition to the company doctor, who just happened to be walking by the flight line and saw me working on my bird. He started yelling at me in front of everybody, and I was pretty embarrassed. He ordered me grounded for two weeks starting immediately. So, I had nothing to do for two weeks except to go to the enlisted man's club and drink. A couple of days later I was in the club drinking when the corpsman walked in. He came over and asked me what I was doing. I said, "Well, I'm grounded for two weeks so I'm drinking." He said, "You can't drink while you're taking those antibiotics. I said, "Okay", and I stopped taking the antibiotics. I saved the pills and used them for guys that had ailments that they didn't want the corpsman to find out about. I became a pretty popular pharmacist. I stayed pretty much drunk the entire two weeks. My arm got better, too.

After my two-week convalescence, I went right back to flying special missions. I always wanted to go on them, but the more special missions I flew, the more bad things I saw. And the more bad things I saw, the more depressed I became. I didn't care about much of anything, not even home. I even started to lose my religious beliefs. I figured God couldn't really be around if there was such a horrible place like Vietnam. How could a loving God allow such suffering to go on. My church back home would send me a package every month that contained some communion wafers. After a while those packages remained unopened. I was turning more and more to alcohol to help ease my pain. I thought that all that I had were my friends there in Vietnam, and booze. And, since all my friends in Vietnam loved to drink, it was easy for me to get lost in a bottle every day.

Most of the missions I flew went smoothly, without a hitch, but with all the missions I was flying there were bound to be those that had problems. There was one day where I was training a new guy. We were making short hops to detachments, delivering supplies and mail. It was just routine stuff, nothing really dangerous. Bill Rutledge, the door gunner instructor, was assigned to my helicopter that day to train the rookie on how to fire the gun. About halfway through the day he got tired or bored or both, and decided he was going back to the barracks to take a nap. He told me that if anything came up I should just send for him and he'd be right there. I was showing the rookie some maintenance routines when a call came through from a riverboat that had been attacked. They requested a medevac for the wounded. I told the rookie to run to the barracks and get Bill. He started pleading with me, "C'mon, Charlie. Let me go. I'm ready." I said, "No way. This ain't no mission for a rookie. Go get Bill." He continued pleading, and by this time the pilot was ready to take off. Because of the urgency of the call, I finally relented and told the rookie, "Let's go."

The riverboat was ambushed by a Viet Cong rocket attack away from its base, so there was nowhere to land but on the bow of the small boat. That was a pretty tricky maneuver, as the pilot had to hover gently over the bow as I got off to help get the injured in. As soon as I jumped out onto the bow, about a half dozen little Vietnamese sailors scrambled by me and jumped into the helicopter. The worst injury I could see was a few scratches. It turned out that the boat was manned by a Vietnamese crew, with one U.S. Navy advisor on board. I wasn't too happy about the situation. We came all the way out there to pick up critically injured when, in fact, they could have been treated with a little iodine and some band-aids. I looked at the Navy advisor and he shook his head and said, "Sorry."

I jumped back on the helicopter, and we were just getting ready to take off when the nitwit who was driving the boat decided he needed to back the boat up. So he starts moving while we're still hovering on the bow. I thought, "Oh great. I'm gonna get wet for sure. We're going in the river." Fortunately, we had about the best helicopter pilot in the Navy that day, and he reacted quickly giving the bird full power. It shuddered and strained and lifted off just in time.

So, there we were. The rookie manning the gun on the right door, and me on the left door, with a pile of supposedly injured Vietnamese sailors in between us. Because of where we were flying, we had a gunship escort for this mission, and, for some reason, he decided to lead us on a shortcut across a rice paddy instead of following the river like we were supposed to do. A short distance from where the riverboat was, we stumbled on the Viet Cong who had done the ambush. As soon as they saw us, they started firing at us. The gunship got hit, taking a bullet through its belly that went through one of the pilot's legs. As our helicopter came over the Viet Cong, they were on the right, out the door where the rookie was. On my side there was nothing, except for a village. I had nothing to shoot at. The rookie got scared and froze. I kept yelling at him over the radio to shoot his gun, but he just sat there terrified. There was no way I could climb over all of the Viet-namese sailors to get over to his side. I just had to ride it out. Fortunately, we weren't hit and we made it back to the base unharmed.

When we landed, the crew from the gunship ran over and started screaming at me. "Why didn't you fire at them. You could have gotten us all killed. What's the matter with you?" I just stood there and took the abuse without making any excuses or blaming the rookie. I figured it was my fault for letting a rookie go out on a potentially dangerous mission, something I would never do again. After the tirade was over, one of my buddies, who had been watching this whole episode, looked at me and flipped me a little pack of cigarettes that came with our "C" rations. I hadn't smoked in over two years but I immediately lit one up. When I got back to the base, I went over to the PX and bought a whole carton of ciga-rettes. I smoked for the remainder of my tour in Vietnam.

It wasn't always bad times in Vietnam. There were good times, too, most of which revolved around the close friendships that developed while we were there. It was more than friendship, really. We were family, and we all looked out for one another. We also enjoyed being together, whether it was on base or off. When one of us would be going home, it was time for a celebration. Sometimes our celebrations got us in trouble, but that was all part of the fun. One time, one of our crew had completed his tour and was going home. On his last night there I told him, "Come on. We're going to town." He was pretty nervous and said, "Aw, Charlie. I don't want to get in any trouble tonight. I'm just staying here. I said, "What can happen? Just a couple of goodbye drinks with your buddies, come on." Reluctantly, he agreed, and we all went to town and had a fine time together, getting a little drunk in the process. We continued our carousing on the bus back to the base. I started singing my favorite song, the "Fixin' to Die Rag". Well, there was this Army guy in the front of the bus that took exception to the singing of a war protest song on a military bus. He got up and started yelling at us. "I'm sick and tired of you Navy hippies and your protest songs. If you don't like this war, then get the hell out of here." I knew that he belonged to the truck pool at the Army base, so I yelled back at him, "We see more action by accident than you truck drivers ever see on purpose." That did it. The Army guy said, "I'm going to kick your ass, sailor." So I stood up and said, "Well come on back here and try." When I stood up, he saw how big I was and he said, "Well, I might not be able to whip your ass, but this will" and he reached in his jacket pocket and pulled out a revolver. He started coming down the aisle threatening to blow my head off, so I jumped behind the guy who was on his way home the next day. He started screaming, "Get out of here, Charlie. I'm going home tomorrow and I'm not going to get shot now. Get away from me and let him shoot you." I jumped back and hid behind a seat thinking, "What are they going to tell my family? 'He was shot on a bus while singing a war protest song.'" Luckily, one of our guys was also carrying a gun, and he came up behind the Army guy and stuck it in his neck. He told him to drop his gun, and he did. We booted him off the bus, but not before I gave him a stern lecture about how it was bad enough that we had the Viet Cong shooting us, that we shouldn't have to worry about Americans shooting us too. Anyhow, I'm sure that the guy who went home the next day has a lasting memory of his last day in Vietnam.

Like most families, there were all kinds of age difference in our group. One of our "kid brothers" was Tony, who was 17 when he enlisted. He trained with us in California, but they held him there until he turned 18 before they sent him to be with us in Vietnam. He was a very likable and good looking kid. We all took great pride in taking care of him and teaching him the ropes. He was going to be sent out on assignment to Det 3, and the night before he left, we took him into town for a night of drinking. There was no drinking age limit in Vietnam. If you were old enough to fight, you were old enough to drink. During the course of the evening there was a little Vietnamese girl that took a special liking to Tony, and was paying him a lot of attention. Later, Tony came to me and said, "Charlie, she wants me to go upstairs with her. What do I do?" I said, "Heck, do whatever you want. We'll wait for you." It didn't take him long to make up his mind, and he bounded up the stairs. We waited and waited for him to come back down. I was beginning to wonder what was taking him so long. Finally, he comes back down and he's madder than a hornet. "They took $25 from me." I laughed. "What did you think, they were going to let you have it for free?" He said "No. They took my $25 but the girl never came back. Now what are you going to do about it?" I started laughing again but I could see that he wasn't going to go anywhere until he got some satisfaction. I said, "Come on. Let's get out of here." We were sitting at a small bar table, and after I stood up, I took my foot and smashed that table into splinters. It made a pretty loud noise and the other people in the bar, sensing trouble, cleared out. I walked out the screen door ripping it off its hinges in the process. When we were outside, I turned to Tony and said, "Well, was that worth $25 to you?" He smiled and said, "Yeah."

I saw Tony only occasionally after that. I'd see him if I flew a mission out to Det 3, or if he brought a helicopter into Bin Thuy for some service. One day, he flew in and I was able to spend a little time with him before I had to leave on a mission. I didn't return to the base until late at night. After we landed, a group of my buddies came over, and I could tell by the looks on their faces that something was terribly wrong. They told me that Tony's helicopter was shot down on the way back to Det 3, and that all four that were aboard had died. I was stunned. I had seen lots of death in my few months in Vietnam, but never had it been so close. He was so young and so full of life. He was my baby brother, and now he was gone. I immediately went to the Enlisted Man's Club and started drowning my sorrows. All my buddies from the base were coming over to me and telling me how sorry they were. I appreciated their concern and their sympathy, but I really wanted to be alone, so I took off into town to really tie one on. I was well on my way to oblivion when my buddy Chuck came running into the bar. Excitedly, he came over to me and said, "I figured I'd find you here. Did you hear the news? Tony got bumped off of that flight this afternoon. He went back to Det 3 later. Charlie, Tony's alive." Now I didn't know what to feel. I was overjoyed that my little buddy Tony was alive. But I still felt terrible that we lost four of our own that day. That's how it was in Vietnam. There was always something bad to temper the good.

One of the benefits of being a Sealord was that I was permanently assigned to the base at Bin Thuy. I didn't have to worry about being assigned to a detachment. There were nine Seawolf Dets, all over the Mekong Delta. Each Det had two or three helicopters, and four or five crews. The purpose of having Dets was to be able to respond to the needs of the riverboats and firebases more quickly. Whenever there was trouble, a call came over the radio, "Scramble Seawolves" and the nearest Det would respond. Det 1 was probably the most remote. It was at the southernmost tip of Vietnam, away from any town or village. I felt sorry for the guys who got assigned there. I remember one time going there and seeing a lone body bag laying by the loading dock. I found out the boy in the body bag committed suicide. The loneliness of Det 1, coupled with a "Dear John" letter from home, sent him over the edge. When I heard this I got angry with everyone back in the States. They had no idea of what it was like in Vietnam. How could they be so insensitive to guys whose only things to look forward to was a letter from home and the day when they would be able to return. I really believed that to most people in the United States we were just forgotten young men.

I tried to do anything I could to make the guys lives at the Det a little brighter. On one mission to Det 1, we were picking up some crates of ammunition and grenades to take back to a firebase. As I was loading the heavy crates in the back of the helicopter, a guy carrying a sea bag came up to me and said, "I need a ride to Can Tho." I told him that we had to get this ammo back to the base, but that we could come back later and get him. He said, "You don't understand. I'm going home, and if I don't make my flight at Can Tho today, it's going to be two weeks before I can get another one." I thought for a minute. With all of the crates I had loaded already, there was no room for a passenger. But the pleading look in the eyes of this sailor really touched me. I went up to the pilot and asked him if he would mind making two trips back to the base. He looked at the sailor standing there with his sea bag, and I guess he figured out the situation. He said, "Whatever you want to do, Charlie." So I started unloading some of the ammo crates and putting them back on the loading dock. All of a sudden this supply officer comes running out, and he's screaming at me. "What are you doing? You've got to get this ammo back to the base." I said, "Don't worry. We'll be back. We're just going to drop this sailor off at Can Tho, and we'll come back and get the rest of this." The supply officer got even madder. "I'm telling you, you're taking this ammo back right now." And I calmly said, "I'm telling you, we're taking this sailor to Can Tho so he can catch his flight home." The supply officer turned to the pilot. "This man's refusing to do a direct order. You tell him he's got to take the ammo." The pilot said, "It's his bird, and I'll do whatever he says to do." We took off leaving a frustrated supply officer standing on the loading dock next to the crates of ammo. We got that sailor to his flight on time, and the appreciation that was in his eyes as he jumped off our helicopter made it worth all the trouble I knew I was going to be in when I got back to the base.

In my letters to home, I never mentioned the bad things I saw and experienced in Vietnam. First, I didn't want to worry them, but also I didn't think that they would understand. About the only person that I thought might be able to comprehend what I was going through was my father. From the little bits and pieces he told me of his war experience, I knew that some of his experiences mirrored mine. One time, I thought that I would unburden myself and write a letter to my dad telling him about what was going on in Vietnam. I wrote it to be read by him alone, and I really bared my soul to him, seeking his advice on how to deal with these war related issues. He never acknowledged receiving that letter. I still don't know if he ever got it. Throughout the rest of his life, I never asked him about it. I never opened up like that to anyone again. I decided I'd have to deal with my problems on my own.

9

Around Thanksgiving, I, along with several other crewmen and pilots, were chosen to go to a jungle survival school in the Philippines. We were all pretty glad to be able to get out of Vietnam for a while. We went to the Subic Bay Naval Base and were pretty excited about it. We heard stories of the great nightlife off the base in town, and were looking forward to going to some bars that had a little more ambiance than the ones in the little village at Bin Thuy. Unfortunately, when we got there the base was in lockdown, which meant we weren't allowed off the base at all. It seems there was an incident that occurred just before we arrived. There was a lot of racial tension in the Philippines, and in the towns there were defined areas for blacks and whites. It was an unwritten law that you did not cross the defining lines. Apparently one young sailor on liberty didn't know about this, and went into a club where he didn't belong. He was thrown out of a third story window and died. So when we arrived we found ourselves stuck on the base. The first night we were there some of the pilots took pity on us and snuck us in to the officer's club. It was really nice, but probably a little too sophisticated for our behavior. While we were there, a group of Australian sailors came in and we struck up an immediate friendship with them. Aussies aren't known as wallflowers, and the more we drank, the more raucous we became. I don't remember a whole lot about that evening. I vaguely recall spilling a few drinks on some officer's wives. I know the pilots were told never to bring us in there again.

I really liked the school. It was only 1½ days long, but I learned a lot. For 24 hours we were taken out into the jungle and taught survival skills by some authentic jungle dwellers. We were taught about edible jungle vegetation and how to make cooking utensils out of bamboo. They taught us how to catch fish using surgical tubing and the firing pin out of an M60. We had a nice dinner of steamed fish and rice that evening. The remaining half of the day was spent learning camouflage techniques. We tried to avoid capture by blending in with the jungle. This time, though, we were not beat up when we got caught.

At the base there was a little Philippino tailor that came on the base with a catalog of clothes that he could make while you were there. You would pick out what you wanted from the catalog, he would take some measurements, and the next day you got your clothes. At that time I didn't own any civilian clothes, so I got myself a couple of outfits. I thought I was really something special wearing my big bell bottomed pants and a jacket with the wide lapel. I looked like something out of "Saturday Night Fever". I was ready to strut my stuff.

Done with the school, we still had a few days left to spend as we wished. Rather than spend it on the base, a bunch of us found a newly built hotel outside the city that was really nice. It had a swimming pool and air-conditioned rooms and good food, too. Some of the guys even found companions that stayed with them for the two days we were there. I was happy just to be in a relaxed atmosphere. I had just been promoted to E4 and, as such, I was unofficially responsible to make sure that the guys didn't get into too much trouble. We were a little late getting back to the base for our flight back to Vietnam and I got a stern lecture from the officers about the responsibilities associated with increased rank. I thought, "Who cares about rank when you're with your friends?" Overall, we had a good time in the Philippines. It was a brief respite from the misery we returned to in Vietnam.

When I got back to Bin Thuy, it was life as usual in Vietnam. I was flying missions and taking care of my helicopter. I was getting pretty used to my life by then. When Christmas came, though, my attitude changed. There was a two-day cease fire and the base was eerily quiet without the sounds of gunfire and mortar attacks. I thought to myself, "If they can cease firing for two days, why can't they just cease fire forever?" It just didn't make any sense to me. Then I got really homesick. This was my first Christmas ever away from home and family. I laid in my bunk and listened to the Bob Hope USO Christmas show on the radio. It was the first time that I cried since I arrived in Vietnam. It had been six months since I saw my wife. I was lonely and depressed and I spent the entire Christmas day in my bunk.

After six months in Vietnam you became eligible for a one week, out of country R & R (Rest and Relaxation). Some of the guys would go to Hawaii and meet their families there. Since Fran didn't fly, that wasn't an option for me. I didn't want to go anywhere alone, so I made arrangements to go with my buddy Chuck Wright. He was nearing his eleventh month in Vietnam and hadn't used his R & R yet. We decided to go to Australia. We heard a lot of good things from guys who went there, and I remembered the fun we had with the Aussie sailors at Subic Bay. Our big plans were thwarted, though, when we found out that you couldn't take your R & R in your eleventh month of service in Vietnam. It was too close to the end of your tour. So, I just gave up on the idea of an out of country excursion. I was content just to take a couple days here and there and spend them drinking in town.

It was around this time that I did another odd thing. I signed up to extend my tour in Vietnam another six months. I decided this on my own. I didn't even discuss it with Fran. I thought it was a pretty good deal. At the end of my 12 month tour I would be given a 30 day leave and I could go back home for that time. Then I would return to Vietnam for another six months. I really loved flying and I thought that the only way I could continue doing it was to stay in Vietnam. I was still going to be in the Navy anyway, so why shouldn't I spend that time doing something I really like?

I was still doing a lot of drinking. Actually, I was doing more and more. Even though we were supposed to refrain from alcohol 12 hours before we flew, I would spend my entire off days drinking and then, when my helicopter returned from a mission, I would go out to do the daily maintenance and drink some more. There were a couple of times when I almost got in serious trouble over my drinking. One time, my helicopter came back and it was pretty dirty inside. I decided to take it out back and clean it up. I had spent the day doing some pretty serious drinking, and I had a bottle of booze with me as I got ready to clean the bird up. I was wearing my heavy jungle boots and, as I was clumsily getting into the helicopter, my foot slipped and my boot got trapped in one of the entrance stairs. In my inebriated condition I fell backwards and was hanging upside down with my foot caught in the stairs and there was nothing I could do about it. Hoping somebody might be around, I started meekly calling, "Help" but since I was way out back, no one was there to hear me. Finally a guy on guard duty came walking by and heard my cry for help. Of course he called some of his buddies over to look at the spectacle I made of myself, and they all had a good laugh at my expense. Fortunately, they didn't report my drunkenness to anybody.

Then there was the day I was scheduled for a mission to Det 1. There was a big First Class Petty Officer out there named Starks who demanded that every time you came to Det 1 you bring milk and mail. If you failed to bring them, he said he would shoot you. Nobody ever tested his threat. We made sure that if we were going to Det 1 that we brought milk and mail. I did a lot of drinking the day previous to the mission, and I was feeling no pain as I did the daily maintenance on my bird the night before. I did my work, and was ready to go at 5:00 in the morning. I got a case of milk and loaded it on the helicopter. The pilots started the engine and were warming the bird up while I went to get the mail. There was nobody in the mailroom due to the regular mail clerk being on R & R, so I had to run to the barracks and get the guy up who was supposed to be doing the mail in his place. We got the mail together, and by the time I got back on board the pilots were already pretty mad at me for taking so long. I just didn't want Starks to shoot me. We took off and got about four feet off the ground and all of a sudden the engine quit and we hit the ground with a thud. Nobody got hurt, and after a quick inspection it was determined that the engine had seized. We actually were fortunate that I delayed the take off because if the engine hadn't been running for so long before we lifted off, it might have taken longer for the engine to seize, and we may have been at a much higher altitude. For now, I had to figure out what caused the engine to seize.

The worst thing that a crewman could allow to happen is to let an engine get "fodded". FOD stood for foreign object destroyed. When the big turbines started up on the helicopters they would suck anything left laying around right into the engine and destroy it. If you, as a crewman, allowed an engine to be fodded by your carelessness, it was the end of your flying career. While doing routine maintenance a crewman always carried a special tool with them in a pocket on the right sleeve of their shirt. The tool was used to get some of the cowling off of the helicopter. As I looked for my tool that morning I noticed it was missing. A cold feeling of dread came over me as I thought that it might have come out the night before while I was working on the helicopter in my drunken state. I was greatly relieved when I was told that the reason for the seized engine was a bad engine bearing. Nonetheless, my close call caused me to swear off drinking before flying.

I had other reasons to quit drinking, too. I started thinking about when I would be going home for my 30 day leave in June. I needed to start to save some money so that Fran wouldn't see me with empty pockets. I also wanted to start working out more. I wanted to look good when Fran saw me. But also, I still had to tell Fran that I signed up for another six months in Vietnam. I didn't think I would be able to convince her that it was a good idea if I had an alcoholic monkey on my back.

So I started the new year, 1971, with some resolutions to take care of myself better, and to do my job more conscientiously. I went into the chow hall on New Year's day expecting the traditional pork and sauerkraut dinner. When I found out that they were not serving it, I was a little upset. I asked the cook if he didn't know that it was bad luck not to serve pork and sauerkraut on New Year's Day. When he ignored my comments I jokingly told him, "Well, if something bad happens to me this year, it's your fault." Little did I know.

10

The new year started with some excitement for the Sealords. The Navy bought some new helicopters, and one of them was assigned to the Sealords. It was a big deal to us since we were flying old, hand-me-downs from the Army. One of my buddies got the new bird and the rest of us crewmen were envious, but glad for him too. On its first mission they were suppose to fly to Det 3 at Ca Mau. A pilot, new to the Sealords, was flying it that day. He was a young Lt. Commander who was bucking for a promotion, and thought that flying in Vietnam would put him in line for a Commander ranking. So, they took off to Det 3, which was a pretty good distance from our base. When they got there they were starting to refuel when they got a call from an LST requesting that they come and pick up something there as soon as they could. It wasn't a life or death situation, but the young pilot, eager to impress everybody he could, tells my buddy that they're taking off immediately and going to the LST. My buddy, aware of the distances involved, told him that they were running low on fuel and that they better continue refueling before heading over to the LST. The pilot, however, thought he knew better, and told my buddy to get in because they were taking off. Well, they made it about halfway to the LST before they ran out of fuel and plunged into the bay. Fortunately, everyone aboard made it out of the helicopter before it sank, and were rescued. The pilot, however, was in hot water back at the base. He had destroyed a brand new helicopter through his own stubbornness. He was grounded for the rest of his career, which delighted us crewmen. However, he was given the assignment as permanent officer of the day, which meant we would have to deal with him on a daily basis. I wasn't happy that this cocky, young officer was going to be deciding where I was going and what I was doing. I just had the sense he was going to be more trouble.

It didn't take me long to get off on the wrong foot with him. I came into the flight room one day to get my orders and found that I was going on a rather boring mission. I wasn't too happy about it and I mouthed off to my colleagues about the new officer of the day. I said, "What does he know about sending me on a mission. He can't even tell when he's running out of gas." All of a sudden it got real quiet in the room. I turned around and saw the new officer of the day standing right behind me. He uttered a few choice words describing me as some sort of big idiot. We were off to a great start.

We came out one day to find new additions to our helicopters. There were some pods installed on either side next to the doors. We weren't told what they were. We assumed they were for some kind of rocket launcher or something. Because of where they were installed, I had to change the way I mounted the guns on my helicopter. I couldn't put them on the outside of the door where they had been. I had to put them inside the door. I got the gun mounts installed and got ready for the day's mission. We were going to Rach Gia, which was a Special Mission 2 and required that we be armed. I was taking Gramps along with me. Gramps was an older, 20 year veteran of the Navy who needed some flight time to get his extra $50 for the month. He was near retirement and he came to Vietnam because he found out if he did, he could move up a grade, which meant more retirement pay. We got loaded up and mounted the M-60s when we saw a jeep headed towards us. It was the new officer of the day. He jumped out of the jeep and started yelling at me, "What do you think you're doing?" I told him we were going to Rach Gia and I was mounting our guns. He said, "You can't take guns on this mission." I said, "Well, you can't send me to Rach Gia without guns." A few months previous, the Seawolves lost a pilot and a crewman when their helicopter was shot down while on a special mission. Since then, we were very careful about with our preparation when we were going to an area where the enemy was known to be active. He proceeded to tell me that the mission was to drop off an underwater demolition team in a canal where a patrol boat had been sunk. It was blocking the canal and needed to be destroyed so that the canal would be navigable again. He said that the gun mounts would be in the way of the demolition team when they would try to exit the helicopter with all their underwater gear on. He said they wouldn't be able to get around them fast enough. Once again I argued that he couldn't expect me to go to that area with no weapons, but I quickly lost that argument and took the gun mounts out. On my way back to my helicopter, after taking the guns to the ordnance shop, I saw my buddy Chuck Wright. By that time he wasn't flying anymore and was working nights in the line shack. I would always try to have some kind of breakfast food to give to him whenever I would see him in the early morning. That day I threw him an apple and said, "I'll see you later on." I got in my bird with Gramps and we took off. It was January 9, 1971.

As fate would have it, I ended up with two rookie pilots that day. It started out that we were going to have one rookie, a Lt. Junior Grade, as the co-pilot and a combat experienced Lt. Junior Grade as the pilot. The young officer of the day decided that we couldn't have two junior grade lieutenants flying together. We needed a full lieutenant as a pilot. The only one that was available that day was another rookie and that's the way we took off that morning, with two rookie pilots at the controls.

Our first stop was an Army firebase, where we picked up a sailor whose boat was the one sunk in the canal. We were going to take him to Rach Gia where we would pick up the underwater demolition team and then he would direct us to his sunken boat. He was hoping that they might be able to retrieve some of his personal belongings off the boat before they destroyed it. While we were at the firebase, an Army helicopter landed next to us which was their "Flying PX". I had a few minutes before we were going to take off, so I went over to see what kind of goodies they were carrying. I was thrilled to find that they had cans of Oreo cookies, something that the Navy never had back at the PX at Bin Thuy. I really loved Oreos and I bought a can to take back with me. We took off and flew to the base at Rach Gia. When we arrived they fed us lunch. They served us nice roast beef sandwiches on hard rolls. After lunch I was having a cigarette with one of the sailors from the base and I told him how I got some Oreo cookies from the Army PX helicopter. His eyes lit up and he said that he hadn't had an Oreo cookie since he left home. I always felt bad for these guys who were stuck out in the boonies on these bases. They never had a chance to go to any PX. So, I gave my treasured can of Oreos to him and said, "You can have them. I can get some more." I knew that probably wasn't true, but what the heck. I had a soft spot for my sailor mates.

At the base our mission was explained to us. We would take the underwater demolition team to the sunken boat, they would blow the boat up, and we would bring them back to the base. It was pretty simple and straightforward. Nothing to worry about. I never even took my new M-16 rifle out of the overhead rack. We were getting ready to go when a Navy officer came up to my helicopter, accompanied by a group of Vietnamese officers. The Navy officer said, "Charlie, you've got to take these officers out to the site first, then come back for the demolition team." It didn't make any sense to me and I asked him why. It turned out that the underwater demolition team we were taking out was the first team of Vietnamese frogmen to be used in the war, and these Vietnamese officers wanted to witness this great event first hand.

We loaded up the Vietnamese officers and took off for the sunken boat site. We followed the canal, flying at about 1500 feet. When we saw the sunken boat in the canal we radioed to the crew on the ground to ask them where they wanted us to land. They radioed back saying they would "pop a smoke" to show us where to land. They ignited a smoke flare, which, in turn, ignited the dry grass field.

The whole landing area was on fire. Gramps and me just started laughing think-ing, "What a bunch of idiots." The pilot went in and hovered over the area and the prop wash blew out the fire. We landed in this big blackened grassy area. The officers jumped out and we got ready to go back to the base to pick up the demo-lition team. The pilot comes to me and says, "Charlie, this is taking too long, and I hate flying at 1500 ft." I explained to him that there were only two ways we were supposed to fly in this area. Either we flew above 1200 ft., or we flew as low as we could, as fast as we could. Both methods made it difficult for the VC to hit us with small arms fire. The pilot decide to try flying low and we took off flying about 8–10 feet above the canal. On the way back we passed a small village and many of the villagers and their children were outside. They all waved at us as we flew by. We made it back to Rach Gia in about 15 minutes.

We loaded up the frogmen and the American sailor and got ready to take off again. The pilot turned around and said, "Man that was fun, Charlie. Let's go back the same way." I wasn't going to argue with him because I really enjoyed the fast, low level flying, too. It was exhilarating to be going so fast so close to the ground standing by the open door. We took off and followed the canal again, fly-ing low. When we came to the village that we passed on the way back, just twenty minutes ago, I noticed something different. There were no villagers in sight. It was as if they all disappeared. As we passed by, the village was on my side of the helicopter. All of a sudden I heard small arms fire. I learned to recognize it as the sound of popcorn popping. My responsibility as crewman was to try to locate the source of the small arms fire and relay that information to the pilot so he could take the appropriate action. Since we didn't have any guns, I assumed that action would be evasive. I thought, that with two rookie pilots, I'd better give them a good reading on where the shots were coming from, so I swung outside the door to get a better look. As I looked at the village, I saw a lone man in the doorway of a hooch, pointing an AK-47 at us. I swung back in the helicopter and was keying my intercom microphone to tell the pilots where the sniper was when a horrible feeling come over me. All I could think was, "I'm hit." Then I passed out.

Before I describe what happened next, I need to go back about two weeks pre-vious. Whenever we flew, crewmen were tethered to the inside of the helicopter by what was called a "monkey belt". It was made out of a web-type of material, much like what a seat belt is made of. It would strap around us and connect to mounts in the floor of the helicopter. This allowed us freedom of movement, while still assuring us we wouldn't fall out. On one practice mission, I was test fir-ing my M-60. When you fired them for an extended period of time the barrels got hot. To prevent them from melting down you would replace them with another barrel using asbestos gloves. I heated up a barrel and replaced it, and carelessly threw the hot barrel on the floor. I didn't notice that it had landed on my monkey belt, and, before I did, it had burned right through the webbing. I was pretty embarrassed about my carelessness, and I didn't want anybody to find out what I did, so I didn't order a new monkey belt. I had to come up with something, though, because the pilots, especially new ones, always checked to see if we were belted in before we took off. So I found several seat belts and rigged them all together so that they made a long tether and allowed me even more ability to move around than the monkey belt did. I could get around most everywhere inside the helicopter and still be tethered. I kept the excess belt material tucked under me, and, when the pilots would turn around to check whether I was belted in, I could show them my connected seat belt without them knowing how long it was. I was pretty proud of my invention and I was using it the day I got hit.

It was bad enough that I had been shot and was passed out, but even worse was the fact that when I passed out, I fell forward out the door and the length of my homemade seat belt allowed me to fall right out of the helicopter. So here I was: shot, unconscious, and hanging by a seatbelt on the skid under my helicopter. Now even though I was unconscious, I can remember that I still was able to think. And what I thought at that particular moment was, "I'm going to die." I actually started feeling euphoric, and thought that dying wasn't too bad, really. Then I caught myself and thought, "You've got to open your eyes." I was probably unconscious only for a minute or so. I forced myself to open my eyes, and when I did, I realized that my situation was even worse than I imagined. Now I knew I was going to die. I looked up and saw Gramps leaning out the door trying to pull me in. I looked down and could see that we were climbing rapidly to get out of the range of the sniper. And I looked at the tail section of my helicopter and it looked like somebody had sprayed it with red paint. Only it wasn't paint. It was my blood.

I knew I was in pretty dire straits. I couldn't move my right arm and I assumed that's where I'd been shot. Gramps didn't have the strength to pull me back in. I remember thinking, "Why doesn't that American sailor give him a hand?" Using my left arm I was able to shimmy up my seat belt enough so that my nose was at the floor level of the helicopter door. When I saw what was happening inside, I realized why the American sailor wasn't helping. The Vietnamese frogmen were all huddled together, frightened and jabbering away in Vietnamese, blocking the sailor from getting anywhere near the door. No matter how hard I tried, I couldn't get enough strength to get myself back in the helicopter. Finally, I thought to myself, "Charlie, you're going to screw around here and you're going to fall." So I called off Gramps from trying to get me in, and I put my left arm around my right arm and shimmied back down my seat belt and just hung on as the pilot flew us back to the base at Rach Gia.

While we were flying to Rach Gia, and I was hanging there, I didn't try to talk or yell to Gramps, who was still hanging out the open door. I knew I could never be heard. Even when you were inside the helicopter during a flight, the noise was so loud that you couldn't talk to one another except over the intercom. I just hung there trying to be as still as I could. For some reason, though, my helmet was bothering me. I thought it was due to the prop wash that was blowing down on me. I felt I would be more comfortable with the helmet off, so I reached up with my left hand and took it off. I handed it to Gramps. At the time I didn't realize it, but the helmet had a small hole near the bottom of the left side and the whole top of the helmet was blown away. Once I got the helmet off I felt more comfortable. It didn't take long to get to the Army base at Rach Gia, but when we got there, it took a few minutes for us to land. There were guys positioned on the ground who had to get me unhooked from my belt while the helicopter hovered a few feet off the ground. Since I was hanging on the skid, if the helicopter had landed it would have landed on top of me. After I was unhooked, they put me on a stretcher. The Vietnamese frogman and the American sailor quickly jumped off and they loaded me back on. The pilots yelled at the sailors on the ground, "Where's the hospital?" The guys said there was no hospital nearby, but that Det 8 supposedly had a doctor. So we took off again for a short hop over to Det 8.

When we got to Det 8, we immediately found out that there was no doctor there, either. All they had was a corpsman, who quickly jumped on board. He said that we were going to have to fly to the Army hospital right next to our base at Binh Thuy. We took off again. My eyes were still wide open and I was fully aware of everything that was going on around me. I was still thinking that I could die any minute, so I kept my eyes open. Gramps put a pressure bandage on my wound back when we landed at the Army base. A pressure bandage is about an eight-inch piece of gauze that is put directly on the wound. When it becomes soaked with blood, you were supposed to put another one on top of the old one. The bandages were never supposed to be removed until a doctor could do it. On the flight to Binh Thuy, I remember that Gramps asked the corpsman how bad my wound was. The corpsman lifted up my pressure bandage, pointed to my wound, and just shook his head. I was furious. I remember thinking to myself, "Why you dumb son of a bitch." Not only had this ignorant corpsman lifted off the bandage when he wasn't supposed to, he had broken one of the cardinal rules of medevac protocol. You never let anyone know how badly wounded they were. You're always supposed to tell them that they were going to be all right. You give them a cigarette, and ask them where they're from, but you never let them know how bad they are hurt.

It took about a half-hour to get to the Army hospital at Can Tho. I was rushed into the hospital and put in a room filled with bright lights. A doctor came in the room and took one look at me and said, "Christ, we can't operate on him." He turned to the corpsman and said, "You're going to have to try to get him to Long Binh." I distinctly remember him saying "try" and I said to myself, "Shit, I'm dead." Arrangements were quickly made for an Army medical helicopter to take me to Long Binh. Before I left they stuck an IV in me and catheterized me (I distinctly remember that part).

Some of the guys from my base at Binh Thuy heard on the radio that I had been hit and was being taken to Can Tho. They came over to the hospital to see me when I arrived. As they were carrying me out of the hospital, I suddenly got nauseous and leaned over the side of the hospital bed and threw up. I don't know why I remember some details so vividly, but I do remember one of my buddies was right there and tried to catch my vomit in his hands to prevent it from getting on me. It really touched me, and still does to this day, that somebody was so concerned for my well being that they were willing to do something like that. Such was the Seawolf brotherhood. One of the young officers from my base, Eric Lauston, wasn't going to let me go on that Army helicopter without another Navy man on board, and even though he had no orders to do so, he went along with me to Long Binh. Theoretically he was going AWOL, and he almost got in trouble over it. Because he had no official orders, nobody would fly him back to Binh Thuy. He ended up breaking into a clerk's office, stealing some orders, and forging them in order to get back. I really appreciated it that he was with me in that critical time.

I remained conscious during the entire one hour flight to Long Binh. By now I knew that I had a head wound, but I still couldn't figure out why I couldn't move my right arm and leg. I stayed awake because I still believed I was going to expire any minute. I kept looking out the open door, watching the scenery pass by, knowing that this was probably my last helicopter flight.

It was nearly dark by the time we got to Long Binh. They rushed me into the operating room and began to prep me for surgery. Some medics put me on an operating table, and the first thing they did was rip my dog tags off of me. When I was in the Philippines, I bought some "love beads" and I wore them around my neck, too, much to the consternation of my officers back at the base. I heard someone say, "Get the beads off, too." I wasn't going to let them rip my beads off, so, when the medic reached for them, I grabbed his hand to stop him. The other medic, who was inserting a needle in my other arm, said, "Don't worry. He'll be out in a second." I thought to myself, "You bastards. I'll show you. I won't go to sleep." That was the last thing I remember of January 9, 1971.

11

I didn't learn until later that I was the first person to have brain surgery Long Binh Hospital. They never had a surgeon there who was able to perform these types of surgery. Until I showed up, what they did with head injuries was to patch them up as best they could, and then fly them to Japan for surgery. It was my very good fortune that a new doctor there could perform my surgery, for I never would have survived the long flight to Japan.

When I woke up from my surgery, I saw a young medic sitting on a gurney beside me. When he saw me open my eyes he said, "Oh good. You're awake." He came over and checked my pulse and heart. He said, "Now I don't want you to get upset, but you've been shot in the head, and the right side of your body is paralyzed, and you can't talk." I thought to myself, "How does this young punk know what I can and can't do? I haven't even tried to say anything." And that's what I was going to tell him, but when I tried, all that came out was a bunch of nonsense sounds. I couldn't believe what I was hearing coming out of my mouth. I knew what I wanted to say, and my thoughts were clear in my mind, and I thought I was moving my mouth correctly to say the words, but all that was coming out was babble. I got very angry and I wanted to swear. I got out, "Shhhhhh-hhhh" and held that sound for quite a while until, finally, I forced out, "..it". That medic just stared at me while I was trying to get that word out, and, when I did, he just doubled over in laughter. He almost fell over the gurney, he was laughing so hard. Later on, as I was getting ready to leave the hospital, he told me that when he heard me get that word out, he knew I was going to be okay.

It didn't take me long to begin to realize how fortunate I was. I thought I was going to die, but I was still alive. It never occurred to me that I could be disabled. I always saw things as black and white. Either you lived, or you died. My recovery began at Long Binh in a big ward, with bright lights that were on all the time, day or night. The people there were very nice to me. The nurses and attendants were bright and cheerful and very understanding about my condition. I was frustrated that I couldn't talk, and sometimes had difficulty communicating what I needed or wanted. The nurses made me a list of eight or ten items that I could request. They told me I could point to whatever I needed. That wasn't good enough for me. When I was left alone, I would take out that list and practice saying the words. It wasn't easy, but I got to where I could say all of the things on the list. I was particularly good at saying, "iced tea", and "ice cream", as they were two of the things I requested the most.

Eric stayed with me at Long Binh for two days. He was always by my side, and it felt good to have someone familiar around. Finally he said, "Charlie, I've got to get back to Bin Thuy before they throw me in the brig." I was sad to see him go, but I appreciated all he did for me. I didn't see him again until we met at a Seawolf reunion, some twenty years later.

Somehow word got to the minister of my church back home about what happened to me and where I was. He knew that the son of another minister in Michigan was stationed in Saigon, and was somehow able to get a message through to the young man. His name was Art Kaun, and he came to visit me every time he was off duty. Even though he didn't know me beforehand, he would just come to the hospital and sit by my bed and talk to me. Sometimes I'd try to talk back and he'd say, "Charlie, why don't you just let me do all the talking." It was nice to be visited by somebody from my church. My faith had greatly diminished during my time in Vietnam, but in the couple of days since I'd been shot, I began to gradually get it back. I felt that God must have something left for me to do that he would allow me to survive being shot in the head. My talks with Art helped to revive my faith, and I was glad to have him around at that time.

After a few days I was put in a wheelchair and allowed to go outside. It was stifling hot, like it always was in Vietnam, but it felt really good that day. Later that day, I was sent to get some X-rays. I wasn't told why. I thought it was just so that they could see how my wound was healing. After the X-ray, a medic came to me and said, "Good news, Charlie. You don't have to have that second operation after all." Since I didn't know that I was supposed to have another operation, I had no reason to feel relieved. It turns out that when they performed the initial operation they were concerned over of the length of time it was between when I was shot and when I got to surgery. Because of that, they wanted to get me closed up as quickly as possible. They were worried that they may not have got all the bone fragments cleaned out before they closed, and that's why I had the X-ray. It turns out that the surgeon did a better job than he thought.

I never got to know the doctor who did the surgery on me. I knew he was a good looking guy, and that the nurses all fawned over him. I would see him come out of surgery late at night, his surgical scrubs all covered in blood, and the nurses would all rush to give him his regular post-surgery treat: a big cup of chocolate ice cream. He never spoke to me, even when he would come and examine me. He always showed up with a group of doctors and nurses accompanying him. He would cut off my bandage, and point to my wound and say, "Look at that, how nice it's pulsating." Then he'd leave, and one of the nurses would bandage me up again. Never once did he say, "Charlie, how you doing today?" or "Charlie, you're recovering nicely." It was like he pretended I wasn't even there, like I wasn't able to understand what he was saying. He acted like he didn't want to know you, and, looking back, I guess that was how he dealt with all the death and misery he had to see up close. He was an amazing surgeon, and certainly performed a miracle on me. I never knew his name, though. I tried to find out later on, but it's Navy policy not to release such information. I was thankful he was there when I needed him.

Every day I woke up at Long Binh, I would smile, and I would wear that smile the whole day. I smiled at everyone I saw. Because I couldn't talk, I suppose everyone was asking, "What's he smiling about?" I was happy, and felt lucky just to be alive. Every morning was an affirmation that I was still alive, and was a reason for me to smile. But in moments of solitude, I was sad. I was sad that I wasn't able to move my right arm or leg, and I was worried about facing the future with a disability. I asked the inevitable question, "Why did this happen to me?" At night, when nobody would see me, I would bury my head under the bed covers, and I'd cry.

I guess I was too caught up in my own situation to consider what my wife and family were thinking back home. They got a telegram the day after I was injured saying I'd been shot and was in critical condition at the Long Binh hospital. They advised Fran to stay at home, and wait for further information. They waited a week without hearing anything more. Finally, my dad got in touch with our Congressman, and he expedited the next message, which told them I was recovering, but it was still not known when I'd be returning to the States. Personally, I had no communication with Fran while I was still overseas. It didn't matter that I wasn't able to phone or send her a letter. I couldn't talk or write yet. Besides that, I didn't want them to know what kind of condition I was in. In my mind, my paralysis was just a temporary thing, and I felt that any day now I would be back to normal. There was no sense in worrying my family over something that wasn't a permanent thing. I actually thought I would return to my Seawolf duties, and complete my tour of Vietnam. I remained pretty optimistic about my recovery.

I got to be good friends with the medics and nurses that attended to me at Long Binh. They all treated me nice. There was one older medic, though, who thought I should be progressing more quickly than I was. I hated using bedpans, and I would do all I could to avoid them. This usually meant that I would wait until the last possible moment before requesting someone to take me to the bathroom. One day I really had to go bad, and called for a medic get me to the bathroom. This older medic comes to my bed and said, "Instead of using the wheelchair, why don't we walk to the bathroom today." Now I hadn't even stood up on my own, at that point. My right side was completely paralyzed, and this guy's telling me to get out of my bed and walk. So I got out of bed, and leaned on him, and hopped on my good leg, and dragged my bad leg all the way to the bathroom. By the time I got there, I was drenched in sweat and I didn't have to go anymore. I was exhausted. He used to tell me that he was going to retire soon, and he was going to become a chiropractor. After he told me that, I've made it a point never to go to a chiropractor.

I also had a bad first experience with physical therapy while I was at Long Binh. The therapist wanted me to do things that were not physically possible for me at that time. I tried as hard as I could, but, for some reason, the therapist felt I wasn't giving it my all. After one session he told me I was hopeless and that he was giving up on me. Needless to say I wasn't too impressed with physical therapy at that time.

Just one week after I was brought to Long Binh was Super Bowl V. The nurses got a TV and set it up at the foot of my bed. I was able to watch the entire game. One of the medics even snuck me a couple of beers. That game, I believe, is considered one of the worst Super Bowls ever. Dallas beat Baltimore 16-13. For me, though, it's quite a fond memory. It felt really good to be watching good old American football on TV.

There was one guy at Long Binh who came in about the same time I did, who wasn't doing as well as I was. He was in a bed at the far end of my ward. He, like me, was also shot in the head. He gave fits to everyone on the hospital staff. Every time anyone would try to do something to him, he would fight them. He would tear out his IV's. He would thrash around in bed if anybody tried to feed him. He was always creating a violent scene. It was like he just wanted to be left alone to die. As nice as the nurses and medics were to me, they were pretty mean to him. I guess they were tired of his outbursts. I got to know his name, Daryl, because of all the nurses that yelled at him, "Stop it, Daryl." I used to watch these episodes and, using my newly rediscovered religious philosophy, said to myself, "I could have had it much worse." Later on I found out that he was an Army officer. I learned that when we both got on the same plane to go to the hospital in Japan, and he was put on a hospital bed, while I was put in a rack on a cot. Daryl ended up following me through most of my rehabilitation.

As dramatic an improvement I had made at Long Binh hospital, I still wasn't in terrific shape. I wasn't able to get out of my bed on my own. I couldn't feed myself, as my left arm, the only one that still worked, was still pretty weak and awkward. I could say a few words, but I was nowhere near being able to hold a conversation. I wasn't eating very well, and the nurses would complain to me about it. I told them to quit feeding me crap, and that maybe I'd eat more. We came to a compromise on that problem. As I started to eat more, the food got better. When they had done all they could for me at Long Binh, and it was safe for me to travel, I was sent to a hospital in Japan. One of the medics, who I had a good relationship with, got me ready for my flight. He took me in a wheelchair to a room with a drain in it, and proceeded to pour buckets of warm water over me while I cleaned myself. The last bucket he put over me was filled with ice water. After I got over the shock, I could laugh about it. I was glad that people still felt they could joke around with me.

On the 20th of January, less than two weeks since I was injured, I was taken from Long Binh by helicopter over to Tan Son Nhut air base, where I was put on an Air Force medical transport plane and flown to the Air Force hospital in Tachikawa, Japan. The plane actually had a hospital room on board. I don't remember much of the flight, as I was lying on my back the entire time. I do remember that the plane was filled with wounded, some less injured than me, some more.

The hospital in Japan was beautiful, especially compared to the hospital at Long Binh. The wards were bright, and even had windows. I was surprised to learn that it snowed in Japan. As I watched it fall outside the window, I was reminded of winter back in Ohio. The staff there were all pretty nice to me. Daryl wasn't on my ward, but he was on the one next to mine, and I could peek in and see him. I noticed that the staff treated him better than the staff at Long Binh did. I was glad about that.

I was still having speech problems, and was finding it increasingly frustrating for me not to be able to express myself the way I wanted. It's funny, but when people would talk to me back then, they would talk very slow, and very loud. I felt like I should hang a sign on me that said, "I'm not retarded. I can understand you. I just can't talk." I would get frustrated when people would talk to me like a little deaf child, and, the more frustrated I became, the worse my speech would get.

Although I now realized that my days overseas were numbered, I still felt like I could get better, and I didn't want to go home until I did. I didn't want my wife to see me as a cripple, and I was more than willing to stay in Vietnam until I could stand on my own two feet. Although the staff there encouraged me to think positively about my rehabilitation, they also tried to make me see the reality of the situation. It was going to be a long, hard road to recovery, and I would be going back to the States to begin that process.

There was one nurse there that worked the night shift. Every night at 10:00 P.M., she would come by my bed, and ask me how I was doing. She would also ask me if I could move my right leg, and my answer was always, "No." It wasn't for a lack of trying that I couldn't move my leg. I would work every day just trying to get the slightest movement out of it. One day, it happened. I strained, and my right leg lifted off the bed about three inches. First, I was shocked. I didn't know if it was just a reflex action, or if I was really making it move. I did it again. It was really me moving my leg. I was so excited I just about drove everyone on the ward nuts. I showed everybody, even people who were visiting other patients. I couldn't wait until the night nurse came by to show her. I practiced all day, and 10:00 P.M. came, but the nurse didn't show. I found out that she was in some kind of seminar, and that she wouldn't be in until much later. It didn't matter. I waited for her. She finally showed up on the ward after midnight. She was quietly checking patients when I saw her, and I yelled out, "Ask me." She looked at me sternly and whispered, "Shhh, Charlie. You'll wake everybody up." I didn't care. Once more I yelled to her, "Ask me." To keep me quiet she came over to my bed. "Ask you what?" she said. I said the only word I could get out at the time, "Move." Fortunately, she understood and said, "Okay. Can you move your leg?" I pulled away my sheet, and lifted my right leg off the bed. I was really proud of myself. A few weeks previous I couldn't have imagined how such a little thing could make me so happy. I was determined to get it working even better, and I worked on moving that leg all the time I was in Japan.

Up until this time in Japan, I had not yet seen what my wound actually looked like. I knew it felt weird, like something was missing on my head. There really was no need for me to look in a mirror. I didn't have any hair to comb, and I certainly wasn't going to try to shave myself at that time. That would have been a real disaster. I wanted to see what it looked like, but I didn't want anyone around when I did. I didn't know what my reaction to it would be. One day, a medic took me into the bathroom so I could wash my face and brush my teeth, and he left me alone there for a few minutes. The bathroom had mirrors over the sinks, but, because I was sitting in a wheelchair, I was too low to be able to see myself in them. I got in front of a sink, and with my left hand grabbed hold of a faucet and pulled myself up to where I could look at myself in the mirror. I didn't look for long, for what I saw devastated me. It was the ugliest thing I had ever seen. My bald head had a huge scar on it, going from the center all the way down the side. My head was misshapen where my skull had been blown away.

Although there was skin over the wound, there was no bone underneath it, so it looked loose and flaccid. I sat back in my wheelchair in shock. I never wanted anyone to have to see what I looked like. From that point on, I wore a skullcap all the time, day and night. The nurses tried to convince me that I didn't have to wear it, that the wound would heal better if it were left uncovered, but I didn't buy it. I thought the wound made me look like a Frankenstein monster, and nothing was going make me take off my skullcap. One night, while I was sleeping, the nurses stole it from me. The next day I was so depressed that I wouldn't eat or respond to anyone. They eventually gave it back to me, and I continued to wear it my entire stay in Japan, and also when I got back to the States.

The hospital in Japan was mainly to prep and stabilize me for the long flight back to the United States. While I was there I was required to go to physical therapy. During my first visit I told the therapist about how the guy at the hospital in Long Binh gave up on me after one session. This therapist told me, "Well, Charlie, I'm not going to give up on you." He worked with me every day while I was in Japan and really made me realize how important physical therapy was going to be in my rehabilitation. I was in Japan less than a week when, on January 26, I was strapped in a military transport plane, and began the two-day journey back to the United States. Although it felt to me that I had been in hospitals for months, it really was less than three weeks. Ready or not, I was headed for the start of my rehabilitation process. It was going to be the most difficult thing I had ever done.

12

I spent the flight back to the USA on a stretcher. There were lots of other wounded guys on the plane, along with guys who were returning to the States after completing their tours of duty in Vietnam. We were the lucky ones. In the cargo bay underneath us were some who were also returning home, after giving the ultimate sacrifice. No matter how I felt about Vietnam and the war, they were, and still are, my greatest heroes.

In typical military logic we didn't land in San Francisco. Being January, our first stop in the United States was Anchorage, Alaska. It was so cold there that no one was allowed off the plane during the layover. We continued on our way, and arrived outside Chicago on Thursday, January 28, 1971. It was also very cold there, and they bundled me all up and carried me to a waiting ambulance, which whisked me away to the Great Lakes Naval Hospital. I was right back to where I began my Navy career.

At the hospital, I was assigned to Ward 8, which was the domain of Nurse Nehr. I liked her right off the bat. She was a career Navy woman and was a Lieutenant Commander. She was a real straight shooter, and didn't hesitate to speak her mind to anyone, which is probably why she never became a full Commander. We got along great. Out of all the nurses that took care of me, she's the one I remember the most. As soon as I settled in, I announced to Nurse Nehr that I was ready to start walking. This was before I had any physical therapy or anything. I had only been there one day, and I thought I was going to have to learn to walk on my own, so I figured out how to get out of my bed and I started walking around it, using the bed as my support on my right side. Of course, I lost my balance and had to be helped back into bed. Nurse Nehr told me to be patient, that once I started my physical therapy, I would be able to learn how to walk. Patience wasn't one of my strong suits, and I had special motives for learning how to walk quickly. I wasn't going to let Fran see me until I could stand on my own two feet. In the meantime, they gave me a wheelchair and I figured out how to get around in it using my one good arm and leg. I wheeled myself all around that hospital, propelling myself with my arm and steering with my leg. I was scheduled for physical therapy starting the following Monday, for three times a week, in one hour sessions.

The first weekend I was there, some Red Cross volunteers came around to help some of us write letters home. I still hadn't contacted Fran since I was injured, so I sat down with one of the volunteers and wrote Fran a letter. I told her I was doing fine, but that the weather was horrible, and I didn't want her driving to Chicago to see me, because she might get caught in a snowstorm or something. I told her that she should just wait until spring, maybe April or May, before she came to see me. I figured that I would be walking and talking pretty good by then. With the letter written, I felt pretty safe that I wouldn't have any visitors for a while, at least until I had the chance to get myself back to normal again. Right after I was done with the letter, a corpsman came up to me and said that there was a good looking, young, blond woman that was waiting to see me. I said "Yeah, right" and ignored him. He came back about a half-hour later, and said the young blond woman was still waiting to see me. I thought that this guy wasn't going to leave me alone until I went out to where this blond woman supposedly was and all the corpsmen could have a good laugh about fooling the cripple in the wheelchair. I already knew that they could get pretty mean with some of their pranks with the patients. So, I wheeled myself to the visitor's area, and I was startled when I saw that the young, beautiful, blond woman was, in fact, Fran. I felt awkward at first, but I got over that as soon as she hugged me. I was glad she came, even though it didn't fit into my plan. She cried a little when she first saw me, but held her emotions pretty much in check. She told me how good I looked, much better than she anticipated I would be. I figured that if she thought I looked okay, that she might as well see my wound, so I took off my skull cap and showed her. She flinched a little, but then said, "You know, even that isn't so bad." That made me feel pretty good. Maybe I was just over reacting about how bad my skull looked.

Later that day I had more visitors. My parents decided to fly in to see me. When they first saw me, they also told me how good I looked. They said they were expecting me to be in some hospital bed, immobile, with all kinds of tubes connected to me. They hadn't received a lot of information from the Navy concerning my condition, and they were really relieved to see that I was awake and up in a wheelchair. I thought I might as well show them my wound, too, since Fran said it wasn't too bad. As soon as I took off my skull cap, my mother started screaming, "What have they done to my boy. This is horrible." I was really embarrassed. My mother later calmed down, but that was the last time I ever gave anyone any sneak peeks of my damaged skull. Fran told me later that when she first saw it, she thought it was the most horrible thing she'd ever seen, but she knew that if she showed her repulsion, that it would have made me feel terrible.

Later on in the day, my parents asked me if I wanted anything. I looked at them and said, "What I really want is a McDonald's cheeseburger and some fries." So, they went out and got it for me. They brought me back a chocolate shake to go along with it, and I still think it was one of the best meals I ever had.

After the weekend, Fran and my parents went back home to Ohio, and I was left on my own again. On Monday I was scheduled to have my first physical therapy session. Up to that point I had no idea what physical therapy was, or how they went about their job. Nurse Nehr told me that they were the guys who were going to get me walking again, and that's all I cared about. I was ready and waiting for them on Monday morning. My therapist was Rich White, who, besides being the major force in my rehabilitation, would also become a very dear friend. He was a Navy guy, an E5, who joined the Navy to get some practical experience, and also to get some financial assistance when he finished up his degree at Northwestern University. He ended up writing one of his college papers about me. We hit it off right away. I guess he recognized in me the determination I had to get better, and my willingness to work hard to achieve it, and I saw in him a knowledgeable, helpful, and caring individual, that also wanted to make me reach my highest potential. From the first session, I loved physical therapy. Although I was scheduled for only three one-hour sessions a week, I was there every spare minute I had. Unless I was scheduled for some test, I could always be found in the PT room working on my various exercises. In order to keep me out of trouble, and out of the way of other patients, Rich devised a system of elastic straps that he hooked me up to, which he called "isometrics". I spent a lot of my time there at Great Lakes hooked up to those straps. Like I said, Rich was not only a great therapist, he was a great friend. The first time I was allowed out of the hospital, Rich took me to his home to meet his wife and to have dinner. I really appreciated that, for not only did I need physical rehabilitation, I also needed some social rehabilitation, too. I was still unsure as to how people were going to react to me being a cripple, and Rich, with his kindness, really helped me out there, too. He was a very big reason I was able to accomplish what I did.

As much help as physical therapy was in helping me to walk, there was no such therapy to help me learn how to talk better. There were no speech therapists at that time, and I was left pretty much on my own insofar as exercising my speech. Ward 8 was filled with patients who were immobile. Some of them were in comas. Some were in traction. Some were in beds that rotated. They all became unwitting practice partners for my speech therapy. I would wheel myself over to their beds, and just talk to them for hours. Most of them were in no condition to make me shut up. Looking back, I'm sure that most of the time they didn't understand what I was saying, but that didn't matter. I think that sometimes it was enough for them just to have somebody by their bed paying attention to them. It surely helped me out.

One of the oddities of my speech was my ability to articulate curse words. I don't know why, but they inadvertently would pop up in sentences, and I would have no control over them. They always came out crystal clear, too. It wasn't that I was thinking of them, or that they even made sense in the context of the sentence. I would just blurt them out. If someone would show me a picture of their children, I might say, "Oh that's a cute baby, shit." Most people were very understanding of this problem, but I had to really concentrate when I spoke to avoid some embarrassing situations.

Although my speech progressed, I still found it difficult to communicate at times. The hospital staff nicknamed me "Jeremiah", after the Three Dog Night song that was popular at the time.

> "Jeremiah was a bullfrog.
> Was a good friend of mine.
> I never understood a single word he said…"

They even put the name "Jeremiah" on my cane. I didn't mind. It was all good spirited.

One of the things I had a lot of trouble with was reading. My uncle used to send me some outdoor magazines, and I could read the words, but I didn't understand the stories. No one ever tested me for my reading ability. I just figured that it was because I had been shot in the head, and that it would eventually come back to me, just like everything else.

I never got any clear prognosis on how much I should expect to recover. At first I was told to expect to be in a wheelchair for the rest of my life. Then, after I started making progress with walking, I was told I might get back 75% of my functionality. In truth, I don't think anyone knew how far I could go. One of the doctors told me that as the bullet went through my skull, it left bone and shell fragments on my brain. Rather than try to dig them out, they just removed a portion of my brain. He told me I probably wasn't using all of my brain anyhow, so I wouldn't miss it. I still expected a full recovery. During the first few months I was amazed that, almost every day, I was able to accomplish something new. At that pace, I thought I'd be back to being good old normal Charlie in short order.

I was prohibited from walking on my own until the physical therapists felt that I had gained more strength and agility. I was okay with that, except for the fact that I still had to rely on a corpsman to assist me with bathing. They would take and put me in a tub, where I would have to clean myself. I always hated baths, and I especially hated them when somebody had to put you in the tub. I wanted to take a shower, and I needed to do it on my own. Finally, I drew the sympathy of one corpsman, who got me into one of those portable toilets on wheels. He got me into the shower room and I was able to take a long, luxurious hot shower, all by myself. It was a great feeling. It also was the end of taking baths.

My favorite part of physical therapy was swimming. When I was in the pool, I didn't feel like a cripple. I developed a side stroke, and I was able to swim around for hours. Where other things, such as walking, eating, and writing were very difficult for me, swimming came naturally and easy. I even got to the point where I could play water volleyball. It was a great form of relaxation for me, and I tried to get to the pool as often as I could.

When things on Ward 8 got a little too boring for us, we would organize wheelchair races. I got to be pretty good at it, although I tended to be a little more aggressive with my racing than I was tactful. Sometimes, we would even have some wheelchair baseball games on the ward. We'd use some old bundled up sock for a ball, and our canes for bats. We were always trying to do something on the ward to take our minds off of our physical problems.

Fran continued to visit me as much as she could. She would load up her little Volkswagen Bug on Fridays, and head west on the turnpike to Chicago. She usually would bring her parents along with her. We had a lot of snowstorms that winter, and sometimes the snow on the turnpike would be higher than the running boards of her Bug, but she always made it. I was always happy to see her, and, being with her on those weekends, made my resolve to get better even stronger. During the week, I was so busy with my therapy that I didn't have time to miss her.

I made rapid progress during the first months at Great Lakes. So much progress, in fact, that the doctors there used me as an example of how effective their therapy program was. The hospital administrators would arrange for me to talk to people about my rehabilitation. I talked to civic leaders, and Senator's wives, and to doctors from other hospitals. Mostly, though, the doctors would have me talk to the wives and families of newly admitted patients. I guess they considered me somewhat of a success story, and they thought the progress I made with my injury might give some other people with similar problems some hope.

One day a young doctor, who had been treating me, came to me and said that he had a patient whose wife thought he wasn't making the progress that he should. He asked me if I would talk to her, and I agreed to. She was a young and very pretty woman, and we talked for a long time. She told me that her husband had a similar brain injury to mine, and I tried to encourage her that his recovery may just take some time. I must have done a pretty good job with my encouragement, because the next day the young doctor came to me and told me that the young woman wanted to have her husband moved into Ward 8 so that he could be closer to me. There was only one problem. It turned out that her husband was an officer, and Ward 8 was for enlisted men only. Fortunately, there was a closed room adjacent to our ward, that we called the "Quiet Room". It was used whenever someone on Ward 8 was having some problems, and was causing a disruption on the ward. The hospital administration agreed to allow the officer to temporarily use that room so that I could keep an eye on him. After he moved in, the doctor asked me to go in and introduce myself to him. As soon as I went in the room, I recognized him. It was Daryl, the man who was so disruptive back at the hospital in Vietnam. When I first saw him, I thought that God was surely trying to tell me something. Somehow, I was supposed to help this man. Daryl didn't recognize me. I don't think he remembered anything about those first few days after his injury. They had him in the hospital bed, and they had a boxing glove on his right hand, the one he used to flail about with. He couldn't talk very well, but then neither could I. Somehow we managed to communicate, though, and we eventually became friends. I would visit him daily, and practice talking with him. Sometimes I'd put a boxing glove on my left hand and we'd do a little hand boxing. His room was situated so that I could see it from my bed, so I kept a watch for any trouble that might occur. I wanted to especially make sure that none of the corpsmen gave him any problems. His parents used to come to visit him, and, whenever they came, he would immediately bring them over to me and they'd have their visit with him by my bed. I guess he just felt more comfortable having me to support him. One time, his parents brought along pictures of him as he graduated from officer's school. When I saw those pictures, I understood why he was so upset about his injury. He looked like a poster boy for Army officers. He was strikingly handsome, and had a chiseled body. He was a nearly perfect physical specimen, but the Vietnam War didn't show any favoritism, and now, he was just like me: a cripple.

Eventually, Daryl got to the point where he would socialize with others on the ward. In the evenings he would come out of his room and watch TV with us. One day, all the regular nurses were gone to some seminar or something, and they brought in some Reserve nurses to cover for them. We always were a little concerned when the regular nurses were gone, because that was when the corpsmen used to try to get away with things. They could get mean and malicious. You really had to keep an eye on your belongings, especially your cigarettes, because some of the corpsmen were known to be thieves. Some of them were good and conscientious about their job, but we always had to be careful when they were unsupervised. That night, we were all together watching TV when one of the corpsman asked Daryl if he needed anything. Daryl was able to communicate that he wanted a cup of coffee, and the corpsman went to get it for him. He must have thought it would be funny to make it extra hot, because when he brought it back, and Daryl took a sip, he burned his lips. He yelled, and dropped the cup, spilling coffee all over the floor. The corpsman didn't think that was funny, though, and he yelled at Daryl, "You dumb nigger." Something inside of me snapped. It was probably partially because I felt responsible for taking care of Daryl. But also, it was due to my intolerance of racism in any form. I grabbed that corpsman from my wheelchair and tumbled to the floor with him. Fortunately, I ended up on top of him and started pummeling him with my good arm. The other corpsman quickly broke it up. I felt bad, because the incident really frightened those young Reserve nurses. I was angry at the corpsman, but I felt a little bit good about the fact that, despite my injury, I was still able to deliver a pretty good punch. The next day, when Nurse Nehr found out about the incident, she wasn't happy. She gave me a good brow beating, telling me that I was never to raise a hand to any hospital staff ever again. She must have understood the situation, though, because I wasn't punished in any way for my actions. And, for the remainder of my stay at Great Lakes, I obeyed Nurse Nehr's order and never put my hand on another corpsman. I used to whack them with my cane instead.

My sisters with me in Dad's car

My favorite outfit: Hopalong Cassidy

A young Davy Crockett

Wedding day 1966

Fran and her sailor boy

Seawolves in Vietnam

Me and my bird in Vietnam

Seawolves UH-1

UH-1 taking off

Telefax

847P EST JAN 11 71 CTA231   [TWO PAGE.]
CT CT WA150 DR '''XV GOVT PDB FAX WASHINGTON DC 11 412P EST
MRS FRANCES MAE MORRIS, REPORT DELIVERY, DO NOT PHONE, CHECK
CLY CHGS ABOVE 75 CTS
    751 GILBERT LAWSTON OHIO   (HEW WILL CALL)
    WITH CONCERN I CONFIRM ON BEHALF OF THE UNITED STATES NAVY
THAT YOUR HUSBAND, AO3 CHARLES JOSEPH MORRIS, JUNIOR, USN,
B46 82 99 WAS SERIOUSLY WOUNDED IN ACTION ON 9 JANUARY 1971
AT KIEN GIANG. SOUTH VIETNAM WHILE A CREWMEMBER ON A COMBAT
SUPPORT HELICOPTER TRANSITING FROM FIREBASE TO A LANDING ZONE
SECURED BY FRIENDLY FORCES. THE AIRCRAFT RECEIVED MODERATE
SMALL ARMS ENEMY FIRE AND YOUR HUSBAND WAS WOUNDED ON THE SIDE
OF THE HEAD. HE IS PRESENTLY HOSPITALIZED AT THE TWENTY-FOURTH
MEDICAL EVACUATION HOSPITAL, LONG BINH, SOUTH VIETNAM. IT
IS ANTICIPATED THAT HE WILL BE FURTHER MEDICALLY EVACUATED
TO THE U. S. ARMY HOSPITAL, CAP ZAMA, JAPAN. HE WAS PLACED

WU 1270 (R 5-69)

Telefax

ON THE SERIOUS LIST ON 11 JANUARY 1971 WITH PROGNOSIS GUARDED.
YOU ARE ASSURED THAT HE IS RECEIVING THE BEST POSSIBLE CARE
AND TREATMENT. WHEN FURTHER REPORTS ARE AVAILABLE CONCERNING
HIS CONDITION YOU WILL BE PROMPTLY INFORMED. THE ANXIETY THIS
REPORT BRINGS YOU IS FULLY UNDERSTOOD AND I JOIN YOU IN THE
WISH FOR HIS RECOVERY. IF I CAN ASSIST YOU PLEASE WRITE OR
TELEGRAPH THE CHIEF OF NAVAL PERSONNEL, DEPARTMENT OF THE NAVY,
WASHINGTON, D. C. 20370. MY PERSONAL REPRESENTATIVE CAN BE
REACHED BY TELEPHONE AT OXFORD 42746 DURING WORKING HOURS AND
OXFORD 42768 AFTER WORKING HOURS
    VICE ADMIRAL D H GUINN CHIEF OF NAVAL PERSONNEL.
    /1010/
AO3 B46 82 99 9 1971 11 1971 20370 42746 42768.(512)

1270 (R 6-69)

Telegram sent to Fran informing her of my injury

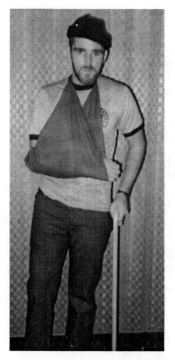

Young family portrait

Returning home from Vietnam

Church youth counselor

First Seawolves reunion, 1987

With Matt at Seawolves reunion

A couple of my favorite things: tennis and golf

The 1973 Ford Torino that Matt and I restored

My strength and support for 40 years

13

After a couple of months I made enough progress that the doctors arranged for me to have a two week leave, where I could go home to Ohio. They wanted to see how well I would adapt to my home environment. I was pretty excited about it. I was walking pretty good with my cane, and, even though I still talked funny, I was able to get my message across.

The week before I was scheduled for my leave, a young man came to the hospital that had a wound much like mine, only he got his a year previous. He came to the hospital to get his skull plate inserted. You had to wait a year before you could have it done to make sure everything in the wounded area had stabilized. I was pretty inspired by the guy. With the same type of injury that I had, he was walking without a cane, and he talked fine. I thought that if he could make such a great recovery, I could, too. I talked to him all the time. I wanted to know everything about what he did to make his recovery.

On the day of his operation, he was sitting on a bed near mine dressed in a surgical gown. A doctor came in and told him that they decided to change the way they were going to operate, and that the operation was being rescheduled. I thought he would be pretty upset, but he took the news calmly. I was watching him as he put his clothes back on, and, all of a sudden, his arm started shaking. Next, his leg started shaking. Then his whole body. Then he went rigid and fell on the bed. The nurses and doctors rushed in and gave him an injection. What he had was a grand mal seizure, something I had never seen or heard of. I was really scared. I went to my doctor and asked him if this was what could happen to me. He tried to be reassuring. He said as long as I kept taking my medication, that I would have no problems. I said, "What medication?" He grabbed my medical chart, and found out that the medication portion had been covered up by something else on the clipboard. I had been there two months, and had never taken any medication. I had been feeling fine. I had no pain or any problems, so I didn't need to take any. The doctor prescribed the anti-seizure drug Dilantin for me, and I started taking it immediately. A few days after I started taking it, I started not feeling so good. I felt tired all the time. I went to the doctor and told him that I thought the medicine was bad for me. He told me that I needed to take it for two weeks before it would start being effective. I told him that in two weeks I'd be at home on leave. He said that by the time I got there that I would start feeling better. So I continued taking it.

When I did get home, I was feeling even worse. Fran had arranged a party for me when I arrived, and I wasn't doing well at all. I felt off balance and I was falling a lot. It wasn't a good first impression for my family and friends. I even fell through a plate glass window and cut myself up pretty good. I guess I put on quite a show for all my guests. Later in the week, I felt even worse. I was barely able to walk at all, and had double vision on top of everything. Fran got nervous, and loaded me up in my uncle's car and drove me back to Great Lakes.

When the doctor asked me what was the matter I told him, "I think this medicine is killing me." He told me he didn't think the medicine was the problem, and arranged for a series of x-rays and neurological tests. After the tests, he still couldn't figure out what was causing my problem. By this time I was very weak, and couldn't walk at all. The doctor was talking to me, and he told some sort of a joke and I laughed a little. He looked at me and told me to open my mouth. He looked at my gums, which had sores all over them, and pronounced, "You're having an allergic reaction to the medication." I said, "That's what I've been trying to tell you all along." He changed my medication to Phenobarbitol, and I never had any more problems. I did, however, have to learn how to walk all over again. That was no big deal for me. It came back quickly, and I didn't mind spending the extra hours in Physical Therapy.

As time went on, I got stronger and more confident of myself. With the confidence came a desire to be independent. I used to ask for weekend leaves, and the hospital would give them to me, assuming that I would have someone pick me up for the weekend. Instead, I would get a taxi to take me to the airport, and I'd get on a plane back to Ohio all by myself. It wasn't easy, because it always seemed that my flight was the farthest one to get to on the concourse. I'd be walking with my cane, with my old heavy sea bag slung over my shoulder. I always got to where I was going, but never very rapidly. I was always amazed that, of all the times I was at that crowded airport, never once did anyone even ask me if they could help me. I realized that anything I was going to do, I would have to do it on my own.

I saw my first Medal of Honor winner while I was at Great Lakes. He was a Navy helicopter pilot who was shot down three times in one day. Apparently he was airlifting wounded out of a battle zone when his helicopter crashed. He was taken back to his base, where he got another helicopter, and returned to the battle zone where he was shot down. Once more he was rescued and taken back to the base. By this time there were no regular helicopters left. All that was there was a small, one-man observation helicopter. He got in that, and returned to the battle zone where he flew as a spotter for the other pilots, warning them of enemy hot spots. Once more he was shot down, this time losing an arm in the process. The Navy used him as the guest speaker at a little USO show. It took place at an auditorium on the Great Lakes campus, and there were a lot of dignitaries present. They invited some of us wounded Vietnam veterans to attend, too. I went there with a corpsman, and we arrived early and got seats near the front row. All of the excitement affected me, and, all of a sudden, I was having trouble breathing and I felt lightheaded. The corpsman helped me out to the bathroom, where I quickly recovered. Feeling better, we went back in to find that our seats had been taken, and we were relegated to the back of the auditorium. During the ceremony there was a beautiful young woman who sang, and, during one of her songs, she came off the stage and sang right in front of a sailor who was sitting in the exact seat I had vacated. That corpsman wouldn't let me forget that. During the actual presentation, I was taken by how beautiful that medal was, all shiny with the wide red, white, and blue ribbon. But as that young pilot held that medal with a hook in place of his arm, I thought to myself, "I'll bet he'd gladly give up that medal to have his real arm back."

In early May I convinced my doctors that, since my first two-week leave home was shortened because of a mistake they made, I should be given another one. They agreed, so I went home again. It was a good visit, without any of the problems of my previous one. While I was gone, Daryl was transferred to a VA hospital in Milwaukee, and when I got back to Great Lakes, he had already left. I never saw him again. To this day, I have no idea how his life turned out. It was amazing that despite the fact that all of us on Ward 8 shared a life altering experience, we didn't make any long term bonds with one another. I even lost contact with the most important person for me at that time, my physical therapist, Rich White. I tried to find him several years later, but I found out he moved to Iowa somewhere.

A week after I returned from my leave, I was notified that I was being discharged from the Navy. I didn't have anything to say about it. I didn't really want to leave the Navy, but I guess I wasn't doing them too much good in the condition I was in. They made sure I was discharged exactly one week before my two-year service anniversary. That resulted in a substantial reduction in my retirement pay. I love the Navy, but I always felt they screwed me a little on that deal. Being discharged from the Navy also meant that I would be discharged from the Great Lakes Naval hospital, as it was for Navy personnel only. I was more upset about leaving Great Lakes than I was about leaving the Navy. I was now going to become a patient in the Veterans Administration medical system. I wasn't looking forward to that, as I had already heard that the care you got from the VA was nowhere near the quality of care you got from the Navy. Once again, there was nothing I could do about it. I was able to negotiate that, after one year, I could have my skull plate installed at Great Lakes. At least I knew that that part of my medical care would be done by a competent facility.

14

So, I left Great Lakes, and was loaded on another plane, and took a zig zag tour all over the Midwest. Several times we landed at places in Ohio, and I would tell them, "Just let me out here. I'll call somebody to pick me up." But they wouldn't let me, and two days later I finally arrived in Cleveland. I was transported by ambulance to the Wade Park Veterans Hospital. I immediately hated it. The first thing they did there was to take all of my clothes and locked them up. I had to wear pajamas all the time. I couldn't leave the facility to go home unless I had a special pass, which was next to impossible to get. The food was terrible, and I didn't have any choice as to what I ate. I felt like I was in prison. As soon as I got there I announced, "I want to go home." I was told that I had to wait until my discharge was official, and that, in the meantime, I would continue receiving physical therapy and that I would also be meeting with some counselors and advisors. Their idea of physical therapy wasn't what I was used to at Great Lakes. It was 15 minutes of electro-shock treatments to my arm. The counselors asked me questions like, "How do you feel about being disabled for the rest of your life?" Needless to say, I wasn't happy about being there. I met with a guy from Social Security who tried to get me to sign up for disability benefits. I told him, "You're wasting your time. I'm not going to be disabled. I'm getting better." He was persistent, though, and finally convinced me to sign up. He told me that it took 6 to 9 months before I would get any benefits, and that if I felt better by that time, I could say that I didn't need them.

Finally, they sent me to a woman who was some kind of therapist. I went to her office and she said, "I hear you want to go home." I said, "Yeah. Get me the hell out of here." She asked, "What do you want to do with yourself when you get home?" I told her I wanted to be a policeman, but I didn't think that was going to happen anymore. I said that I'd been thinking about being a high school teacher. I thought I'd like to work with kids. She asked me if I minded if she gave me some tests. I agreed, and I took the tests. A few days later, she called me back to her office. She told me, "Charlie, you can't go to college, and even if you did get into a college, you could never be a high school teacher." I said, "Why? What's the matter?" She told me that my aptitude tests showed me as being only average, and that I only had a seventh grade reading ability. I was floored. I knew

I was having trouble reading, but I had no idea that it was this bad. I didn't know what to think. She looked at me and said, "I could work with you here, but you say you want to go home. What do you want to do?" I said simply, "Fix me."

So, as much as I hated being in the VA hospital, I stayed for an extra month. I worked with that therapist every day doing reading exercises and taking tests. Part of the program was that I had to continue with the physical therapy while I was there, too. I put up with the shock treatments on my arm, even though it wasn't doing any good. After a month, I was discharged from the hospital and continued my reading therapy as an outpatient. All through the summer I traveled the 40 miles one way to the VA hospital twice a week. I was determined to raise my reading level, and worked hard to do so. At the end of the summer, my therapist brought me in her office and sat me down. "Guess what?" she said. "You've gone from a low 7th grade reading level to a 13+. You can go to college now." I was pretty happy about that.

My therapist helped me to fill out the paperwork for my college admission. It was already too late for me to get into the fall semester, but that didn't bother me. I had already decided to wait until the following fall to begin college. I still planned to have my skull plate put in that winter and that would have disrupted my studies. So I decided to continue working on some of the physical aspects of my rehabilitation. By this time, I was walking pretty good. I still carried a cane, but didn't rely on it as much. The only problem was that I concentrated so much on making my bad leg work, that I had ignored my arm. I figured that I would be able to live with one arm, but I didn't want to rely on a wheelchair to get me around. Walking was my main priority. Now that I was walking, I could start working on my arm. At that time, I kept my right arm in a sling, rather than have it just hanging lifelessly from my shoulder. I didn't have much movement in it at all. I had long since given up on the VA physical therapy and their shock treatments that didn't accomplish anything. I started working on it at home on my own, but progress was very slow.

My reading abilities got better, but I still couldn't write legibly with my left arm, and I thought I should work on that before I started college. I decided to take a shorthand class at the University of Akron. To me, shorthand looked a lot like my handwriting: just a bunch of scribbled lines. I figured shorthand would be a breeze. I stuck with the class for the whole term. At the end, I really never did learn much shorthand, but my teacher told me, "Have you noticed how your handwriting has improved?" After she pointed it out, I did see that I was writing much clearer. All the repetitive exercises in shorthand had really helped my left arm with its new writing responsibility.

I wish I could say that the progress I made with my walking, reading, and writing abilities matched the progress I made in adapting to life at home. I was having a lot of trouble there. As much as I wanted out of the VA hospital and to get home, once I got there I was very uncomfortable. At the hospitals I fit right in with the rest of the patients. I wasn't any different than anybody on the ward. Everyone was like me. When I got home, though, I felt like a freak. I felt like everybody was staring at me. I really hated being around people. Through all of this Fran was very supportive. She would drag me to public parks and to shopping malls, just to get me used to interacting with people. It wasn't working though. When kids would stare at me I'd scare them by going up to them and growling. I had grown a full beard by this time, so I looked pretty menacing, especially to a small child. One time, Fran and I were in a store and I noticed a middle aged woman staring at me. I shouted at her, "What's the matter lady? Ain't you ever seen a cripple before?" Fran was pretty embarrassed over that episode. The worst, though, was one time when we were in a department store. I was walking down a clothes aisle, and I guess I wasn't walking fast enough for some big, fat guy, who got impatient with me, and shoved me into a rack of shirts as he barreled by me. If I could have caught up to him, I probably would have killed him. That's how angry I was. Instead, all I could do was curse him so loudly that everyone in the store could hear me. After that, Fran decided not to take me shopping anymore.

In the United States, about the only way you can truly be independent is to drive your own car. I certainly didn't want to have to rely on public transportation to get myself around. I also didn't like asking people to take me places. And I didn't like waiting until Fran got home from work to be able to go somewhere. So, I taught myself to drive. Nobody ever said I couldn't drive, and I never asked anybody if I could. I first tried driving Fran's little Volkswagen Bug, but that was a disaster. First, it was too small, and second, it was a stick shift. It was hard enough to learn how to drive with one leg, and the wrong one at that, without trying to use a clutch, too. So, I went out and bought a big, old, 1965 Oldsmobile Starfire. It was shiny black with a white interior. There was plenty of leg room, so there was no problem crossing over my left leg to operate the gas pedal. As soon as I got it, I made a solo run out to my parent's home. I'm barreling down Main Street, thinking that there's no problem, when I came to a street I had to turn on, and I couldn't transfer my left leg from the gas to the brake pedal fast enough. I made that turn with my tires squealing, but the car was so big and heavy that it wasn't going to tip over. I eased up a little after that.

My driver's license had expired while I was in Vietnam, so I had to go to the license bureau to get it renewed. It seems funny now. I hobbled up to the counter using my cane, my arm in a sling, barely able to talk intelligibly. The woman behind the counter looked at me and said, "Do you have any disabilities that could prevent you from operating a motor vehicle?" I looked her in the eye and said, "Nope." She said, "Okay" and gave me my license.

Later that summer, I got a letter from the VA saying that they would like to help me buy a new car. They authorized $2800 towards the purchase of a vehicle with the equipment I needed to accommodate my disability, things like automatic transmission and power steering. I was so excited that I went right out on my own and took that letter to the nearest Ford dealership. They asked me what kind of vehicle I was interested in, and I pointed to the brand new, maroon, Ford pickup truck they had on the front row of their lot. Before I knew it, I had traded in my big Oldsmobile and was the proud owner of that new Ford truck. When Fran came home from work that night, and found out what I had done, she wasn't entirely pleased. She thought that I should have at least consulted with her before I went out and spent that amount of money. She also thought that maybe a nice family car would have been more practical. None the less, I was pretty happy with my purchase. It wasn't the first time I did something without her approval. It wouldn't be the last, either.

For the most part, Fran never bothered me about anything I did. She was very patient with me, and was my biggest help in adjusting to my disability. Whenever I got crabby over something I was having trouble with, she would leave me alone until I got over it. She never treated me like a cripple. In fact, most of the time she didn't even consider that I had some physical limitations. Each morning, before she left for work, she'd write down some things that I was supposed to do that day. Sometimes I'd get angry with her, because she'd give me jobs to do that I couldn't possibly do. She wasn't being mean. She just forgot that I had a disability, and, to her, there was nothing I couldn't do. She was a great motivator in that regard.

Driving wasn't the only thing I taught myself how to do. Just because I was stuck with half a body didn't mean I was willing to give up doing some of the things I loved to do. I still loved the outdoors, and I wanted to get back to the woods and fields and do some hunting. My old hunting partner and cousin, Denny, accommodated me. He'd take me with him when he went hunting. At first, I just would follow him around, just happy to be outside. After a while, I figured out how to make a sling so I was able to hold and shoot my shotgun. I got to be a pretty decent shot, too. Eventually, I was able to bag my share of quail and pheasants. One of my favorite things to do was coon hunting. One time, Denny took me with him, and we ended up coon hunting through most of the night. The next morning I had an appointment with the physical therapists at the VA hospital. I came in looking pretty ragged. They looked at me and said, "What happened to you? You look terrible." I told them I was out all night coon hunting. They all started laughing hysterically. I guess they found the idea of a crippled man with a cane chasing raccoons through the woods all night quite humorous.

Another thing I wanted to do was to take up golf. I thought it was another great way to spend some time outdoors. Seeing as how I had to do everything left handed now, I went out and bought myself a set of left-handed golf clubs. I spent hours at the driving range trying to learn how to hit a golf ball. Eventually I did, but I never was too good at it. I got frustrated, and went to the owner of the driving range, Mr. Kosar, and told him that I had no idea what I was doing wrong. He said, "I can help you." He told me that golf was a game meant to be played by right handers, and said that the first thing I should do is get rid of the left handed golf clubs. He made up a small set of used right-handed clubs for me. Then he taught me how to hit them back handed. It was a little awkward at first, but soon I was hitting the ball farther and straighter than I ever had before. Eventually, I got good enough to graduate from the driving range to the links. Golf went from being a frustration to something that I enjoy even today.

Besides doing things that I enjoyed physically, I also learned to take care of my spiritual being, too. I started going to church three times a week. With all the problems I had, I didn't want God mad at me too. From the beginning of my rehabilitation, I never asked God to help me to become well again. I figured He'd already done a lot by letting me live. I would have felt stupid asking for more. I'd say to him in my prayers that if He wanted to help me, I'd appreciate it, but, mostly, I just wanted the strength to do what I was capable of doing by myself. I felt fortunate enough just to be alive.

I even joined the choir at church. I found out that I could sing a lot better than I could talk. I used to listen to the radio a lot. I thought it was odd that I could sing along with most of the old rock and roll songs, but I couldn't carry on a sensible conversation. I still haven't figured out the reason for that. I really enjoyed singing in the choir. The only problem was that sometimes I'd get a little exuberant, and I'd start to sway with the music. It was easy for me to get off balance, and I'd end up bouncing off the poor soul who happened to be standing next to me. One of my fellow choir members used to say that he always had bruises the day after he sang next to me in choir. People learned to give me a little extra space.

In February, 1972, I made arrangements to return to Great Lakes Naval Hospital to have my plate put in. I had to pay my own expenses to get there, but it was worth it to have it done at a facility that I trusted. When I walked into the hospital, the doctors who had worked on me were fascinated by the progress I had made. I put on quite a show for them, too. I walked tall and straight, and talked slowly and clearly. I even filled out my own paperwork. I was proud of how far I had come, and I wanted to show off a little, especially to those who thought I'd never make any progress.

There were two reasons for having the plate installed. The most important was that since there was a large portion of my skull gone, my brain had no protection from outside forces in that area. Even a slight bump to that area could be very dangerous. The doctors even wanted me to wear a football helmet for protection whenever I was riding in a car. Needless to say, I never followed that advice. I had enough problem being noticed without being seen wearing a football helmet in a car. The second reason, and pretty important to me, was the aesthetics of my head. With my bare head showing there was a large indentation where the skull was missing. Some Marine at the VA hospital nicknamed me "soap dish", because he said that's what my head looked like. I could take the harassment from a fellow Vietnam vet, but I wasn't going to take any abuse from the general public. Since Fran didn't like me wearing my skull cap in public, I had taken to wearing a wig to cover up my flawed head.

I was pretty excited about getting my plate. It was made out of plastic, and, a few days before the operation, they came in and shaved what little hair I had and formed this plastic mold over my skull so that the plate would match the contour of my head. After they finished making the plate, they let me hold it for a while and show it to anyone who was interested. They told me that the plate would actually be stronger than my skull was. I didn't care how strong it was. I just wanted it to make me look more normal. Although I was anxious to have the plate put in, I also was a little nervous about the operation. I was afraid of what might happen with them cutting into my head again. Any surgery close to the brain is always dangerous, and I admit I was a little scared going in to the operation.

For some reason my operation was postponed for a week. Aside from the added anguish of having to wait another week for the operation, I didn't mind. I liked being back at Great Lakes, on my old familiar Ward 8. It was a lot more comfortable than being out in public back in Ohio. I had a pretty good time during that extra week. I did a lot of visiting, especially with my old pals in physical therapy. I even got to try some of the new equipment they got since I left.

The operation went off without a hitch. Well, almost, anyhow. I should mention that up to this time I never had any pain associated with my injury. From the time I was shot till just before the operation I never had to take so much as an aspirin because of pain in my head. That all changed as soon as I woke up in the recovery room. I had never felt pain like that before. Fluid would build up in between the new plate and my scalp, and the result would be a throbbing headache like I couldn't even imagine. Once a day, the surgeon would come in and take a stitch out of my incision and he would press down on my scalp to get rid of the excess fluid. The pain was excruciating. I would tell the doctor, "Are you sure you know what you're doing?" He would reply, "Who do you think put the plate in?"

It was during this time that I got acquainted with codeine. At first, they gave me a shot of it every four hours. I liked its effect. It allowed me to sleep, but, even when I was awake, it kept me feeling mighty fine. But the headaches would always return. After a couple of days, the doctor said that the liquid form of codeine might actually be causing me to have a hangover, which is why I was having headaches. He put me on codeine tablets, which I could take every three hours, and I always made sure that I got them on schedule. After a few more days, I was lying in bed and I yelled to a corpsman, "Give me my pills." He left for a while, and when he came back he didn't have any codeine pills with him. He told me that the doctor said that I had enough codeine in me already that they could have amputated my entire head and I wouldn't have felt a thing. The corpsman handed me two aspirin, and that was the end of feeding my codeine jones.

As much as I wanted to stay in the safety and comfort of the hospital at Great Lakes, I was sent home two weeks after my operation. Fran and I were still living with her parents, mainly because we had no money. For some unknown reason, my Navy retirement pay had been delayed. After I got home from Great Lakes, my dad took me to downtown Cleveland to see what could be done about getting me my retirement pay. The man we talked to there was very apologetic, and assured us that we wouldn't leave there without a check of some sort. As it turned out, they cut me a check for all the back pay they owed me. We used that money to get an apartment of our own. I think Fran hoped that being on our own would help me to adjust more to fitting in. I did, too, but I wasn't too optimistic about it.

With my newly repaired head, and a new apartment, I was ready to start the next phase of my rehabilitation: getting my college degree. The VA had a program of vocational rehab that would pay for all my college tuition, books, and expenses. It covered more expenses than the GI Bill would have so I decided to try to get into the program. My therapist, who helped me with my reading, also helped me fill out all the necessary paperwork to apply for Voc Rehab. I sent it all in and waited for a response from the VA. In the meantime I applied for admission to Kent State University and was accepted as a full time student. I was to begin classes in the fall of 1972. I waited all spring and through most of the summer to hear from the VA, but all my letters of inquiry seemed to be ignored. In August I decided to make a personal visit to the VA in downtown Cleveland to see what the holdup was. I went there without an appointment or even a name of somebody to see. The VA was in the Federal Building and I was able to find out where the Voc Rehab department was. I went to the floor they were on and for several minutes I was totally ignored by everyone there. Finally my patience wore thin and I shouted out, "Does anybody work in this damn place?" The prospect of having to deal with an irate crippled veteran got their attention and I was told that I needed to see a Mr. Feingold. They ushered me to his office and found my application and gave it to him. He looked over my paperwork and said, "Yeah, we got your application here. We don't feel you're being realistic in your goals." I asked him what he meant. He went on to tell me that he felt that someone in my condition couldn't be an effective high school teacher. He said that I would never be able to control the students. I got defensive and stubborn and told him, "Well, if I can't be a high school teacher then I'm not going to do anything at all. I'll just sit on my ass and you can pay me for doing nothing." He said, "That's a bad attitude." I said, "It's the only attitude I've got." He shook his head and said, "Well, before you can go to college you have to take some tests to see whether you're qualified. If you pass them, you can go to school." I said, "Fine. Give me the tests." He said, "They'll have to be scheduled." I explained that I planned on starting school in September and that it was already August. He assured me that they would get them scheduled as quick as they could. With that he ushered me out of his office and told me to wait until they contacted me.

So, I went home and waited. Finally, one week before the end of late registration at Kent State, I got a letter from the VA that my testing was scheduled for October. I was pretty angry and decided to take matters into my own hands. I went to Kent State and signed up for my classes and got my books, and paid for everything with my own money. Before I registered I talked to my neighbor at our apartment building, who was also a high school teacher. I mentioned to him that I wanted to be a history teacher. He said, "Charlie, history teachers are a dime a dozen. You need to get into something else." He gave me a booklet, "The

Twenty Most Wanted Teaching Positions" and I discovered that one of the most in demand was Business Education. I had an interest at one time in becoming an accountant so I thought that business might be a good major for me. I talked to a counselor at Kent State about it and we came up with the plan that I would major in Business Education and have a minor in Economics. I was pretty satisfied with my choice and, even though I had to go through late registration, I was able to get all the classes I wanted.

I started my classes and adjusted pretty well to them. October came and I got ready to take my tests at the VA. Unfortunately, I came back from Vietnam with some pretty bad teeth and a few days before my scheduled tests I developed an abscess in one of them. My dentist couldn't extract it until the swelling went down so he gave me some antibiotics and some painkillers to get me through until he could pull it. Although I felt horrible I didn't want to reschedule the test knowing how long it took to schedule this one. So, I went down to Cleveland to take an eight-hour test with a swollen face and taking painkillers every four hours. About halfway through the testing my face was throbbing. I was having a lot of trouble concentrating and I didn't know how well I was doing on it. After the testing was over, I explained to the test administrator about my tooth problem and how it may have effected my test results. She said that she could see how swollen my face was, and she would be sure to make a note of the situation should another test be necessary. I set up an appointment with Mr. Feingold for the following week to go over the results of the tests.

The next week I went back to Cleveland for my appointment with Mr. Feingold. As he called me into his office I could tell he didn't look happy. He said, "Well, you passed, but I still don't like it." According to the tests I was better suited to become a forest ranger. He still felt I wasn't being realistic in my goal of becoming a high school teacher. I said, "It doesn't matter. That's what I want." Reluctantly, he had a check made out to cover all of my first quarter's school costs. I was on my way to getting a college degree.

15

My first quarter at Kent State I took just enough credits to be considered a full-time student. I knew school was going to be difficult for me and I didn't want to be overwhelmed right off the bat. At first, I had a very hard time getting used to school again. My terrible high school studying habits didn't do anything to prepare me for the more intense college courses. I had never learned how to be a good student and I had to figure out how to be one real quick. The other problem I had when I first started college was self-inflicted. I was determined to look like just any other student, which was very hard to do considering my physical problems along with the fact that I was a lot older than the standard 18 year-old freshmen. In order not to get noticed, I would arrive for class well before its scheduled starting time and would be in my seat before anyone else arrived. I also would stay until everyone else left. I thought I was doing a pretty good job of covering up my disability and fitting in as one of the guys until one day in class I was sitting at my desk and I dropped a pencil on the floor. Of course it fell on my bad side, and, as I leaned over to pick it up, I tumbled out of the chair and hit my head against a heat register on the side wall. When my head hit the register it sounded like a loud gong. I wasn't hurt, as by this time I was pretty used to falling, but it kind of shocked the rest of the students and the next day, and for the remainder of that quarter, no one would sit anywhere near me.

Getting to and from school was another adventure. At first I didn't drive to school because the student parking lots were a pretty good distance from my classes and, with the way I walked, it would have taken me a good while to get from my car to class. Of course I was eligible for a handicap parking permit, which would have allowed me to park right next to my class buildings, but the parking sticker had a wheelchair on it and I wasn't going to allow any image of a wheelchair to be put on my truck. So, I rode the bus. It came by the street where I lived and dropped me off right in front of my classes. Every day I'd get on the bus toting all of my heavy textbooks in a drawstring plastic bag. A backpack was too difficult for me to get on and off. I'd put the drawstring through my good arm and lug it around like that. Usually that was no problem, but some days the bus would get crowded and there were no seats. I'd have to stand in the aisle, trying to hang onto a post and my books with my one good arm. One day, the bus was very crowded and I was stuck standing in the aisle. Then the bus was held up by a train at a crossing, and it took a while for the train to get through. The heavy book bag cut off the circulation in my arm, and, just as I was setting the bag down to give my arm a rest, the bus took off. I lost my balance and, for some unknown reason, there was a reflex action in my bad arm and it shot out and hit a young girl standing next to me right in the ear. It really smacked her, too. I felt absolutely terrible about what I had done. The girl fought back the tears as best she could, but I could tell that she really got stung. I apologized profusely and she was very understanding. That didn't help me to feel better, though, and I certainly never wanted it to happen again. I was so upset that the next day I went and got a handicap parking permit and I never rode the bus again.

Insofar as my actual classes were concerned, I was doing okay. I wasn't making the Dean's list or anything like that, but I was holding my own. Taking notes in class was pretty difficult for me. The VA offered to buy me a tape recorder in order to tape the lectures but I didn't want to do it that way. Nobody else in my classes had one and I didn't want to do anything different than anyone else. So I took notes using my chicken scratch handwriting. I'd take a lot of notes, and the only problem was that when it was time to refer to them when I was studying for a test, I couldn't tell what I had written. I got by, though.

During my first quarter I had a History class. History was one of the subjects I really enjoyed in high school and I was thinking that I was going to do okay in it. However, this was the history of Ancient Civilization and I was bored to death with it. I'd fall asleep while I read the textbook. To top it off there was a teacher's aide from Africa that taught the class and I had a lot of trouble understanding him. He'd explain something and, while everyone else in class seemed to understand him, I'd raise my hand and say, "What?" He thought I was making fun of the way he talked, and I considered myself lucky to get through that class with a "C".

Then I had an English class taught by an Indian lady. I saw that as a problem right away. She started giving us writing assignments the day the class began. She wasn't impressed with my illegible handwriting and eventually told me that I'd have to turn in my papers typed. I had Fran type them for me, but I had to be right next to her when she did because she couldn't read my writing either. Nothing I did ever impressed that teacher until one time she gave us an assignment to write a paper and then talk about it in class. I guess she realized that I would have double trouble with this assignment because it involved both writing and speaking, so she told me I could write about anything I liked. I decided to write about coon hunting. I took all the funny stories that had happened to me and my cousin Denny through all the years we'd been coon hunting, and I wrote them like they all happened in one night. I was pretty proud of myself when I turned it in. I ended up getting a "B₁" on it and I would have got an "A" had I not misspelled so many words. She told me later, "I had no idea what you were talking about, but it was the funniest thing I ever heard."

I also took an Economics class, which was a subject I was interested in, and I thought I could do well in. I liked the teacher. He was a World War II veteran and he was very knowledgeable and a good speaker. But I had no idea what he was talking about. It seemed like everyone else in the class did, but I just couldn't grasp things like gross national product and other economic terms and concepts. He did give credit for speaking up in class and I was always looking out for something intelligent to say. Driving to class everyday I'd listen to my regular rock and roll station on the radio. During my commute time the commentator Paul Harvey used to come on. Usually I'd just block him out, but one day I recognized some of the words he was saying were economics terms. I went into class that day and I talked about what I had heard on the radio. I just didn't mention that I heard them on the Paul Harvey show. I just pretended that they were some of my own ideas. The teacher was very impressed and, everyday thereafter, I talked about what I had heard on Paul Harvey that day. I really should have sent Mr. Harvey a letter thanking him for the "B" I got in my Economics class.

Outside of school my life was starting to come together, too. The VA finally made a ruling on my disability compensation. They ended up classifying me as 230% disabled. I was 50% disabled because of my leg, 50% for my arm, 50% for the hole in my head, 50% for a nervous condition, and 30% for my speech. Now that didn't mean they paid me 230%. The most you could get was 100%. After that they went by letter, starting with "A". I ended up being 100% "M". I had to choose between getting VA disability payments or my Navy pension. I wasn't allowed to get both. It wasn't much of a decision. The disability payments were much greater than I would have gotten from my Navy pension, especially since they kicked me out before I had two years in.

I got a nice check for the disability payments I was owed since I became disabled. Fran "advised" me that I wasn't to do anything stupid with that money like buy another pickup truck. So, for the first time in my life I made a sensible financial decision and we bought a house. We found a nice little bungalow in Kent that had a big yard. The yard was what I was most interested in, because, by this time, I already had two dogs. My cousin gave me a coon hound and a friend of mine gave me a bird dog. Since I couldn't keep them at the apartment we were living in, I had to keep them at my in-laws. I think they were the happiest of anyone when we announced that we had purchased a house.

My favorite place to hang out was a little ice cream store called Isaly's. I spent a lot of time there before, after, and in between classes, and I was pretty well known among the regulars there. A lot of the regulars were construction guys who knew I liked to pick up a little extra money by doing some odd construction work here and there. One time there was a bricklayer there who asked me if I could dig a footer for him for a house addition he was working on. He said that he couldn't get his backhoe in where he needed it and it would have to be dug by hand. I was pretty good with a shovel, so I agreed to do it. With the new house and everything I needed a few extra dollars. While I was working there I met the owner of the house and, apparently, someone had told her that I was injured in Vietnam. She told me that her son was the president of a chapter of the Vietnam Veterans Against the War and that he would really like to recruit me to join his group. I told her, "Ma'am, nobody hates the Vietnam war more than I do, but as long as my buddies are still over there fighting, I can't protest against it." She never brought the subject up again.

There were people on the other side of the debate on the war that tried to get me to join them too. There were a lot of Vietnam veterans going to Kent State at the time. Having returned from their tours of duty, they were taking advantage of the GI bill and getting their college education on Uncle Sam. One day, I was walking on campus when a pretty mean looking guy with a gruff voice and a bum leg comes up to me and says, "You a Vietnam vet?" I told him yes, and asked him why he assumed I was. He said, "Most cripples our age are Vietnam vets." He went on to tell me that he belonged to a group of veterans that were going to an anti-war protest rally that weekend. He said they were going there to beat the crap out of those hippie protesters. He said, "You should come along." I found the guy to be pretty scary, so I said, "Yeah, sure. Sounds great." I made sure that I came up with a bona fide excuse for not showing up just in case I ever ran into him again.

I had some issues with other veteran's groups, too. On the first Veteran's Day since I came home from Vietnam I felt like doing something with some other veterans. I couldn't come up with any ideas of what to do when Fran suggested that I go to the American Legion hall that was down the road in Stow. She said there was bound to be a bunch of veterans there that I could hang out with. I headed over there and rang the doorbell. Someone inside opened the peephole in the door and in a rough tone of voice said, "What do you want?" I explained that I was a Vietnam veteran and that I just wanted to spend Veteran's Day with some veterans. He said, "Well you can't come in here without a sponsor." I told him I could show him my retired Navy ID card. He said, "Don't make any difference. You can't come in." With that he shut the peephole. I cursed him vigorously through the closed door and went back home.

When I got home, Fran asked me what had happened. I told her about being rejected by the Stow American Legion. She said, "Why don't you try the one in Kent?" I said that they're all probably the same. She said, "Why don't you try anyhow." So off I went again, and I rang the doorbell at the Kent American Legion hall. An older man opened the door and in a friendly voice said, "Can I help you?" I told him I was a Vietnam veteran looking for some other veterans to spend the day with. He said, "Come on in." I said, "But I don't have a sponsor." He said, "Well, you do now." He brought me in and bought me a beer and I spent several hours there that day listening to all kinds of stories about World War II. I thoroughly enjoyed the time I spent there. Years later, the Stow American Legion was having a recruitment drive. They called me up and invited me to come down and visit them. I told them that because of the way they treated me that I would never set foot in their hall again and I hung up on them. I never got over that.

Eventually, I started reacquiring my old drinking problem. As I became more comfortable in social settings, I starting hanging out with my old buddies. It seemed that all that my old buddies wanted to do was to go bar hopping, so, on weekends that was my regular activity. It got to the point where that was all that I wanted to do. I knew that I really wasn't supposed to be drinking any alcohol in my physical condition. I especially wasn't supposed to drink while I was taking my anti-seizure medication. So, I stopped taking it. I'd stay out until all hours of the night, coming home in the wee hours of the morning. And, to top it off, I was driving in this condition. Let me tell you, a drunken, one arm, one leg, hole-in-the-head driver is not something you want to run across out on the road at dawn's early light. Fran hated the fact that I was drinking. She really hated drinking, period. She never drank and still doesn't to this day. On the rare occasions when we would go out to dinner I'd say I had to go to the bathroom and sneak off to the bar for a quick screwdriver. Fran never yelled at me, or gave me any ultimatums about my drinking, but I could tell it was really straining our relationship. It's the closest we ever came to splitting up.

It's funny how things work in my life sometimes. My beliefs are that a higher power seems to take over whenever I'm in serious trouble. And so it was when I was on the verge of destroying my relationship with Fran, a miracle happened that turned me around 180 degrees. One morning Fran woke up very sick. She was so sick we decided to see a doctor right away. He did some tests and sent us home. The next day he called and I answered the phone. He said, "The test came back positive." I said, "Positive for what?" He laughed and said, "Positive that your wife is pregnant." I was stunned. I couldn't believe that I was going to be a dad. We had been trying to start a family ever since I came home but nothing happened. I began to think that part of my disability was that I was unable to father any children. Just a few weeks previous I told Fran, "You know if we can't have children it's okay. I'd rather be a rich uncle than a poor father." Now I learned that my worries were unfounded. I was going to be a father and, as proud and happy as I was, I gave up drinking immediately.

I also immediately became a doting father-to-be. I wanted to be with Fran all the time. I guess I kind of smothered her. It even got to the point where she suggested that I start spending some evenings with my buddies again. But I didn't want to. After all, I was going to be a father. There was no time for foolishness. After some of the initial excitement wore off I began to get worried. I was concerned about what my child was going to be like. Even though my disability had nothing to do with genetics, I was worried that my child was going to be disabled like me. Although I was very happy about my impending parenthood, I was also scared to death about the health and well being of my child.

I think those nine months were the longest of my life. I was extremely anxious for the birth to take place and I was fit to be tied when Fran was 12 days late going into labor. It was December 21 when she finally did. I was just like most nervous fathers when she told me it was time, and I loaded her up in the car and drove her to the hospital. Back then, birthing classes weren't so popular and we didn't attend any. It was my intent to drop her off at the hospital and I would remain in the waiting room. So, I was kind of surprised when, after getting Fran registered and into a wheelchair, the nurses told me to follow them to the labor room. Now there was nothing in the labor room that I wanted to see, but I followed them anyway. They got Fran into a bed and told me to put towels on her head and to massage her stomach. Then the nurses left us alone as they went off to some hospital Christmas party. This was a lot more involved than I wanted to be, but I continued my duties while Fran moaned in pain. This went on for hours with only an occasional visit from a nurse, who would come in and check Fran out and then announce, "Not yet." Finally, after 12 hours, the doctor came in and looked at Fran. He said to the nurses, "We can't wait any longer. We're going to have to take the baby now or else we may lose both of them." Those weren't exactly words of comfort to an already overwrought, soon-to-be father. They asked me to leave, which I gladly did, and they prepped Fran for surgery. I went to the maternity waiting room and waited while Fran had a caesarian section. I was scared out of my mind. I sat in that room all alone and waited and waited for what seemed like days. Finally, the doctor came in and started talking to me about baby care. I said, "Wait a minute. What about my wife?" He looked at me strangely and said, "You mean nobody's told you?" My heart started racing. He continued, "I'm sorry. Your wife is fine. Everything went well. You've got a beautiful son." To say I was relieved is an understatement. I was relieved and overjoyed. The doctor took me to the maternity ward and motioned for the nurses to hold up my son so I could see him. I watched as a nurse struggled to get a blue blanket around a very big baby. It wouldn't fit around him. Finally, she held him up to me, naked as a jaybird. I never saw anything so beautiful.

My son, Matt, weighed over nine pounds when he was born. There was no way that tiny little Fran was going to bring anything that big into the world with a natural childbirth. Both mother and child were healthy, but Fran remained in the hospital for four days to recover from the ordeal. It was after Christmas by the time I got them home. Fran's mom stayed with us for the first few days to help out. I didn't know anything about how to take care of newborn babies. On top of that, I was afraid to hold Matt, worried that I'd either drop him trying to hang on to him with one arm, or I'd lose my balance on my one good leg and fall on top of him. It took a while before I got up enough courage to hold him, but once I did, I held him all the time. After a few days I sent Fran's mom home telling Fran that I could take care of both her and Matt. One of the first things I had to learn was to change a diaper, a daunting task even for a man with two arms. There was no way I could use the standard cloth diaper with the safety pins. I was glad that there were things such as Pampers back then and, after a few tries, I was able to do a credible job changing Matt. About the only problem I had was that I used to spread Vasoline on his butt and it would get on the sticky tabs of the Pampers and render them useless. It was a small price to pay for the joy I got taking care of my new son. It was really odd. Whenever Fran changed Matt, he would constantly be fussing and fidgeting and wouldn't hold still, but, whenever I would put him on the changing table and put my hand on him, he would lie perfectly still until I was done. I always felt that right from the start Matt understood that his father had some problems and he wanted to make it as easy as he could for me. I was greatly appreciative for that, too.

I tried not to let my new responsibilities as a father interfere with my education, but, all of a sudden, some of my classes were becoming difficult for me. I started taking some accounting classes as part of my curriculum. I thought that since accounting was based on math, and I was good with math, that I would do well in accounting. Then I found out that accounting was mostly based on concepts and procedures and, even though I had some great professors, I had no idea what they were talking about a lot of the time. The accounting classes started to bring my grade point average down because the best I could do in those classes was to get a "C". I began to wonder whether the program I chose was going to work out after all.

I had to take a college algebra course and I was pretty sure I wasn't going to have any problems with it. It was the one course that I did well in at high school. But, when I started the class, I found that I couldn't remember what I had learned back in high school algebra. I started getting migraine headaches, something I had never had before even with my brain injury. The headaches were so bad that I was getting nauseous from them. I started taking aspirin by the bottle to relieve the pain. When they didn't go away, I naturally thought I had some sort of brain tumor and was going to die. I figured I was living on borrowed time anyhow. Finally, I went to the VA hospital to get myself checked out. I told the person at the admission desk the problems I was having, and they sent me to a room to wait for a doctor. When the doctor came in he told me he was a psychiatrist. I blew up. I yelled at him, "I've got headaches and I probably got some kind of brain tumor. I need a real doctor, not a shrink." The psychiatrist told me to calm down and he went out and came back with a couple of doctors, both M.D.'s. They examined me, and talked to me for a while, and sent me to have some neurological tests done. They told me that they would call me when the results of my tests came back.

The following week they called, and I went back to the hospital to talk with them. They told me that the tests confirmed that there were no tumors whatsoever. I was greatly relieved to hear that. Then they told me that it was their opinion that my problem was that the loss of the portion of my brain during my surgery had reduced my capacity for learning. I had been pushing myself so hard at school that my brain had reached its limits, and I was now trying to go beyond its capabilities with the result being severe headaches. Basically, they told me that there was no way physically I could continue with so many difficult classes. They wrote a letter to Kent State explaining my situation, and that allowed me to withdraw from the accounting and algebra courses without getting a failing grade. Now I had to figure out what I could change my major to.

One of the courses I had taken as an elective was a marketing class. At the time, I had no idea what marketing was, but, as the class progressed, I found that I really liked it. Maybe it was because I had a great professor, but I found that the concepts of marketing came easy for me. Everything about it just seemed logical.

I particularly liked when the professor divided the class into teams and we had to come up with a marketing plan for a fictitious business. It ended up being a little competition between the teams to see who could come up with the best marketing plan. I liked being part of a team, and I used some of my old Navy training as a squad leader and became sort of the unofficial director of our team. I did quite well in the class, and, when I started looking for a new major, I looked for one that was marketing based.

I went back and looked at the list of the most in-demand teaching positions and down the list in about 15th place was something called Distributive Education. I looked into it and found that what it did, basically, was to teach students marketing skills. I thought that it was the best of both worlds. I would get to teach high school and I'd also be involved in marketing. I went to my counselor at Kent State and told him I wanted to change my major to Distributive Education. He looked over the credits that I already had and found that all my classes could be transferred to the new major so I wouldn't lose any hours. So, I made the decision and changed my major.

Right away I started taking more marketing classes than I had to. I filled up my electives with business classes. It was all part of my grand plan. I thought that if I didn't like teaching I would have a back up plan where I could go to work for some big company in their marketing department. I figured that there would be lots of large corporations lined up to hire a disabled Vietnam vet for the public relations value. They could hire me as a token cripple. I wouldn't mind.

I really enjoyed all my business and marketing classes, and I had no trouble doing well in all of them. I also had to take Education courses and, while I found them interesting and liked them, I had a difficult time with them. One of the classes I had a particularly bad problem with was a speech class. It wasn't only because of my physical problem with speaking, either. The class was taught by some new age flower child, who came to the classroom with her dog and sat down on the floor and said, "Okay. I don't want to talk. I want to hear what you've got to say." For some reason she rubbed me the wrong way. I spouted off, "Lady, I didn't come to this class to hear myself. You're being paid to teach, so teach." I guess I rubbed her the wrong way, too, because a couple of days later my counselor called me into his office and told me that with my speech problem and all maybe the speech class I was in wasn't in my best interest. He suggested that I transfer to an alternative class, Interpersonal Communication. I didn't know if I was supposed to read into something there or what.

I adjusted well to my new college major and school in general. I got to the point where I could determine almost immediately whether a class was going to be too difficult for me to handle, and I could drop it before it became a problem. I also knew when I was taking too many credit hours in a semester, and I could reduce them before my brain got fried. Insofar as my education was concerned, I was learning to be in control.

At home, however, a new problem was cropping up. I don't know whether it was the more isolated environment of our new house, or the feeling of being responsible for the protection of my wife and new son, but I started getting very fearful during the night. My fears were unfounded, but, to me, they were very real. I was getting paranoid about someone breaking into our house with the intent of harming me and my family. It got to the point where I put a loaded gun underneath my bed and put a large hunting knife on the nightstand next to the bed. This, of course, frightened Fran. With the slightest disturbance I would be instantly awake. Fran was always worried that something she might do would startle me and end in disaster. I'd wake up in the middle of the night sure that I heard the noise of someone trying to break into our house. Eventually, I wouldn't sleep at all during the night. I'd stay awake and on guard until dawn when I'd get a little sleep until it was time to get up. I wasn't having any nightmares or flashbacks to Vietnam. I wasn't dreaming at all because I wasn't sleeping. This went on for months and it took its toll on me physically. I thought I was going nuts. Compounding my anxiety was the fear that eventually Fran would have me committed to the psychiatric ward at the VA hospital in Brecksville. Through it all, though, Fran never once suggested that I visit a shrink. She probably thought it though.

It was during this time that I was taking a psychology course at Kent. During one class the professor talked about this thing called apprehension. It was when somebody had unsubstantiated feelings that someone was out to get them. During that lecture I had a "Eureka" moment. I said, "That's me. I've got apprehension." From that point on when I woke up in the night fearful, I would tell myself that it was just my apprehension and I would feel better. Eventually, I overcame my fears and was able to sleep through the night. I was saved by my psychology class. I still kept the knife by the nightstand, though, just in case.

16

My first experience with teaching came when I was assigned to take part in what was called the Junior Participator program. It was designed to give education students some exposure to teaching early on in their college degree program. I tell you, it almost made me change my mind about a teaching career. I was sent to a junior high school in Parma, a suburb of Cleveland. There, I was assigned to assist an English teacher. It was ironic that I had to teach the subject that I was worst in. The teacher decided that I should have my own little group to tutor, so she singled out all of her worst students and told me to work with them. So, while her class was rid of problem children, I was basically thrown to the wolves. I didn't mind, though. After all, I was just like them when I was their age. I wasn't even given a classroom. I had to teach them in the hall. As soon as they got out there they started acting up. Two girls started giggling and got up and raced down the hall to the bathroom. A few minutes later I saw smoke coming from the bathroom door. I went down there and yelled through the door for them to come out. They said, "Come and get us." There was no way I was going to go into a girls bathroom, so I told them I was going to report them to their teacher. They replied from inside, "You wouldn't do that." They were right. I didn't, and after a while they came out and rejoined us. Those kids saw in me a vulnerable young man with no real authority and they took as much advantage of the situation as they could. Study halls were the worst. The kids would come in at the front of the auditorium and sneak out right through the back. I'd spend the entire period just chasing kids down. I could see how these terrible kids affected the permanent teachers there. There was one teacher there who was only 23 years old and had only been teaching for a year. I swore he looked forty. I heard some of the teachers talking about a fellow teacher who was in a hospital after having some kind of nervous breakdown. To say the least, the situation there was chaotic. I did my best to maintain my cool for the six weeks I was there, but there were times when I thought I was going to explode. After that experience I vowed that I would never ever work in a junior high school again, not even as a substitute for a day. That age group is just uncontrollable.

My experience with the junior high kids caused me to question my motives for pursuing a teaching career. In fact, I could have asked why was I pursuing any career at all. I didn't have to work. It certainly wasn't for the financial rewards that I wanted to be a teacher. I could have stayed home and collected my disability benefits and I would have had no money worries whatsoever. My dad actually thought I was nuts for not just sitting back and let the government take care of me for the rest of my life. He thought they at least owed me that for what I'd been through. Realistically, I could have really lived the life of Riley. I could have just done the things I loved to do. I could have spent my days hunting and fishing and playing golf and tennis. For some reason, though, I never considered that option. Right from the time I was in the hospital in Vietnam I started thinking about what I would do when I got home. Of course, I always thought that my paralysis was temporary and that one day soon I would be back to normal. Because I thought I was going to be normal, I also thought that I would return to working in the factory at Massey Ferguson, doing the same job I did before I left for the Navy. I really didn't like that job all that much, so, while I was in the hospital, I started thinking of alternatives. My original plan was to complete my time in the Navy and then come home and be a policeman. I didn't want to be a regular patrol cop. I wanted to be on some sort of youth division where I could get involved with helping troubled kids. After my injury I realized that passing the physical tests to become a policeman would be improbable, so I shelved that plan. I still wanted to do something with young people, though. I wanted to do something with public service. I thought back to the time when I was training at Jacksonville and I was the class leader. I really enjoyed being involved with the teaching of that class, even though I mostly did menial tasks. I thought teaching high school was the perfect way for me to fulfill my desire to help young people and to be doing a job that I enjoyed, too.

My education background certainly didn't point to a teaching career. I was a bad student. I got bad grades and I hated being in school. I was a troublemaker. It was kind of funny. When I was getting my college application ready I had to go over to my old high school to get my transcripts. The principal then was a history teacher that I had when I went to high school. When he gave me my transcripts he said, "So, you're going to college, Charlie. What are you going to be?" When I told him I wanted to be a teacher he doubled over in laughter. He said, "You old hellraiser. I hope you get back everything that you gave out when you were here."

Some of my motivation for becoming a teacher stemmed from my intense desire to be just a regular, normal guy. I got angry with people who would tell me, "You can't do that" before they even gave me a chance to try. I didn't want to be the crippled guy that everyone looked at and said, "Wow. Look at all the things he can do despite his disability." I wanted people to see me as just plain old

Charlie, nothing special. I wanted to be just like I was before my injury. I practically drove myself nuts trying to fit in unnoticed. Sometimes I'd even go off by myself and cry. I'd ask myself, "What do they want from me? I'm doing everything that regular people do. What more do they want me to do?" After years of therapy I learned that "they" didn't want anything. It was what I wanted that was driving me crazy. As far as I had already come in my rehabilitation, I still wasn't happy with myself.

While there were a lot of people who supported me after my injury, there were a lot of people who doubted my abilities. Sometimes my motivation was to prove these doubting Thomas's wrong. There were times when I felt like the guys I hung out with at Isaly's looked at me like some sort of retarded guy who thought he was a college student. One time, I came in and sat down and started to unzip my jacket. Under my jacket I was wearing an old University of Akron sweatshirt and the guy sitting next to me noticed it and reached over and opened my jacket for the rest to see. One of the guys piped up, "Hey, what school is Charlie going to this week?" That drew a big laugh from the rest of the guys. Maybe I was being oversensitive, but that hurt me. It hurt me enough that I still remember it thirty years later. Even some of my family doubted me. Some of them, when they would call, and I would answer the phone, would ask to talk to Fran. I always thought it was because they felt I was too stupid to remember anything, or to take a message, or to carry on an intelligent conversation. Even after I started college, they still treated me like I was a little bit "off."

My prime motivators, though, were my wife and my son. I never wanted to be a burden to Fran, and I never wanted my son to look at me as some cripple. Outside of school I was doing good. I had no physical problems whatsoever, and I was keeping myself in pretty good shape with all the exercising I was doing. There weren't many physical activities that I couldn't do. Somehow I'd figure out how to do everything with half a body. After I started playing golf, Fran told me that she always wanted to learn how to play tennis. Occasionally, we would go to a park and whack a few balls back and forth but nothing real serious. I told her that if we were going to play tennis we were going to learn how to do it right. As part of their continuing education program Kent State offered classes in tennis so we both signed up. It was like instant love. We never could get enough of it. Our garage door was all beat up from us practicing hitting balls against it. When Matt was just a little baby we would take him to the park and set him up with some toys in a corner of a tennis court and, while he occupied himself, we would play for hours. My biggest challenge in tennis was learning how to serve with only one arm. Fortunately, I have pretty large hands and I was able to hold a ball and my racket in one hand. After lots of practice I was able to toss the ball over my head while still holding on to the racket and, eventually, developed a pretty decent serve. We joined a local indoor tennis club so that we could play year round. My Friday nights out with the boys now was playing tennis on stag night at the tennis club. As in all the sports I participated in, I was highly competitive. It was another arena where I didn't want to be viewed as a cripple trying his best at an activity that was difficult for him. I wanted to beat people. I met an older gentleman at the club who was 64 years old and had taught himself to play tennis. We would practice together every morning at 6:00 A.M. at the club. Occasionally we would find a couple of guys to play doubles with. We played pretty well as a doubles team and I took particular delight in beating players that were younger. More than once there were players that left the court after playing us muttering to themselves about being beaten by a old man and a cripple. I liked that.

Another activity I got involved in was karate, although my motives for learning it were less than pure. Believe it or not, I still had revenge on my mind for the fat guy that shoved me into the clothes rack at the department store. He humiliated me and needed to be taught a lesson. It didn't matter that I didn't know who he was, or whether I would even recognize him if I ever saw him again. The point was I was not going to allow myself ever to be shamed like that again. I wanted to learn how to handle myself. Once on Wide World of Sports I saw a wheelchair bound Vietnam vet who was an expert in karate. On the show he did a demo and I was amazed at all that he was able to do. I figured that if he could do karate out of a wheelchair, I should be able to do it standing on my one good leg. Once again I found that Kent State was offering a continuing education course in karate and I signed Fran and myself up for it. I really liked it. As with all things I learned to do, I practiced a lot at home. I got a kicking bag and worked out with it all the time. The class taught mainly the art of karate as opposed to actual fighting techniques. The instructor was especially helpful to me. Every once in a while he would bring to class some of the experts from the karate club he belonged to. They would work with me in adapting some of the traditional karate moves to be done one armed. We even developed some new moves for me. I eventually got to the yellow belt level. Then my instructor was injured in a karate competition and wasn't able to teach anymore. I found a private instructor that lived not too far from me. He started teaching me how to fight, and I loved it. There were some teenage boys that were also being taught, and sometimes he would let us fight. I never felt any pain while I was fighting, but I would always come home with bruises all over my arms and legs. One day, he had me fight one of the smallest boys in our group. This boy was always leaving himself open to be kicked. I waited for a while and when he left himself vulnerable again I kicked him right in the shin. He immediately fell down and started crying in pain. I was worried that I had done some serious damage to him and I really felt bad about it. I realized that this wasn't the person I wanted to hit. I came home and never went to another karate class.

I still loved to swim, too. I would spend summer days at the swimming area at Munroe Falls Park. Occasionally I would see some of my students there and they would always ask, "Mr. Morris, can you swim?" I used to tell them, "Yeah, but only in circles." I don't think they ever got it, but it was my little attempt at humor. Although I was a pretty good swimmer, there was one thing that I couldn't do in the water, and that was water skiing. Before my injury I was pretty good at it. One summer day, my cousin and some of our buddies took his boat to a nearby lake. We got there early in the morning and the air was still pretty cool. Nobody was anxious to get into the water. I called them a bunch of sissies and told them I was going water skiing. I hopped into the water and found a way to get the skis on. I got to the end of the tow rope and gave the signal to take off. I was able to get up using my good arm to pull me up. As soon as I got up, though, my bad leg gave out, and the right side ski went off at an angle and I tumbled into the lake. Undaunted, I kept trying but with the same results every time. I kept trying until I was so exhausted that a couple of my buddies had to help me back into the boat. I just accepted the fact that there were a few things that I just couldn't do.

I didn't have much success at snow skiing either, although I could make it down some of the beginner hills without falling. My problem with snow skiing was getting off of the chair lift. The first time I tried it, a friend instructed me as to how to do it. She told me that when I got to the top of the lift, just to lean forward and slide away on my skis, away from the chair. She said to use my poles as support. Since I only had one good side, I figured that two poles were useless, so I skied with one. The first time I got off of that chair lift, I planted my one pole and found that it couldn't handle all of my weight. It buckled in half and I kept going right on down that hill. I kept my balance, but found that I picked up a lot more speed than I had on the beginner hill. My stop was less than graceful at the bottom, as I ended up with a snowy tumble. I wasn't hurt, but I decided that I didn't like snow skiing enough to jeopardize breaking my one good leg. I never liked winter sports that much, anyhow.

One of the things they say you never forget how to do is riding a bike. I decided to give that theory a test. I found an old stationary bike at a garage sale and I rigged it up with a coat hanger on the right pedal to hold my foot in place while I rode it. I worked out on that contraption until I felt comfortable, and then tried riding Fran's bike. I rigged up the same coat hanger system and found that it worked. Since I knew then that I could ride a bike, I went to Sears and bought a new three-speed model. I had it equipped with leather straps on the pedals and I became pretty proficient on it. Occasionally I'd fall down, and I'd have to roll over on my back to try to kick my feet loose from the pedals. I suppose I looked like an injured turtle or something, but eventually I would get back up on the bike again. I used to ride it to the golf course, which was five miles away. I had a yearly pass to the course so I left my clubs there. I'd play a round and then hop on my bike and come home. I really enjoyed the good exercise it provided me. I started feeling pretty cocky about my bike riding ability, and when I heard that there was going to be a bike race nearby, I signed up for it. It was only a ten-mile race, and I thought I'd have no trouble with that distance. I showed up at the race with my trusty little three-speed Sears touring bike and immediately noticed that everyone else was riding lightweight ten-speed racing models. Right then, I knew I was in trouble. Before I even completed the first lap of the race, the rest of the field came up and lapped me. I decided that that was enough embarrassment for one day, and pulled off the course and watched the rest of the race from the sidelines. I came back the next year riding a specially adapted ten-speed model with all the gear changing controls on the left side. I finished the race that year.

With all of my physical activities, I can't even begin to count how many times I've fallen. It seemed like I've always had scrapes and scabs on my knees and elbows. My neighbors used to watch me running down the street and were aghast at some of the tumbles I took. The smallest bump in the road would send me head over heels. I know that some of my falls probably could have made the intro to "Wide World of Sports" in the "agony of defeat" segment. I just accepted the fact that it was part of my life. There were times I was going to fall. One thing I've never accepted, though, is help getting up. People learned quick that when I fell just to leave me alone. Looking back, I realize that sometimes I wasn't too polite when I rejected their help. I got mad at myself when I fell, and I got even more mad when someone tried to help me. Once I even yelled at my minister when I fell on the sidewalk at his house. As he reached out his hand to assist me to my feet, I said, "Get away from me. I can do it myself." He looked pretty shocked, but I think he understood. My friends learned to warn people when I fell. They'd tell them, "Just stay away. He don't want help." Sometimes, when I'd fall, it would hurt like hell. But I would just pull myself up and keep going. For me, that was the only way to do it.

Sometimes my pride caused me to miss some of the things I enjoyed. For example, I really like steak, but it's very difficult for me to cut it. So, whenever we went out to eat, I would order chicken or fish, something that was easy to cut with a fork, rather than have Fran cut my meat for me. I didn't want anyone to see that. Eventually I learned to let people do little things for me. I realized that people sometimes got uncomfortable around me, and their offers to help were really to help ease their awkwardness about my disability. They were just trying to be nice. So, once in a while I'd let them open a door for me, or help me find a page in my choir book, little things like that. I still never let anyone help me if I fell. That was still off limits.

Sometimes I'd get a little discouraged. When I first got injured, things came back to me relatively quickly. As time went on, things came back much slower, and with much greater effort and difficulty. Even though I always believed I would someday be back to the way I was before the injury, I was beginning to have my doubts. Sometimes I felt that maybe I'd gone as far as I could go.

I was very self-conscious about letting anyone see me fail at anything I tried. For that reason, I would always try to practice something by myself before I would display it in public. My basement became my test laboratory. I had my weights down there along with my karate bag and other equipment related to physical exercise. I even set up a little track down there so I could practice my jogging before taking to the streets. I didn't want anybody laughing at me.

After the bad experience with teaching at the junior high school, I was a little leery when it came time for my official student teaching semester, which was in the spring of 1977. I was assigned to the Distributive Education class at my old high school in Stow. As soon as I found out, I started going over there during my free time between and after classes at Kent. I thought that the better I was acquainted with the students and the better they knew me the better the experience would be. I sat in on some of the classes there and I helped the teacher out whenever I could. He was a very nice man who was actually younger than me. He had been teaching there for two years. We got along great. By the time my actual student teaching started I was familiar with the class and the class was familiar with me. They were already used to my disability, and accepted me. I really enjoyed the student teaching there. My experience removed the doubts that I had about whether I could be effective as a teacher, and also whether I liked the job. By the time the semester was over, I was anxious to graduate and to get a permanent position.

I even helped out a little with some of the graduation activities at the end of the school year. I thought the kids behaved well, but apparently there were some parties that got a little out of hand with drinking. Some of the parents got into an uproar about it and the school administration needed a scapegoat. They chose the youngest member of the faculty, the young Distributive Education teacher, to put the blame on. Rumors started flying that he not only allowed drinking at some of the graduation parties, but that he also supplied some of the parties with alcohol. I felt bad because I knew he was just a good teacher that got along with the kids. I began to see some of the school system politics at work.

After I finished my student teaching assignment, I had completed all of the requirements for my bachelors degree. That spring I started getting notices from Kent State that I should sign up for graduation. I didn't realize what that meant. I knew I had enough credits to graduate, so I just ignored those notices. It wasn't until it was too late that I learned that the notices were to sign up for the commencement exercises. It didn't really bother me that I didn't put on a cap and gown and march across the stage. I wasn't interested in the graduation exercises. I was only interested in getting my diploma. I was proud of my accomplishment, but I didn't feel the need to show it off. I knew Fran was proud of me, too. I tried to convince her to go on a trip to California as my graduation present, but she felt that Matt was too young to travel, and suggested that we postpone the trip until he was older. That was okay with me. I still had to find a job that summer, anyway.

17

I signed up at the job placement center at Kent State and I got some offers for jobs I wasn't really interested in. I continued doing some part time construction work during the summer. A few weeks into the summer I got a phone call from the young man I student taught with at Stow. He told me he was quitting his position there and wanted me to be the first to know. The pressure over the graduation party debacle had got to him and decided to move on to another career in real estate. He thought I would be a good fit for his old job, and suggested that I apply for it as quickly as I could. I was sorry to see him leave, as I thought he was an excellent teacher. On the other hand, my dream job was open and I was pretty excited about that. I worked all night on my resume. Obviously, I didn't have a lot of work experience aside from the gas station and the Navy. I filled up the resume with all of my hobbies; hunting, fishing, golf, tennis, weight lifting, etc.. All of them were physical so that they wouldn't think I was disabled. The next morning I went to Stow High School and personally handed them my resume. I was very hopeful. I figured I had a leg up on any competition since I had just finished student teaching there in the spring and was familiar with the program.

It got to be late in the summer and I still hadn't heard anything about the job. I knew that they'd have to hire someone before school started in September. In my impatience I called them and was told that they hadn't made a decision yet, but as soon as they did, they would let me know. I was beginning to have some doubts as to whether I was going to get the job. I even had a dream that I didn't get it. I told Fran, "I don't think I'm going to get this job." She told me not to give up. I found out that my main competition for the job was a guy that I had gone to Kent State with. He graduated the winter before I did and had been working in a Distributive Education program in Canton. I didn't think that six months of experience meant more than my six months of student teaching in the actual school system we would be working in. I tried to keep positive.

It was about two weeks before school was scheduled to start. I still hadn't heard from Stow about the job and couldn't understand why they were taking so long to make up their minds. I was in Isaly's one afternoon and I had little Matt with me. The principal of Stow High School came in and came over to me when he saw me. He said, "Sorry that you didn't get the job, Charlie." He must have noticed the shock on my face. He said, "Nobody's notified you yet?" All I could do was shake my head. He said, "I feel really bad about this." He didn't feel nowhere as bad as I did, though. I tried to contain my emotions since Matt was there, but I was completely devastated. I felt like the rug had been pulled out from under me. By the time I got home I was furious. I was sure that the only reason I didn't get the job was because I was crippled. For me, there was no other explanation and I was really angry about it. It just so happened that the next day I got a call from a school system in Greenville, Ohio that needed a teacher right away. I started yelling at the person, "If you have any reservations about hiring a disabled person, just let me know right now so I don't waste my time with you." They assured me that they didn't, and set up an interview for the following week. By then, I was so embarrassed about my outburst that I never even went for the interview. Within another week I started thinking clearly again, and signed up for substitute teaching for the fall semester.

I discovered that I was in demand as a substitute teacher. I was so much in demand that I was able to stipulate, "Don't call me for any junior high school jobs." I still didn't want anything to do with that age group. There weren't many teachers that had a degree in Distributive Education and also a certificate in Business Education. I got called in a lot to teach accounting classes. One time I taught a class for three straight weeks. I got to know the kids pretty well during that time and built a good rapport with them. I got to be known around the school, especially since at that time I was driving a red, white, and blue van. One of the teachers asked me not to park my van in front of the school because when his students saw it they were disappointed if I wasn't teaching their class. I was enjoying my work, but I still really wanted my own class on a permanent basis.

I didn't have to wait long until I got my second chance at the job I really wanted. The man that was hired over me for the Distributive Education program at Stow High School lasted only two months before the kids, and the job, got to him. He decided he hated it and quit to pursue what I heard was a career in the men's clothing department at J.C. Penneys. What was odd was that even though I had been substitute teaching at Stow High School, and that just a few months previous I had been in contention for the position, no one from the administration informed me that there was going to be an opening again for that position. One of my teacher friends finally told me. When I found out, I hurried home and redid my resume adding the two months worth of substitute teaching experience I now had. I thought it was funny that I had to go through the entire application process all over again. But I did, and this time I had an interviewer who I thought was pretty honest. He confronted me with the questions: how did I think that the students would act towards a teacher with a disability, and, how did I expect to control the students? I was ready with my answer. I told him that I felt that sometimes we just didn't give the kids enough credit for their ability to see past someone's shortcomings. I told him that I had been the youth director at my church for five years and in that time not once had my disability even come up. I said, "The kids look at me and they just see Charlie. You look at me and see a disabled person." I don't know if that was the answer he wanted to hear, but that's the answer I gave.

A lot of my teacher and counselor friends from Stow were pulling for me to get the job. A few weeks before the position was to be filled the principal called me. He said that the DE teacher was going to take a week off and that it would be a good time to see if I could handle the job by substituting for him. I quickly accepted the offer. I also found out quickly that the job was going to be a challenge. I knew that the kids were obviously difficult, seeing as how they drove a teacher from the job in just two months. I wasn't prepared, though, for how bad they really were. They were undisciplined, unruly, and uncooperative. They were constantly testing you to see how much they could get away with. I wasn't afraid to get into their faces though and set down the law. There was one boy who was particularly terrible. After a couple of days of putting up with his nonsense I grabbed him and took him outside the classroom. I put my finger in his chest and said, "If I were you I'd be praying that I don't get this job permanently, because, if I do, I'm going to really enjoy staying on your back all the time." I think he understood my point.

It was kind of cute. During my substitute teaching I had made friends with several of the big athletes from the school. If they heard I was having trouble with a student they would come to me and ask, "Do you want us to take care of him for you, Mr. Morris?" I'd tell them, "No, I think I can handle it myself." I thought it was kind of neat, though, to have my own little group of enforcers at the school.

I made it through the week without any major problems, and I still wasn't dissuaded from my desire for the position. Once more I waited in nervous anticipation for the school's decision. My cousin Denny invited me to go deer hunting with him down in southern Ohio, and I was looking forward to that at the end of November. I hadn't been deer hunting since my injury, and I thought a few days out in the woods would be good for me. A week before we were supposed to leave, I got a call from the principal. "If you want the job it's yours." I was ecstatic. As much as I wanted to go hunting, I wanted this job even more.

Overall, I was feeling pretty good about myself. I felt like I had proved all the naysayers wrong, especially those who thought I'd never make it through college, much less become a teacher. Although I did a lot of things on my own, I knew I never would have made it on my own. I had a lot of help along the way. I had my faith and I felt God's hand pushing me along all the way. Without His help, I wouldn't have gone anywhere. But my faith involved more than just my belief in a higher power. The church I went to, and the members of my congregation, were a great support to me in my time of need. By allowing me to become a youth leader, I was able to gain the confidence I needed to pursue a teaching career. The kids I had in my youth group never looked at me as some cripple. They respected me, and I got along with them even better than I could get along with adults. Of course my family was instrumental in my recovery. It goes without saying that my wife, Fran, was always there when I needed her. She gave me the space I needed to figure things out for myself, but yet she seemed to always show up when I needed her support. She never really pushed me, but she never let me quit. There were times when college was so hard for me I thought I would go crazy before I ever would graduate. Fran was always there with words of encouragement. Most of the time those words were simply, "No, you're not quitting." Somehow we were able to tough it out.

Friends also were a big help after my injury. I felt that many of my old friends shied away from me after I came back from Vietnam. I wondered why, and I once asked my cousin Denny about it. I could always count on Denny being honest. He told me, "You know Charlie, sometimes you do sound a little retarded and it scares people a little." Fortunately, I was able to make a lot of new friends. I had friends at college, friends at church, and friends from my neighborhood. They all helped me in redeveloping my social skills, and made me feel more comfortable about myself out in public.

My Navy experience, even though it was short lived and nearly ended in tragedy, was a great source of strength during my physical rehabilitation. When I was in the Navy it was the first time in my life I was ever proud of myself. When I became a Seawolf, I felt like I was something really special. In a little over a year I was transformed from an overweight machine operator in some dingy factory to being in charge of my own helicopter. I had a lot of great leaders while I served in the Navy. I respected them and I always tried to do the best job I could for them. They, in turn, respected me. Being part of such a good organization, and having such good leaders, had a lot to do with my motivation to always try to do my best.

18

It didn't take long for the excitement of getting my dream job to wear off and the reality of what I was about to attempt set in. I was worried whether I could stand the heat. The job had taken two guys out already, in very short order. I felt like I was back in Vietnam going out on another special mission. I didn't know what was going to happen. I decided that I would try my hardest to do a good job, but if I went down, somebody was coming with me. Early in the year I bought a pocket calendar from one of the kids who was selling them at school. Each month had a different saying that was at the top of the page. The saying for December, the month I was starting my new job, was "Nobody knows what they can do until they try." I decided to make that my class motto. I bought some poster board and had Fran paint the words on it. I hung it right at the front of the classroom, right over my desk, so that everyone in the class would have to notice it.

Starting in at the new job was interesting to say the least. I was fortunate in that I had a good idea of what the students were like from my previous experience with them. I knew which ones were interested in learning and which ones to keep my eye on. My first conflict came as no surprise to me. It was with the boy I warned during my week of substitute teaching. He was the type of kid that was always picking at you, always trying to get your goat. He was just a bad student and I really didn't want him in my class. During the first two weeks as his teacher I sent him to the office several times for various kinds of misbehavior. It didn't have any affect on him. The classroom didn't have desks, but rather we had tables that were arranged in a "U" shape around the room. I taught the class from the center of the "U". One day he started mouthing off to me and I decided that it was time for a showdown. I walked up to the front of the table he was sitting at and grabbed a corner of the table with my good arm and flipped it right out from under him. I was pretty strong when I got mad. Now there was nothing between him and me. The rest of the students watched in complete stunned silence. I stood over him and said, "Go to the office now. I'll be there in a minute." He knew I meant business because he was out of that chair and out the door in a flash. By the time I got to the office he was already seated with the assistant principal. As soon as I walked in he started bad mouthing me again. I yelled out, "That's it" and I took a couple of steps in his direction. The assistant principal stopped me before I got any further. He told me that he would take care of the matter. He kicked the kid out of my class permanently, which is all I really wanted in the first place. I felt I had a better chance with my class without that nuisance there.

He wasn't the only bad one in my class. There were several more, but I was able to deal with them on my own, mostly on a one to one basis. Some of their behavior was very shocking though. One time a boy and a girl in my class got into some sort of argument and the boy hauled off and slapped that girl right in front of me. I was enraged. That was something I wasn't ever going to tolerate under any circumstances and I wanted him to know it was unacceptable. I grabbed him and dragged him out to the hallway and threw him up against a locker. I told him in no uncertain terms that he was never to do anything like that again, and that if I found out that he did, I would come after him and there would be hell to pay. I know he got the message because by this time he was fighting back the tears. I told him sit in the hall for the rest of the class that day. I went back into the classroom to find that several students had gathered in the back of the room and were smoking pot. Right then I knew that it was "game on". I was ready.

The Distributive Education class was part of a work experience program. Students in the program would attend classes in the morning and then work at jobs associated with the program in the afternoon. The course was meant for the student who was unsure whether they would be attending college or going right into the workplace after graduation. It was designed to give them training in sales, advertising, marketing, and business, so that they would become better employees or maybe start their own business. The course was only offered to students in their senior year. It was supposed to be for goal-oriented kids, but a lot of times it was just kids who wanted to be out of school at noon each day. My job was to teach the kids in the mornings and then go to their places of employment in the afternoons to observe them and to get reports from their employers. Part of my job also was to arrange for companies to participate in this program by offering jobs to students. The students were paid while they worked so it was a pretty good deal for them.

I have to mention that I took a pretty good pay cut when I accepted the full time position as teacher. With me working full time, I was no longer eligible for Social Security Disability benefits, and the monthly checks to Fran and Matt stopped too. I hired in at my teaching position at a salary of $10,000 a year. Since I was getting the maximum benefit from social security, that represented a sharp reduction in my annual income. I lost some other benefits as well, such as some tax breaks, reduced home heating cost, and some lower cost government services. My dad thought I was nuts. He thought with my college education I should start some sort of business and put it in Fran's name so that I could continue getting my Social Security money. But I wouldn't hear of it. I thought it was just another way to prove to everyone that I wasn't disabled.

I settled into teaching pretty well and I enjoyed my work. Some of the bad kids really tested my patience, but, over all, I liked being around the kids. I even got involved in some extra-curricular activities. There was a national organization for Distributive Education programs called the Distributive Education Clubs of America (DECA). Twice a year they would have competitions among schools where students would develop business plans, marketing strategies, and advertising campaigns, and submit them for presentation and judging. Schools competed on the regional, state, and national level. Being highly competitive in nature, I promoted the DECA competition with my classes and worked with the students after school hours to help develop their entries. Some years we did pretty good, making it to the state level of competition in Columbus. One year we even made it to the national level, and I escorted the kids down to Miami.

My real interest was in sports, though, and I tried to help out where I could with those activities, too. Though certainly not one of the glamour sports, I helped out with the golf team, and even took over for the coach for a few weeks when he was ill one time. I got to be the Junior Varsity tennis coach, too. I mostly worked on developing the basic skills of the young players, and, as soon as they were halfway competent, they moved into the Varsity program. I enjoyed running the players through drill sessions and helping them learn the fundamentals of the game. My secret desire, though, was to somehow get involved in football. I didn't care at what level or what grade. I still loved football. I even took a course in coaching football at Kent State. There weren't many opportunities for me to get involved, though. For the most part, I just hung around the practice field when I could.

One day the high school football coach, a young man whom I had become friends with, came to me and told me that his 8th grade football coach had quit, and they needed someone to fill in right away. He asked if I would be willing. As much as I wanted to, I was a little hesitant. I thought that I could be a pretty good assistant, but I didn't know if I was ready to be a head coach yet, even at the 8th grade level. I asked him if he was sure I could do the job. He told me, "Don't worry. I'll help you out." With that, I accepted the job. I was a mile high. I was finally going to get to do something that would show people that I wasn't just a cripple. I was so excited I went right home and told Matt, who was only four years old, "Your daddy's going to be a football coach." My joy was very short lived, however. When I went back to school that afternoon I found out that the other coaches had convinced my young friend that I was not the right person for the coaching position. They already had offered it to another teacher, and he accepted. Football coaches are not really known for their tact, and one of them came to me and said, "How would you ever be able to show a kid what to do out on a football field?" Once more I was hurt and angry. I should have been getting used to it by then. I went back to my golf and tennis leaving football coaching to the physically whole. I did get to work out with the wrestling team once in a while. The coach used to have me wrestle with some of the heavyweights on the team. I guess my disability must have just been more noticeable on a football field than on a wrestling mat.

Although I obviously wasn't too popular with some of the football coaches, I felt I had a good rapport with most of the students. I liked the good kids and I could deal with the bad kids. It was the marginal kids that I took a special interest in. I tried hard to push them to do their best. I especially tried to look after the kids who were in my class. I tried to treat them as my own. I really felt bad for some of them as they came from some pretty tough life situations. I hated to see any kid messing up their life with drugs or alcohol. Although I didn't realize it, I was told later on that I was much harder on the boys than I was on the girls. I probably shouldn't have got so involved in some of my student's situations. When they failed, I took their defeats personally. Eventually it would take its toll on me.

I felt good about being a teacher. Although it was not the policeman career I had planned on, I still felt like it was a job where I was giving something back. I wanted to be a good teacher and I wanted to have an impact on student's lives. Aside from teaching I also wanted to be a good example to other disabled people. I wanted to share my belief that with hard work we could do anything that regular people could do. I didn't join any support groups or anything like that, but I still had a soft spot in my heart for anyone with a disability, and if I had the chance to offer them an encouraging word, I would. One time, shortly after I got my full time teaching position, and I was feeling pretty full of myself, I was brought back down to earth by a 10 year old girl. I was standing with Fran in a line at a grocery store and there was a little girl in line next to us that kept staring at me. At first I thought it was another child staring at me like I was a freak, but then I noticed that her right arm was non-functioning, just like mine was. I said hello to her, but she said nothing and just kept staring at me. Finally, her mother noticed what was going on and apologized. She said that her little girl had never seen anyone older with the same disability that she had. She told me, "She's only ten years old and she's already wondering what kind of future she's going to have." I couldn't believe it. Here was a ten year-old girl already worried about what was going to happen to her as she gets older. When the mother asked me if I would talk to her daughter, I jumped at the chance. I told her, "You know we can do anything we want to do. I play golf and tennis. I hunt and go fishing. I swim, I run, and I ride a bike. I'm even a high school teacher." The little girl looked up at me and said, "So what?" I had to laugh. Those two words really put me in my place. Although I was humbled, I was also glad that someone in this world looked at me as just plain old Charlie.

I thought I had overcome the odds. I thought I was well at last. I thought I had made it by overcoming my physical handicap. I learned that physical scars healed, and that, with work and determination, you can get over your physical limitations. I had been disabled for seven years, and I now was a teacher and was able to do most everything I had done before my injury. I felt I had overcome everything. Little did I know the battles that were to come.

19

My relationship with my son Matt was great early on. I read a lot of books on raising children and one of the things I learned was that as boys grow older they tend to favor their mothers. I figured I wanted to make the most out of the years he was going to like me. Having the summers off was definitely an advantage. We spent a lot of time camping and traveling and, fortunately, Matt loved both of those activities. We took trips out west to Yellowstone Park and horse ranches in Wyoming. We went to Florida and Disney World. We also had a permanent campsite at Atwood Lake, a state park about an hour from where we lived. When we weren't traveling, we were out in our trailer at Atwood. Matt inherited my love for the outdoors and he really enjoyed fishing, hiking, and swimming.

My infatuation with sports and physical activity led to me pushing Matt into all kinds of organized sports teams. He got his first set of golf clubs when he was 3 ½ years old. By age 5 he was playing on a regulation golf course. He had a natural swing that was a thing of beauty to watch. I can't really take credit for that. I can take credit for the intensity with which he played sports, and also the frustration and anger when he lost at them. He would get particularly angry whenever I beat him at golf. I also taught him how to play tennis and he was pretty good at that too. During the summer out at the lake I wouldn't allow him to do anything else until he hit balls for 1 to 2 hours a day. That may have been why Matt never developed a great love for the game.

I was a very bad sports parent. I would get very agitated when Matt didn't do well. I had very high expectations for him, and when he didn't meet my expectations I would tell him about it. After games, most of the time I would tell him about all the things he did wrong, instead of praising him. I was quite entertaining in the stands, too. I would attend every football and hockey game he played in, and I was quite vocal with my opinions about how the game was officiated, or who wasn't doing what they were supposed to. I remember one elderly grandmother that used to come to Matt's hockey games. She told me, "I really don't like hockey. I just come hear to see you screaming at the referees." Even that didn't inhibit me.

In some ways, I was living vicariously through Matt, especially in sports. During my school athletic career my father never came to any of my games. I was the direct opposite with Matt. I not only went to all of his games, I went to all of his practices too. People told me that I couldn't live my life through Matt, but I believed I could. When he was playing football I could feel every hit as though I was out on the field. Although I was a constant support to him with my physical presence, I wasn't much of an emotional support for him. I wasn't big on praise, but I was big on criticism. If they lost I never said anything like "great game" or "you tried your best". Instead, I would tell him what he should have done to avoid losing. Although I was very proud of my son, I never let him know it.

My classes at school were going very good. I seemed to be getting better students every year. I guess I started getting a little cocky and I stopped recruiting kids for my class. I thought that kids were lining up to get into Mr. Morris's Distributive Education class. It all came to a crashing halt in spring of 1982 when I found out that only 13 students had signed up for my fall class. I was required to have a minimum of 15 students and the principal told me that unless I had that number of students signed up, that my class would be dropped and I would be out of a job. I was pretty shook up about it. I started having bad dreams and sleepless nights. Sometimes I'd sleep only for about an hour a night. I was tired and cranky at school. I'd come home from school at night and I'd sit in a dark room all by myself all evening. I was having panic attacks and I was worrying about everything. I had headaches all the time and I was taking so many aspirin that my ears started ringing. I was somewhat relieved when, after weeks of hard sell recruiting at school, I found two students who signed up for my fall class. I was safe for another year, but my feelings of job security were never the same.

In the late 1970's there started to be news reports on Vietnam veterans who were having difficulty dealing with the memory of their personal experiences from the war. Some were displaying strange behaviors, and some were just having trouble adjusting to life after the war. Some vets even committed violent acts for no apparent reason. The media began to apply a name to these behaviors. They called it post traumatic stress disorder. I thought it was a bunch of baloney. I avoided hearing about it at all costs. If there was an article in the newspaper about it, I wouldn't read it. If a news report about it came on the television, I would turn it off. I just figured it would be one more thing I'd worry about me having. Then, in 1984, a book came out that took my blinders off. The book was "Long Time Passing: Vietnam and the Haunted Generation" written by Myra MacPherson. I don't know why I bought it, but I did and I spent a summer reading it at the beach while I watched Matt. I found it very interesting. It was a large book, over 600 pages, and it included a variety of topics pertaining to the Vietnam war. Each topic was researched using personal stories from those who had experienced that era. It not only dealt with those who fought in the war, but also those who resisted fighting in it, such as the draft dodgers. It dealt with people with differing viewpoints on the war including two brothers who were at opposite ends of the arguments. What I found particularly interesting, though, was the section devoted to the mental problems some Vietnam veterans were suffering, and to post traumatic stress syndrome. I read about the Vietnam vets who were having trouble sleeping, who had nightmares, who were having a hard time coming to terms with their feelings over what they had experienced in the war. After I read it, I told Fran that the guys with PTSD sounded just like me. She immediately dismissed it and convinced me that I was just fine. I read the book and then forgot about it. I did get a better understanding of what PTSD was, though. I also knew that there were treatment centers set up in different parts of the country to deal with the treatment of PTSD. We even passed one in Florida one time when we went down there to visit my grandmother. It was a beautiful place in a beautiful location, but all I had to know was that it was part of the Veteran's Administration to know that I didn't want any part of it.

Meanwhile, I was changing the way I dealt with my students at school. When I first started teaching, I was pretty physical with the students. I wanted to show them that I wasn't going to take any crap from any of them. As time progressed, I realized that a lot of the kids in my classes had some serious problems. They had drug, alcohol, and family problems the likes of which I couldn't believe. Most of the teachers had a built in mechanism to be able to let the kid's problems go in one ear and out the other. It wasn't that they weren't sympathetic, or that they wouldn't offer advice. It's just that, for them, at the end of the day, those problems remained at school. It didn't work that way for me. I'd feel terrible about what some of my kids were going through. I'd take their problems home with me and I'd think about them in the evenings when I should have been paying attention to my family. I felt like if a kid signed up for my class they were entrusted to me, and I would do whatever I could to make sure they got through my class with a passing grade. I had one principal tell me that he never knew whose side I was on, the kids or the teachers. I never considered it a matter of sides. I just wanted everyone to be able to reach their potential despite the obstacles they had to overcome.

I found it hard to deal with the kid's problems. If they hurt, I hurt. Not until years later did I learn about the psychological term of transference, where their problems became my problems. In my years of college they didn't prepare me for all the things that were coming my way. If I listened too much, I'd want to do too much. One of the tougher problems I had to deal with was when one of my students had an abortion. She was one of my better students, and when she didn't show up for class three days in a row, and I didn't know why, I badgered some of her friends to tell me what was wrong. One of them told me that she had gotten pregnant and decided to have an abortion. Now I had a moral conflict, too. My Christian beliefs taught me that abortion was wrong. But I also knew that this girl was a good kid, and that her decision to not have the baby might be the right decision for her. When she finally came back to class, it looked like all the life was out of her. I spoke to her after class and told her that I knew what had occurred. At first she was mad at her friend for telling me, but then she opened up to me. Any adult who thinks that these kids make the decision to have an abortion with no thought about it, or any conscience, is totally wrong. Through the remainder of the school year I tried to help her get through her issues. It took a lot out of my heart to see the kids suffer.

Shortly after that episode I had to deal with my first class pregnancy. The girl was pretty large and was able to keep the fact that she was pregnant from everyone, including her family and friends. One night, her parents took her out to eat at a local chicken restaurant, and that night she complained of severe stomach pains. Her dad took her to the hospital thinking it was food poisoning. Instead, he became a grandfather. When I found out about it I told my class and I asked them to be especially considerate to her when she came back to school. When she did come back, we had a little baby shower for her in the class. I really wanted her to make it to graduation and I tried to support her every way I could. After class I would drive her to the day care center and then to her job. I heard that some of the teachers, when they found out what I was doing, suggested that I was the father. I just laughed it off although I was quite proud that she named her daughter after my favorite country singer, Crystal Gayle. I was very happy when that girl did graduate. It was a little success story for me.

Sometimes my interest in my student's well being got me in trouble with my superiors. One time, there was a boy in my class who came from a single mother home. The boy would have to drive his mother to work on occasion, and, when that happened, he would be late for school. I understood that, and was lenient with him insofar as applying the school's attendance policy to him. But when the assistant principal found out, he disciplined the boy by taking away his school parking permit. When the boy told me what had happened, I went to the assistant principal and stood up for the boy. I explained the situation and told him that boy deserved a break. The assistant principal relented, and, in a less than sincere voice, told me it was good that the kids had me to be their advocate. That incident was the beginning of a bad relationship with that assistant principal.

I had some special moments with my classes, too. One class, knowing that I loved fishing and that my birthday coincided with the end of the school year, gave me a gift of a beautiful rod and reel. Up until that time I had to use specially designed reels for the disabled that had electric motors built into them to reel in the fishing line. When the kids saw how awkward I was handling this new rod and reel, they realized that my disability prohibited me from using a regular reel. I could see that they felt bad. They started apologizing for making such an error, and offered to take it back. I told them that it was okay, that I would learn how to use it. I really loved that gift, but what made me happiest was the fact that I realized that these kids didn't think of me as being handicapped. They thought of me as just being a normal person who used a normal rod and reel to go fishing. I liked being viewed as such. By the way, that summer I worked on learning how to use that rod and reel, and by the end of the summer I was fishing with it exclusively. I never went back to using specialized reels.

By the end of each school year I was mentally exhausted, and I really needed the summer to recuperate. At first, the summers rejuvenated me, and by the time school started again in fall, I was filled with vigor and enthusiasm once again. By Christmas vacation I was starting to wear down, and from there it was a downward spiral to the end of the school year. It got to where I didn't look forward to the holidays for I knew I'd be in a sad mental state by then. I still loved teaching, though. I used to tell my kids when they graduated that I hoped they would find a job they could love as much as I loved mine.

What I thought was job strain started leading into me having trouble sleeping nights. I started getting less and less sleep each night until I ended up getting only a couple of hours a night. The little time I did sleep was filled with nightmares. The nightmares I could remember were always about Vietnam. I wasn't flying, though. I always was on the ground and I ended up being surrounded by the enemy and trying to run away. I would wake up soaked in sweat, heart pounding, trying to catch my breath. Some of the other bad dreams I had were called night terrors, and they would be so horrible that my subconscious mind would not allow me to remember them. Fran grew numb to my problem. She figured that as long as I was able to keep plugging along, that I must be okay and that eventually these problems would pass. When I would go to work in the morning, I was able to put on my Charlie the Teacher face, and I could fool everyone that I wasn't having any problems. When I came home from work, though, my problem would rear its ugly head. I tried to do anything I could to make myself tired so that I would sleep at night. I worked out harder than ever, hoping that physical exhaustion would solve my problem. When that didn't work I tried taking some

Valium that was prescribed for my dad. That didn't help either. I fought hard to hold myself together during the school day, but in the evenings I would allow myself to let my guard down. I knew that work was contributing to my problem, but it was my home life that suffered the most. I even started secretly drinking again in hopes that the alcohol would help numb my pain. I was looking for anything that would help, but nothing did. I thought I was going nuts.

I had the added strain at work of having to always line up enough students for my class the following school year. I only had a year to year contract with the school, so, if I didn't have enough kids signed up, my contract would not be renewed. Towards the end of the school year I would work myself into a frenzy trying to get my 15 minimum students signed up. I also was subjected to the administration coming to my class to observe my teaching methods in order to give me my yearly review. Normally I didn't have any problems with this, but when my relationship with the assistant principal started to sour, I began to have problems whenever he came into my classroom. I would just fall apart. The kids would notice it and they would start misbehaving. Before long my classroom was in pandemonium. I ended up getting some bad reviews. Fortunately, they weren't bad enough for me to lose my job.

On top of my sleepless nights and my nightmares, I started having panic attacks. When they first started happening I thought I was having a heart attack. I had chest pains and felt light headed and had trouble breathing. A couple of times I ended up going to the hospital emergency room. They would run all kinds of tests, and then reassure me that my heart was fine. Eventually, I was able to recognize the symptoms as being a panic attack, but then I would worry that one time I would dismiss my problem as a panic attack when, in reality, it was a heart attack. I always had something to worry about.

I tolerated things at school, but when I came home it was a different story. It wasn't a very good situation. I had no patience with my growing son. Nobody could do anything good enough for me. I got mad when Fran or Matt couldn't do something. I figured that if you had two good hands you should be able to do anything. I know I was guilty of verbal abuse with Fran. I also was getting more physically abusive with Matt. The older he got, the harder I was on him. The smallest thing would set me off. If he was wearing a tie dye shirt or was listening to a group that I associated with druggies, I would go after him. If I would hear Fran yelling at him, I would go after him, even though I didn't know why he was being yelled at. Then, during my tirades, I would realize, "What am I doing?" I'd back off, and try to explain myself to Matt. I'd tell him, "Your dad is sick." I

knew I was getting close to going over the edge. I thought that suicide was imminent. I felt like my wife and son would be better off without me.

Trouble seemed to be seeking me out. When a teacher resigned in the middle
of the school year, I was temporarily put in charge of the student council in his
place. I figured it wouldn't be a problem seeing as how the student council was
made up of good students, not the misfits I had in my class. I was wrong. The
kids on the student council were terrible and didn't take kindly to any discipline
from a disabled teacher. One thing I wouldn't tolerate was cursing in my class. At
my first student council meeting there was a boy who started using some bad language. I told him that he couldn't use that language in school. He mouthed off to
me and went right on using curse words. I said, "That's it. You're gone." I took
him out to the hall and told him that his student council days were done. He told
me he was going back in. I told him he wasn't. He tried to push his way past me
back into the classroom. I knew that if he got back into the room that I would
lose all my credibility with the rest of the kids, so I went on the offensive. I said,
"Well, I guess there's only one thing to do. One of us is going to have to beat the
crap out of the other one, because the only way you're getting back in that room
is if you walk over me. So, let's go at it, right now." I had no intention of ever
fighting with the kid. I just hoped that he would be intimidated and he would
back down. It was working, because he started backing away. I followed him, step
for step, still telling him, "Come on. Let's go, right now." All of a sudden he
starts screaming in the middle of the hall, "Get off of me. Leave me alone." I said,
"I haven't even touched you yet." He kept on hollering until one of the teachers,
who was on hall duty, came over to see what was going on. He grabbed the kid
and told him to get to the office. The kid broke free and ran out the door crying.
I thought that was the end of that, and was happy that nothing more had come of
it. What I didn't know was that the boy's mother was a teacher at the elementary
school next door, and that's where he ran to. He told her that I had dragged him
out of class and beat him up. His mother never bothered to talk to me to see what
had really happened. Instead, she called the police and tried to press abuse
charges against me. I had to be questioned by detectives. Fortunately, the teacher
who was the hall monitor was also questioned, and told them that I had never
touched the boy. It was determined that the boy was a liar, and the charges were
dropped. That was my first and last day at student council. It was just some more
crap that I had to come to terms with.

At school, I paid particular attention to the student athletes, and always had
good relations with them, whether they were in my class or not. It really bothered
me when I would hear of one who was using drugs or alcohol. It disgusted me to

think how someone could abuse a young, healthy body. Whenever I would learn that someone was taking drugs I would seek them out and try to sit down and talk to them. I noticed that as time went on the problem became more prevalent. Watching these kids throwing away their lives had another effect on me. It caused me to become even harder on Matt, who now was reaching his teenage years. I never really sat down and talked to him about the dangers of drugs and alcohol. I just became increasingly intolerant of any behavior by him that had the slightest connection to being drug or alcohol related. It was another strain on our relationship. Matt once told me that I spent so much time focusing on the bad kids, that I forgot that there were good kids, too.

I got a new principal at school and he was very complimentary of the work I did with my classes. He spent a lot of time observing my class and took particular note of some of the success I had with bad students. He was a former teacher at the school, and even had taught some of the kids that I had in my class. He told me that he couldn't believe how I was able to turn some of the kids around, something he wasn't able to do. Although I was happy to have his praise and support, it also meant that I started receiving more and more bad students to "rehabilitate". I liked the challenge, but it was becoming overwhelming.

Meanwhile, it had been several years that I had been having my sleep and nightmare problems, and it was taking its toll on me mentally. I was fine physically and continued my daily workout routine, but I was becoming increasingly impatient and intolerant of any minor everyday problems I encountered.

Handicap access issues were starting to come up with public buildings, and, since Stow was building a new high school, the administration wanted to address these issues and to be able to incorporate them into the new building. I was asked to be on the committee looking into these issues. Before the first meeting I wrote down some of the problems, as I saw them, and also some of my suggestions for solutions to these problems. I went into that first meeting ready to state my case. I was met at the meeting by the head of the committee, an old principal of mine, now an assistant superintendent. He told me that the committee had already met once, and had already drafted a report to be turned in to the administration. He said all I needed to do was to sign it. I told him that I had written down some of my ideas and wanted to present them to the committee. He told me that they would look over my suggestions, and, that if needed, they could make an addendum to their report at a future date. At that time all he wanted me to do was to sign their report to show my concurrence. I realized that this committee didn't want any of my ideas. They only wanted the signature of a disabled teacher on their report. I don't know why I relented and signed that report. Maybe it was because I believed that they really were going to consider my ideas. More likely it was that my job stability was fragile at the time and I didn't want to rock the boat. I never did find out if the committee ever looked at my ideas.

That incident was the beginning of my mistrust of administration. I also started to have little disagreements with my fellow teachers. One of the things that caused some of the teachers to become miffed with me was that I became a staunch anti-smoking advocate. They say there's nothing worse than a reformed smoker, and I was fairly fresh from quitting the habit. I was in favor of a no smoking policy anywhere on school grounds. It was hard to convince kids that smoking was bad for them when they saw their teachers smoking. My vigilance did not win me many friends. Some teachers also didn't look favorably on my relationship with my students. They thought that there should be some distance between the student and the teacher. I tried to be a friend to my students along with being their teacher. A lot of teachers were none too pleased when one of my classes called themselves "Charlie's Angels" and wore t-shirts proclaiming the fact. I thought it was pretty neat myself.

There were days when I was a good teacher, and there were days where I was just hanging on. I honestly always tried to do my best, but if I couldn't connect with a student I'd lose my enthusiasm. I had one boy in one of my classes that was a star soccer player. He had everything going for him. He had scholarships lined up to good colleges. He was popular at school. But, he also smoked a lot of marijuana. Sometimes he'd show up for my class stoned. I tended to be a little more patient with athletes and would give a little more effort to get them reformed before I would give up on them. I also cut them a little extra slack in class in order that they could continue participating in their sport. Several times I tried talking to this boy, but he just kept right on being a stoner. Finally, one day in class he was a little high and smarted off to me. I took him out to the hall and really lit into him. I told him, "If God was fair, He'd give me your perfect body and you'd get mine. That way you could go on screwing it up, and it wouldn't matter at all." I thought I reached him because he started to cry and ran away. He came back the next day, the same as ever, and never changed. I don't know what ever happened to him. He wasn't one of my success stories.

In the fall of 1987, we moved into the new high school, and right away I started having problems. The old school had tiled floors and I never had any problem dragging my bad foot across the slippery surface. The new school, however, had carpeting, and my toe would get hung up on it as I dragged it, causing me to stumble a lot and, sometimes, even fall. It got to be pretty embarrassing. Up until that time, none of the kids had ever said anything about my disability because I was able to get around pretty good. Now I was stumbling around, and the kids started to make snide remarks behind my back. I had good hearing and I knew what they were saying. It angered me, but I was able to keep it in for a while. But then it all came undone.

There was a boy and a girl in my class who must have had a little thing going on, because they were always together. At the beginning of class each day, the boy would take his chair from the back of the room and bring it to the front where his girlfriend sat. I put up with it for a while, but when he stopped paying attention in class, I had to put a stop to it. I gently told him to take his chair back to where he belonged. He gave me one of those, "But Mr. Morris…" but I just pointed to the back. Then, one of the bigger, smart mouthed boys piped up, "Don't worry. That just makes it farther for him to limp to get to you." I don't know exactly why, but all of the past six years of frustration came out all of a sudden. I yelled at him, "You get the hell out of my class, now." He knew I meant business and he got up immediately and left the class. But I wasn't done. I followed him out of class and into the hallway. I grabbed him and started yelling at him, "You little asshole. You think I want to be like this?" I had him up against a locker and I kept putting my finger into his chest. He was bigger than me, and I was hoping that he would take a swing at me so that I would have an excuse for fighting him. Instead, he ran away and into the principal's office. I stormed back into my classroom and got behind my desk. By this time I've worked myself into a frenzy. I screamed at the kids, "For ten years no one at this school has ever made fun of me. But ever since this class started, you kids have been talking behind my back." I then grabbed a pile of books and papers that were stacked on my desk and I threw them across the room. By now I was so mad I didn't know what I was doing. I yelled, "Fuck you", and stormed out of the class.

When I got out to the hall the principal was already on his way to my class. He stopped me and said "What's going on, Charlie?" I told him what the boy had done, and then I told him what I had done. I fully expected to be fired on the spot, but I guess that the principal had a soft spot in his heart for veterans. He told me he'd take care of it. He went back to his office leaving me alone in the hall outside my class. I didn't know what to do. I was going to leave for the day, but then I decided to go back into my class. I went in, picked up the books I had thrown, and conducted class for the remainder of the day as if nothing had happened. The kids were still too stunned to give me any more trouble that day.

When I got home that night, I started thinking about the events of the day. I told Fran what had happened, but she didn't make a big deal about it. I, however, was deeply disturbed about my behavior. I cringed when I thought about what could have happened. I knew that I was mad enough, and out of control enough, that I really could have hurt that boy. I realized that no matter how hard I tried to hold myself together on a couple hours of sleep a night, that I had reached the end of my limits. At that time there were a lot of stories about crazy veterans who suddenly snapped and went on rampages killing and hurting people. I didn't want to become one of those crazy vets. I also didn't want to do anything that would tarnish the image of Vietnam veterans. I didn't want to dishonor those who had served there. I decided to take a couple of days off of work and check out the Brecksville VA hospital, the place I feared the most I would end up at.

20

Through a friend, I knew that the Brecksville VA had a Center for Stress Recovery. The next morning I drove there, and, without an appointment, walked into the center and said, "I think I need some help." After I filled out a few forms I was introduced to some doctors and therapist who were on the staff there. I was given some tests, one of which had over 700 questions on it. It asked things like, "Do you see things that others don't?" and "Do you think that God is watching you?" They would ask the same question several different ways just to make sure you were consistent with your answers. It took most of the day to complete all the testing. When I was done, I met with a therapist who talked to me for a while. I went into the center that day as Charlie the Teacher, the in-control, calm guy. I must have at least fooled that therapist. She told me that she thought I would be okay with just a little outpatient work. She told me that they would be in touch with me after they analyzed my test results.

I went home and the next day went back to work. I only had a week to go before Christmas break, and I thought I could make it until then, at which time I would have a couple of weeks to get myself back together. The next week, the therapist called me to ask me if I could take off some time at work. I told her that I had quite a few sick days saved up so it shouldn't be much of a problem. She hesitated, and then told me, "The doctors have determined that you would benefit from our eight-week inpatient program." I was a little shocked. My worst fears were being realized. I was going to be committed to the loony bin at the VA. I told her I would get back to her.

That evening I talked to Fran about it. Always supportive, she agreed to abide by whatever I decided to do. I think she realized that our home life, especially my relationship with Matt, needed some help if we were to survive. The next day I went to my principal and asked for a leave of absence so that I could get treated at the Brecksville VA hospital. He was surprised at my request. He told me, "Charlie, you're about the only sane one we got here." He approved my leave of absence, and I was scheduled to enter the hospital right after the first of the year.

People were very surprised when they found out that I was going for treatment at the Brecksville VA. Up until my recent outbursts at school, no one ever saw the side of me that needed help. Nobody but my family, that is. People couldn't believe I was having problems. They thought that since I was able to overcome my physical disability, that I was some sort of Superman or something. I hid that side of me pretty good. Heck, I was a youth leader at church and a Sunday school teacher. I organized Christmas programs and youth getaways. Instead of getting rid of things to do and easing my stress level, I'd end up volunteering to do more. Nobody realized what was happening to me. All the things I was volunteering for were wearing me down to the point of exhaustion. If somebody needed something, and I thought it should be done, I'd volunteer for it. Sometimes it got ridiculous. I mean, whoever heard of a one-armed choir director who doesn't even know how to read music. But there I was, when no one else volunteered for it, in the front of the choir, waving my one good arm around. I was obsessed with making everybody happy. In reality I should have said, "Enough is enough." Only one time did I show off my temper at a church activity. I was trying to get the Sunday school children to sing a song, without much luck. Nobody wanted to sing. Matt was being particularly obstinate, so I used him as an example. I went and grabbed him by the ear, and pulled him to the front of the church where I made him sing in front of the whole Sunday school. There were some pretty shocked looks on the faces of the kids, and also the few parents that were there.

I don't know if Fran ever really understood why I was going to Brecksville. I made the decision to be admitted to the program mostly on my own. She abided by my decision, and even went to the orientation that they had there for family members. I think she knew I needed some help, but she was also worried as to what Matt was going to think about it. I was concerned that Matt might have felt responsible for putting me in the hospital, which was far from the truth. I tried talking to him about it, but, by that time, my communication skills had diminished somewhat with my teenage son.

I really didn't know what to expect from the Post-Traumatic Stress Disorder program at Brecksville. I didn't do any research on PTSD because I still thought it was basically some nonsense somebody dreamed up to apply to Vietnam vets who were going over the edge. Now I know different. PTSD is a psychiatric disorder that can occur after experiencing, or witnessing, a life-threatening event. These events include military combat, natural disasters, terrorist incidents, serious accidents, or violent personal assaults, like rape. People who suffer from PTSD often relive the experience with nightmares and flashbacks. PTSD often occurs along with other disorders such as depression, substance abuse, problems with memory, and other problems of physical and mental health. PTSD is also associated with the person's inability to function in social or family life, including job instability, marital problems, family discord, and difficulties in parenting.

PTSD is not something new, although diagnosis and treatment of it is. There's evidence in historical medical documents that PTSD-like symptoms were seen in Civil War veterans, along with veterans of World War I and II, and Holocaust survivors. In those days it was sometimes called shell shock. It was after the Vietnam war, however, when actual research and treatment began in earnest for PTSD. In 1988 it was estimated that 30% of all Vietnam veterans had experienced the disorder at some point since returning from Vietnam.

Most people who suffer from chronic PTSD have periods where the symptoms increase, then go into remission. For some individuals the symptoms are constant. Some have mild symptoms that increase following events such as retirement, severe physical illness, or reminders of their military service (reunions or anniversaries of war events).

So far, the best way to diagnose PTSD is with structured interviews and psychological testing and assessment. There are various forms of treatment for PTSD. The most effective treatments involve cognitive-behavioral therapy, group therapy, and exposure therapy. Exposure therapy is where the patient repeatedly relives their frightening experience under controlled conditions. This is supposed to help them work through their trauma. There also have been medications that may help ease PTSD symptoms in some patients. At present, the cognitive-behavioral therapy seems to be more effective than drug therapy, but recent research on biological changes associated with PTSD may result in the development of more efficient medicines.

I didn't think I had PTSD. I thought I was just plain crazy. Still, I was hoping that the program would make me better somehow. I went into it with an open mind and the resolve to listen to everything they told me. Whereas with my physical disability I was able to do a lot on my own to improve myself, here I was totally reliant on someone else to guide me along every step of the way. Nonetheless, I was pretty optimistic about getting better. I fully planned to return to teaching after the eight-week program was completed.

I checked in at the Stress Recovery Center at Brecksville on January 25. I was interviewed by a nurse, who seemed nice enough. She tried to explain some of the program details to me, but she used a lot of terms that confused me. She told me that for the duration of my stay I would be restricted to the ward, except for meals and one hour a day at the gym. By the time I got checked in, the rest of the guys in the program were already in their first session of the day, so I was shown to my room and told to get unpacked, and I could join the group later for lunch.

I shared the room with two other guys. It was a pleasant enough room. Fran bought me some Cleveland Browns posters that I hung up on the walls. She thought it might help me personalize my space a little, and I have to say that it did. I was done unpacking just as the group was getting out of their session. I was introduced to Gary, who was sort of the group leader. He in turn introduced me to the rest of the group. There were 18 of us. We then went to lunch and the first thing I noticed was that the entire group stuck together, even at the cafeteria. They all seemed like nice guys, and I had a good feeling about being able to fit in with them.

Later in the day, I met my therapist, Kathy. She was young and very thin. I had my first one on one session with her, but, pretty much, it was only her explaining the program to me. She used some more confusing terms, but I figured I'd learn about them as time went on. After our one-hour session I went to dinner with the group. I got to know them a little better and realized that we all had something in common. We all thought we were nuts, and were going to end up in a loony bin somewhere. We were all reacting the same way to stress. I was relieved to know that I wasn't the only one with problems. I was, however, the only one with a physical disability.

Our ward at the hospital was made up of many small bedrooms surrounding a central day room. There were three patients in each bedroom. My roomates were Sonny, a big, black man and an Army Vietnam vet, and Don, a Korean War vet. There was no bathroom in the bedrooms. We had a large shared bathroom and shower. Everything in the ward was painted gray, an appropriate color. We ate our meals at the hospital cafeteria. The food there was awful and I was always complaining about it. I was elected as the spokesman for the group at the administration meetings discussing food. I went to one meeting and got into a pretty hot argument with one of the staff over the quality of the food, and was told that I was never to attend any more meetings. Subtlety was never one of my strong suits. I ended up bringing a lot of instant soups and noodles from home to help me make it through the week. On weekends at home, I would return to the hospital on Sunday night with a couple of large pizzas and a bucket of chicken from a local pizza place in Kent. The guys always looked forward to my return.

The day room had a TV and a ping pong table, and I spent a lot of time there with the rest of the guys. Most of them were heavy smokers, and there was always a blue haze in the day room. By this time, I was a reformed smoker and had trouble adjusting to being in a smoke filled room frequently. After the first week, I developed a pretty nasty cough and was given a prescription for some cough medicine. Although I didn't like to take it, I felt I had to, because if I didn't hang out with the guys, they'd feel bad.

There weren't many requirements to be admitted to the program. There were, however, strict rules regarding any drug or alcohol use. We were all subject to urine testing every time we returned from being away from the hospital, and any positive result were grounds for immediate dismissal from the program. You didn't get any second chances. There were a couple of guys in our group who failed the urine tests and were sent home the same day. There was another requirement that you remove all weapons from your house while you were in the program. This was a little harder to enforce, and I kind of got around it by putting my hunting rifles and shotguns in the attic for the time being.

As with a lot of programs at the VA, once you were admitted to them, you were eligible for 100% disability payments. There were always a few guys that took advantage of this. They were mostly the guys who were unemployed, and saw the program as a way to get some easy money for a couple of months. Our group, however, were all guys with legitimate and serious problems. We all needed help a lot more than we needed the money.

Everyone in the program was there voluntarily. Although the program required you to get a pass if you left the hospital, our ward was not a locked setting. We could leave whenever we wanted to, if we felt that the program wasn't doing us any good, or we just had enough of it. Once someone left, though, they weren't allowed to return to the group. They would have to wait six months and then reapply for admission to another program.

We weren't with the same 18 guys throughout our eight-week program. Guys entered and left the program on a weekly basis. On Mondays there were always a couple of new guys in the program, and on Fridays there were always a couple that finished their program. It was a lot like a unit in Vietnam, where new guys would come in and old guys would go home. There would be a little graduation ceremony on Fridays where the guys who finished the program would get their certificate and the rest of the guys would get a chance to say nice things about the guys who were leaving. It was all designed to be a part of the program, because one of the big issues with Vietnam vets was that they never had the chance to say goodbye to their buddies when they left Vietnam. I don't know whether they thought these graduation ceremonies would compensate for that or what.

A normal day in the program is a series of group sessions in addition to one-on-one sessions with your therapist. The group sessions include the Community Meeting, where the group can discuss activities and policies, and the Psychotherapy, Autobiography, Communications, and Relaxation sessions. One of the first things I had to do with my therapist was to develop a recovery plan for me. I didn't have much trouble with this. It was a lot like making the lesson plans I made as a teacher. I had to come up with my goals, and how I was going to attain them. During my first week in the group sessions I mostly kept quiet, and just listened to the others. Some of the stories that they told, especially in the Psychotherapy group, were really gut wrenching. Some of the stuff was so damn gory and awful that, within a few days, I had worked myself into the worst depression I ever had. I learned quickly that you were not supposed to react in any way when someone was talking about their experiences. You were supposed to sit there, stone faced, and not make any comment at all. I got in trouble right away. My roommate, Sonny, was always making me laugh. That was good during our free time, but not in the Psychotherapy group. While one guy was telling about one of the horrible experiences he had in Vietnam, I happened to look over at Sonny, who was making a funny face at me. I started laughing, which immediately drew the ire of the group leader, who told me I was being aggressive towards the group. I made up some poor excuse as to why I was laughing, but it didn't make any difference. I was already marked as a troublemaker.

After hearing some of their stories, I really started feeling sorry for some of the guys. They had experiences of war at its absolute worst, and some of them had strong guilt feelings about some of their actions. Some of them had guilt feelings about making it through their tour of duty alive. The group sessions got pretty intense. As one guy would talk about his trauma, it would cause the others to think about their own traumas. Pretty soon the whole group would be lost, reliving their own personal time in hell. In a way, I felt out of place with these warriors.

I got through the first week without any major problems. I mostly observed at the group sessions, trying to get an understanding of what was going on and the rules and regulations. I was surprised that I was given a weekend pass home after my first week. I looked forward to being with Matt and Fran, and maybe I got a little too anxious about trying to have a good weekend with Matt. I went to his basketball game, and on the way home I felt like he was being a little standoffish towards me. He continued to be quiet at home, and I asked him if there was any problem. He just shook his head and went to his room. Well, I got upset and I went after him. I started yelling at him, "How am I supposed to make our relationship better if you won't even talk to me." I worked myself into a real tirade. Then, in my anger, I said the one thing that I most wanted not to say. I told him that he was the reason I was in the hospital. I left his room and it only took me a minute to realize what I had just done. I was ashamed of myself. I immediately went back to his room and begged for forgiveness. I tried to explain to him that I was sick, and that my sickness sometimes caused me to say things that were not true. I told him how much I loved him, and how much I wanted to get better so that I wouldn't do these things anymore. I told him how much I needed his help, too. Matt was quick to forgive, and we got along great for the remainder of the weekend.

When I returned to the hospital, the first thing my therapist wanted to know was how the weekend went. I had to tell her about the episode with Matt. I certainly wasn't proud about what I did, and telling her about it only made me even more ashamed of myself. It gave me one more thing to work on in the program.

During my second week at the hospital I was given my turn to tell my story in the Psychotherapy group. I was pretty nervous about talking about myself, and I have the bad habit of smiling whenever I'm nervous or embarrassed. So, all the time I'm talking, I'm smiling. While I was talking, one of the therapists confronted me. "Why are you smiling?" I said, "I don't know." She said, "That behavior shows that you are very aggressive towards the group." I tried to assure her that the smile was there because I was nervous, not because I felt anything aggressive towards the group. Needless to say, that made me even more nervous, which caused me to smile even more. I didn't understand this psycho-babble. I didn't like it either.

The more I listened to the stories of the guys and their experiences in Vietnam, the more I felt like mine were different. The hardest thing for them to deal with was coming to grips with being thrust into a situation where they were forced to kill, or be killed. That was something I never had to deal with during my Vietnam tour. There were times when I really felt out of place with these guys. I felt I needed to express my feelings, so one day, in a group, I got up and told them that I never killed anyone, and I didn't want to kill anyone. I told them how, after the Kent State shootings, that I requested not to have to handle any guns, and that the reason I flew with the Sealords was that they didn't use gunships. I told them I felt like I didn't have the right to be in the group. I didn't know how the group would react to my statement, and I was pleasantly surprised as to how supportive they were towards me. They told me that I had just as much right as any Vietnam vet to be in their group, and that even though our problems were all different, the important thing was to be able to work them out with the help of other Vietnam vets. That made me feel good, and I felt like I was officially a member of the group after that.

You have to remember that the treatment of PTSD at this time was in its infancy. Therapists were using different methods, trying to find out which one was the most effective. There weren't many long-term results available in which to base the therapy's effectiveness. When I was in the program in 1988, the therapists used a very confrontative method. They believed that the first thing that had to be determined was, "What was the trauma that was the cause of our PTSD?" They also felt that one of the best ways to have someone bring out their trauma was in a group setting. That was hard for a lot of us, to have to open up our most profound life experience in the presence of a group of virtual strangers. Unfortunately, at that time, they also had some preconceived ideas as to what types of trauma could cause PTSD, and if your trauma didn't fit their profile, they told you that you must be hiding something. Such was the case with me. Naturally, I thought that my trauma was being shot in the head. But when I told my story in the group, I was told by my therapist that just being shot wasn't a reason for PTSD. I must either be hiding something, or I was suppressing a horrible memory. I told them that I could remember every day I spent in Vietnam, and that I knew that I didn't do anything horrible to anyone, nor did anyone do anything horrible to me, aside from shooting me in the head. My therapist told me I was wrong. There was no way that I was remembering everything. Their job was to discover what it was I was holding back. After a couple of weeks of intense group and one-on-one sessions, I began to believe that they were right. Something else must have happened to me that I wasn't remembering. As I listened to the other guys tell their horrible stories in the group sessions, ideas began to creep into my head. Maybe I did do something really bad. Maybe I pushed someone out of my helicopter. Maybe I strafed a village with my machine gun. Maybe I shot a child. The more I thought about it, the more depressed I became. Finally, I felt I had a revelation. Why would an unarmed helicopter crew chief stick his head out of the open door of his helicopter while it was under fire? After two weeks of having a therapist pound me with the idea that I did something wrong, I now believed it wasn't because I wanted to locate the source of the sniper fire so that the pilot could take evasive action. I came to the conclusion that the only reason that an unarmed man would do that, was that he wanted to die. I believed that on January 9, 1971, I tried to commit suicide.

Now, I thought I knew the real reason why I had PTSD. My therapist didn't disagree with me. But instead of feeling a sense of relief at getting to the bottom of my problem, I was now even more depressed. I felt that if, indeed, I had tried to kill myself, that no therapy in the world was going to be able to help me. As far as I was concerned, I was done, a hopeless case. Basically, I gave up on myself. For a couple days after my eye opening revelation I moped around, feeling sorry for myself. I didn't participate in the groups, and was pretty despondent with the guys after hours. Gary, our chosen group leader, took notice and confronted me. "What the heck's the matter with you?" he asked. I said, "Nothing. Just leave me alone." He said, "I thought you were strong, but you're just a quitter." I told him to get away from me, but he kept coming after me. "I can't believe that after all you've been through, and all you've accomplished, that now you're going to quit." At that time I didn't need anyone telling me how wrong I was, especially another PTSD victim. I walked away from him and went into the bathroom. He followed me in and started yelling at me. "You're nothing but a quitter." By this time my anger was getting the best of me and I felt my fist begin to clench. Gary saw it. "Go ahead and hit me, but you're still a quitter." I stormed out of the bathroom and went to my room and shut the door.

That night, I had the most restless sleep I ever had in my life. I woke up screaming, "I'm not a quitter." I was soaked in sweat, and my bed looked like a war zone. My sheets and blankets were thrown all over the room. After composing myself for a few minutes, and thinking back at what Gary told me the night before, I told myself, "Dammit, I'm going to make it through this program. Maybe I don't fit their profile, but I still can get something out of it." With that resolve I went through the remainder of the program.

By the third week I was feeling more comfortable with the guys. It was easier for me to talk in the groups and to express my opinions. I listened intently to the therapists as they talked about PTSD and its symptoms and the way to deal with it. I found it particularly interesting when they talked about the sons of men with PTSD. They said that it was common for sons to take on the same symptoms as their fathers when they reached their teenage years. The young boys would copy their father's behavior. They called it Contact PTSD. Thinking about Matt, I realized that he was displaying some of the same tendencies as me. Maybe there was something to this PTSD thing, after all.

Most of the guys were in pretty bad shape when they started the program. Some of them, after the eight-week program was complete, ended up in worse shape than when they started. There was one guy in our group who, when he began the program, never talked to anybody, at any time. He would never make a sound. We found out that he had a passion for Dum Dum suckers, and one of the guys went out and bought a big bag of them. Gradually, the guy warmed to us, and we got to know his story. He served with an Army reconnaissance unit in Vietnam. His job involved being dropped behind enemy lines and performing scouting missions. During these missions his unit was not allowed to make a sound, and communicated solely by hand signals. During one mission, his whole unit was wiped out, except for him. He didn't do much talking after that. Eventually, he started talking to us, and by the end of the eight weeks, he was doing good. About a year later I went back to Brecksville for an outpatient session and I saw him there. He was in another program. I asked him what happened. He told me that before the program he would never leave the house for any reason. After the program his wife was so proud and happy that he was talking and socializing that she convinced him that some outside excursions might be good for him. She took him to a mall, and when he was confronted with all the people there, he went nuts. He went back to his silent ways, and he was back for another try at the program.

Some of the things that came out in the group therapy sessions were so shocking that I found them unbelievable. I got in trouble once when one guy was talking about how he collected ears and noses from captured Viet Cong soldiers. For me, that was bad enough, but the therapist wanted to know more. She asked him what he was planning on doing with these ears and noses. He replied, "I was going to build a head." I immediately burst out laughing. I thought the guy was just making a joke at the expense of the therapist. But then I looked around at the group, and saw that everyone else was sitting there completely stone faced. The therapist started scolding me. "Charlie, this is a terrible thing that happened. How can you laugh at it?" I shook my head and said, "That's the stupidest thing I ever heard." Some of the things were just so sad that I felt that if you didn't laugh, you'd have to cry.

Some of the best therapy for us came after the therapists went home, and we were left by ourselves. We'd congregate in the day room, watch some television, and just talk. It was in these informal sessions that we'd really open up to each other. It was with each other that we were most at ease. We came from different ways of life. Some were successful businessmen, while some could never hold down a decent job. We were whites, blacks, and Latinos. We all had different stories to tell. But we were, above all, a brotherhood. We had a common bond in that we all had lived through the horrible experience of fighting in the most unpopular war that the United States ever entered. Outsiders may scorn us for what we had done, but amongst ourselves we found understanding, compassion, and great strength. Just learning that we were not alone in our struggles was probably the greatest comfort of all.

At the end of the eight-week program I felt that I had gotten as much as I could out of my stay. Although I was going to miss the camaraderie of being with my fellow Vietnam vets, I was anxious to get back to my home and family. I learned that PTSD was not a bunch of nonsense, but that it was a very real and serious problem, especially amongst Vietnam vets. But I still didn't believe that I had it. I got over my notion that I tried to commit suicide. In the end, it was just an excuse to get the therapists off my back. I did take some valuable ideas out of the program, though. I felt that what I had learned about anger management techniques would serve me well when I got home. I learned to recognize things that triggered my anger, and also learned ways to stop myself before I exploded. I learned some very effective relaxation exercises that I felt were going to be a great help in my day to day living. I couldn't wait to get home to Fran and Matt and see how these techniques worked in real life. After all, the main reason I got into the program was that I wanted to be better for my family.

21

One of the immediate results of getting through the PTSD program was that I started sleeping better at home. I wasn't bothered by nightmares anymore and my nights were very restful. That, by itself, was worth the eight weeks of being at Brecksville. I also felt that my relationship with Matt improved. We seemed to be getting along better, but he still knew what buttons to push to get me going. I was able to recognize this now, and I could deal with it in a more appropriate manner using my anger management techniques. One of these techniques was to realize when I was getting out of control. When this happened, I was supposed to tell myself that I was about to engage in some inappropriate behavior, and that I needed to walk away until I was able to deal with the problem in a more rational manner. I figured it might work even better if I let Matt know exactly what was going on at those times. So, instead of just saying them to myself, I would say them out loud to Matt. Many times Matt heard me say during the heat of an argument, "Matt, I really feel like killing you right now, so I'm going to take a break and we'll finish this discussion later." I'm sure that's not exactly what they had in mind for me to manage my anger, but it was better than the way we handled it before.

I jumped right back into the frying pan by going back to my teaching job on the first Monday after ending the program. I returned to the same class that had caused the meltdown that had sent me to Brecksville. The kids knew where I had been. I didn't try to hide it. I even wrote letters to some of the students while I was at Brecksville to keep them informed as to my well being. I was pretty optimistic that I would be able to continue my teaching career. For the most part, I think the kids respected me for returning to the class. I felt like some of the kids, though, looked at me like I was some sort of time bomb that could explode at any time. I'm sure that some of the boys thought of me as another crazy Vietnam vet that would kill them if I was antagonized. I didn't want the kids thinking I was some sort of monster, but if it helped with discipline, then so be it. I tried to explain to the class that some of the events in my past caused me to have some problems now. I don't know if they understood, but, for whatever reason, I was able to get through the remaining three months of the school year without any major problems. The administrators were very understanding, too. They told me that they would help me recruit a smaller class with better students for the following year. I was all for that.

By June I was ready for summer vacation. We decided to go to Myrtle Beach right after school was over. I needed to get away for a week of beach lounging. Unfortunately, our vacation coincided with the annual Senior Week there. The whole town was filled with kids who just graduated from high school. It wasn't exactly the perfect environment for a teacher who had just finished a very exhausting and troubling school year. I was able to survive though.

During that summer I began to question whether I wanted to continue teaching. I wasn't sure whether I had the stamina to make it through an entire school year. I thought that maybe I could retire with a small disability pension. During one of my outpatient sessions at Brecksville, I brought the subject up to my therapist and asked her what she thought about it. She told me that initially she had some doubts whether I should return to teaching, but, since I had made it through the remainder of the previous school year, she felt that I had cleared a major hurdle. She told me that I should be able to continue as a teacher with no problem.

My class that began in the fall of 1989 was smaller than usual. It only had 16 kids in it. They were mostly good kids, too, so getting through the days at school were pretty easy for me. While my job was going well, the same couldn't be said for Matt, who was becoming increasingly troublesome. He began high school in Kent, and started out as a seemingly well-adjusted and active student. He played football and hockey. I was trying to be a better sports parent, and tried to be more positive in my remarks to him and less critical. I found myself using a lot of phrases like "I'm proud of you" and "Everyone makes mistakes" and "It was a good try". He also sang in the school choir and continued taking piano lessons. It seemed, though, that as I lessened my criticism, he was becoming increasingly more critical of himself. He made it through the first part of his freshman year okay and played on the freshman football team. By the middle of the school year, his grades began to decline. He was playing on the ice hockey team and the coach was a stickler on maintaining a good grade point average. Towards the end of the hockey season, mid-term report cards were coming out, and Matt knew his grades were not going to be good enough to stay on the team. He asked me what he should do, and I told him to go to his game and enjoy playing in it because it was going to be the last one he would be able to play that season. I took him to his game on a Friday night, and he went into the locker room and I got my seat in the stands. After a few minutes, he came into the stands carrying his hockey equipment. He looked like he was pretty upset. I asked him what happened. He said that the coach kicked him off the team. I said, "But grades haven't even come out yet." Matt just shrugged his shoulders. Being the dutiful parent, I went into the locker room and confronted the coach. This man wasn't even a teacher or counselor at the school. He was just hired to be the hockey coach. I asked him why Matt was cut from the team. He told me that Matt's grades were not good enough. I asked him how he knew what Matt's grades were, seeing as how they weren't going to be out for two more days. He said that he went into Matt's file in his guidance counselor's office and saw them there. Now, I got pretty upset. I couldn't understand how a guy who wasn't even a teacher could have access to a student's personal file. Unfortunately, it wasn't my school, or even my school system, so there was nothing I could do about it. I called him a jerk, and left.

Matt got over this episode pretty quickly. In fact, his grades improved the remainder of the school year, and by the following fall he was eligible for school sports again. He played on the varsity football team and had a great season. Encouraged by his success, he decided to try to get back on the hockey team, so he went to the coach and apologized for the previous season, and asked for another chance. The coach agreed, although I had misgivings about it. I went to his first practice and I could see that the older players were all picking on him. They were tripping him and hitting him into the boards every chance they got. Some of it was pretty vicious, especially for a practice. The coach, rather than discipline the older players, started yelling at Matt. I could see that Matt was getting angry, and, after a while of this treatment, he boiled over. He got a puck and slapped it high into the stands. Then he took his stick and threw that into the stands, too, as he skated off the ice. I said to myself, "This is going to be trouble." A few minutes later he came to where I was sitting and he said, "Did you get my stick?" I said, "No, I figured you didn't want it." He said, "Well, I do." I told him, "I'm not going after it." He stomped off, got his stick, and we went home.

I didn't say anything to him on the way home. I thought I'd let him cool down for a while. That evening, in my ongoing efforts to be a more supportive father, I made one of the worst mistakes of my life. Because of budgetary restraints at school, none of the teachers got a pay raise that year. As a kind of concession, the school board told us that our children could attend the Stow schools without tuition. I went into Matt's room that evening and, seeing how despondent he was, blurted out, "If you want to transfer to Stow, you can." As soon as I said it, I wanted to take it back, but immediately Matt's eyes lit up and he said, "That'd be great." I didn't think he was going to respond so quickly. As far as I knew the only problem he was having at Kent was with the hockey team. His teachers really liked him, and he was doing much better with his grades. I thought that at least he would wait till the end of the school year before making a move. But I was wrong. He wanted to transfer to Stow immediately. Since I already told him he could, there wasn't much I could do.

He finished the remainder of his sophomore year at Stow. I was pretty nervous about it and, although it was pretty tenuous at times, he got through it okay. I have to admit that it was pretty nice having him accompany me to and from school each day. I certainly didn't want him in my class, but having him at the same school made it easier to keep an eye on him and to get lots of feedback on his schoolwork from my fellow teachers. By the following fall he had adjusted quite well to Stow High School. He decided he wanted to play football and was going to try out for the team. I didn't have a good relationship with the football coach, which dated back to the time he offered me the junior high coaching position, and then rescinded it. He didn't think much of Vietnam veterans. He had avoided the draft by being a student and then going directly into teaching. One time he made an off-color remark about one of my Vietnam buddies, which strained our relationship even further. I didn't want Matt to know this, but I thought that being my son, he might have a difficult time with this coach. I told Matt that I didn't think that he would like football at Stow, but that didn't do anything to dissuade him. He started practicing with the team and, just as I had predicted, he wasn't doing too well with the coach. I could see that he wasn't happy, but since he had started it on his own I didn't want to suggest that he quit. He continued to practice until the day that an exhibition game was scheduled with Massilon, one of the greatest high school football teams in the country. A lot of Matt's friends showed up for the game, and he was very embarrassed when the coach never let him play in the game. After the game, he made some smart remark to the coach, and then quit the team. Personally, I was glad that he was done playing football for that coach. But for Matt, it was a failure that caused him to become even more down on himself.

To fill the void left by football, Matt started to work out with the wrestling team. I was happy to see that because the coach was a good friend and fellow teacher. I know the coach was thrilled to have someone of Matt's size joining his team. He was doing well in this new sport, but, outside of wrestling, I could tell that things weren't well with him. He was acting very strange. He always looked like he was depressed. He spent a lot of time alone in his room. His grades started to slip once more. I tried talking to him but got nowhere. One of the counselors at school tried talking to him, but also couldn't get anywhere with him. She suggested that I make an appointment with a psychologist that she knew, but when I called his office, I was told he was going to be out of town for a couple of weeks.

I decided that things weren't that urgent, and that in two weeks we might have a better feel for what was happening.

Shortly thereafter, Matt had a wrestling match where he pinned a very good opponent in a matter of seconds. After the match, I thought he would be happy with his performance. I told him how impressed I was with his victory, but he just kind of sloughed it off. The next day, when I came home from school, I found him in his bedroom lying on his bed. I asked him, "What are you doing? Why aren't you at practice?" He just laid there and said, "I don't want to do anything." I tried to be encouraging. "Hey, come on. Quit your whining and get back to practice." He looked at me and said, "I don't know. Maybe I should just kill myself." I thought he was just making a flippant remark, and I got pretty angry about it. I told him, "Don't talk to me about killing yourself. You don't know anything about death and killing." Suddenly, he reached under his bed and pulled out my shotgun. He said, "Well, maybe I'll kill myself right now." Seeing that gun in his hands made me panic. I screamed, "No", and I lunged for the gun. I was able to grab the barrel as we tumbled to the floor. We started wrestling on the ground. All I was concerned with was to make sure that the barrel of the gun was pointed at me. Matt started hitting me with his fists, but I wouldn't let go. After a few minutes of intense fighting, I finally was able to get the gun away from him. He just curled up on the floor and started sobbing. It was as if he was heartbroken. I took the gun and left the room.

I didn't talk anymore to Matt that evening. I didn't know what to say. I didn't even tell Fran about it. I don't know why. Maybe I thought she would blame me for driving Matt to this point of desperation. After all, I believed I was the cause. I was still too stunned to think clearly. I realized now that Matt had a serious problem. It wasn't just a case of teenage angst. I just wanted to make it through the night. I didn't sleep much, as I stayed alert for any unusual sounds coming from the bedroom next to ours.

The next morning, Matt and I acted like nothing had happened. We still hadn't talked about it. I took him to school with me. It was one time that I was glad that he was in the same school as me. I could keep an eye on him, and I made sure that he showed up for all of his classes. I tried once more to get an appointment with the psychologist, but he was still out of town. I'd have to hold on for another week. Although he got through the day, and appeared to be somewhat normal, I still was on pins and needles as to when his next outburst would be. All I could do was watch him constantly, and be ready to react should the need arise. I knew that I couldn't trust him on his own.

A couple of mornings later, I was waiting for him to get ready for school. When I saw him, I was pretty surprised. He looked awful, just like a bum. His hair was a mess, and it looked like he hadn't washed for days. He was wearing some crumpled up clothes. I told him, "You can't go to school looking like that." He said, "Well, I'm going to." I was in no mood to argue with him, and I didn't want to antagonize him, so I calmly said, "Okay. Let's go. I don't want to be late." So, he got in the car and I drove him to school. When we got there, I started to get out of the car. He said, "Leave me the keys. I want to go home." Now there was no way I was going to let him drive away, but I wanted to give him the chance to explain his purpose. I said, "Why? What do you want to do?" He said, "Either I'm going to change my clothes, or I'm going to kill myself." That was all I needed to hear. I knew that something had to be done immediately. I said to him, "Just wait here a minute." I took the car keys and went into the school office. I told the principal, "I'm not going to be able to teach today." He could tell by the look on my face that something serious was going on. He didn't question me. He just told me that it wasn't a problem. I went back out to the car and drove Matt directly over to Akron Children's Hospital. It was where the psychologist I was trying to get an appointment with worked.

I went right to the emergency ward. I explained the problem and we were referred to a counselor. She asked if I was willing to commit Matt to a two-week program. I wasn't sure, as I still hadn't said anything to Fran. She took me on a tour of the facilities, and both Matt and I were impressed. Of course, next to VA facilities, everything looks great. The counselor went over the program's schedule with me and we both felt that it was something that might help Matt. I asked Matt how he felt about staying in the hospital for two weeks, and he was agreeable. So, I signed the papers, and left Matt there to get settled in while I went home to get him some clothes and essentials. I felt good about getting him in the program. I didn't know what else I could have done. I didn't know what was bothering him. His problems had far outgrown my ability to help him.

When I got out to the car, the impact of the whole situation finally hit me, and I began to cry. I cried harder than I ever had in my life. I felt entirely responsible for Matt's problems, whatever they were. A sense of overwhelming guilt came over me. I was a terrible father, and Matt was now paying the price for it. My only hope was that the damage I had done was not irreversible. I went home and started packing a suitcase with Matt's clothes. Fran came home and came into Matt's bedroom. She said, "Where's Matt." I sat her down and told her the whole story. When I was finished, she looked at me with an anger in her eyes that I had never seen before. She started screaming at me, "You son of a bitch. You put my baby in the nut house." It was the only time that my wife ever swore at me. I deserved it. I just let her get it out. We drove in silence back to the hospital. I think she expected to see Matt in a padded cell wearing a straitjacket. When she saw the pleasant surroundings of the ward, and she talked to Matt and found out that he wanted to be there, I could see that she was relieved. I wasn't off the hook, nor did I expect to be. Fran realized that Matt needed both of our support, and that he also needed to see that we supported each other, too. She just never knew how serious Matt's problem was, but she quickly adapted to dealing with it appropriately. I was really glad and appreciative of that.

It was hard to keep the fact that Matt was in a hospital from the kids at school. I had to tell the teachers, because part of his program was that he was required to keep up with his schoolwork, so they had to provide him with his homework. After they found out where he was, several of them admitted to me that they had been having trouble with Matt in class recently. I don't know if they had told me earlier that it would have made a difference. Hearing about it, though, strengthened my belief that I was doing the right thing.

The two weeks went by slowly for me. The doctors determined that Matt was suffering from severe depression. They told us that it was a condition that was hereditary. They taught Matt some anger management techniques, and also how to recognize and deal with depression. The psychologist was very positive about Matt's progress, and, at the end of the program, assured us that Matt was ready to return home. We were overjoyed to have our little family back together again. While I kept my eye on Matt, Fran kept her eye on me to make sure I didn't do anything that would cause Matt to have a relapse. I was very cautious with him in the weeks following his homecoming.

I was worried that he might have some problems coming back to school, explaining his whereabouts of the previous two weeks to his classmates. My concerns were unfounded as the kids treated him as if nothing had happened. I did have a problem with one kid, though. He was a big boy that was a troublemaker in my class. I had to discipline him, and he decided that to get back at me, he would go after Matt. I found out that he was constantly picking on Matt, trying to get into a fight with him. Even though Matt was a big kid and pretty strong, he wasn't a fighter, and he just ignored the kid's provocations. Normally, I let Matt fend for himself, but I felt this kid was taking advantage of Matt's fragile condition. I got the kid alone in the hall, and I got right into his face. I told him, "My son is going through some rough stuff right now, and he doesn't need you bothering him. You don't want him, anyhow. You want me. So let's do it." I was ready to fight, but to my surprise, the kid started apologizing. He said he didn't know that Matt was having problems, and said he was sorry for picking on him. He never bothered Matt again. I was happy for another bloodless victory.

22

Matt adjusted well to life after his hospital stay, but the same couldn't be said about me. Even before Matt's problems, I could feel myself getting edgy. I was starting to have trouble again. I was thinking that maybe I should go back to Brecksville. But now, I felt I couldn't do that because I was afraid that Matt would think that he drove me back there.

At that time I had no contact with Brecksville. I wasn't attending any outpatient therapy. I was on my own, trying to deal with my problems through physical exercise. Even though Matt was doing all right in school, and our relationship was okay, I was still worried that he might have a relapse. I was always nervous anytime anyone came into my class with a message. I thought the message would be that Matt had killed someone. I was just trying to hang on, but I felt wore out, and I knew I needed some help.

Then came another day that I'll never forget. It was towards the end of the school year. Matt came into my class after school grinning from ear to ear and holding his class schedule for his senior year, beginning the following fall. When he put it down on my desk, and I saw what was on it, I nearly fainted. His counselor had assigned him to my distributive education class. It was the one thing I vowed I would never let happen. I handed him back the card and said, "No way." His grin disappeared. He said, "Well, if I can't, then I'm quitting school." Once again my hands were tied. I guess I should have looked at it as a compliment that my son would want to be in a class taught by his father. Instead, I saw it as one more thing to be anxious about, in a life that was filled with anxiety.

As it turned, out my worries were mostly unnecessary. In fact, the school year, with Matt in my class, turned out to be pretty uneventful. I think that it had a lot to do with the fact that the class was made up of primarily good students. I was getting more and more students in my class that were going on to college instead of right into the workplace, so the kids were concerned about maintaining good grades. Matt's class, instead of being a conglomeration of misfits, were goal oriented, good students. Although it was unnerving at first to see my son in my class everyday, I gradually got used to it. He didn't give me too many problems. Occasionally, he would try to take advantage of me by not turning in assignments on time, but once he found out that I was not going to treat him any different than any other student, he didn't try it any more. He tried to be the class clown, and sometimes caused me minor embarrassment. Like the time I assigned the class to prepare a sales pitch, on a product of their choosing, to be given before the class. I didn't ask Matt beforehand what product he chose, and I was more than a little uncomfortable when he stood up in front of the class and gave a sales pitch on condoms. He also liked to harass the girls in the class, for some reason. Maybe it was his teen-age hormones kicking in, but he teased them a lot. Sometimes, the girls would complain to me about it, and suggest that he be grounded for his behavior. I used to tell them, "If I ground him, that means he's going to be home with me. Why should I punish myself for something he did." Overall, he turned out to be a pretty good member of the class, and, although I'll never admit it to him, I enjoyed having my son in my class. It's one of the more fond memories I have of teaching.

By the time Matt graduated, I was worn to a frazzle. Even my summer vacation didn't help much insofar as calming me down. I started the school year in the fall of '93 with trepidation. My fears were heightened when I saw the class I had. It was larger than usual, and I guess the administration felt I was ready to tackle the more difficult kids again, because this class was full of them. The class was even worse than I had imagined it to be. I didn't know how long I could put up with them. Shortly after the school year began, I started having panic attacks again. The symptoms were different this time, though. When they came on, I would sweat profusely. There was no way I could hide it from the students or my fellow teachers. I'd start feeling anxious, sweat would start forming on my forehead, I'd get even more nervous, then moisture would start gushing from all over my body. Before long, I was soaked. I couldn't figure out how to stop them. It got to where I didn't want to teach classes anymore for fear of having one of these attacks.

Another sign that I was falling into another state of depression was that I started using curse words more frequently. They often peppered my speech at home, but now it was extending to my class, and found myself using them more and more whenever I had problems with a student. I had learned from my program at Brecksville that increased cursing was a warning sign for me that I was headed for trouble. My nightmares returned, too, after a four-year hiatus. Now, they were not just of Vietnam. I was having nightmares about bad students. In my dreams I'd be cursing at the kids so loudly that it would wake me up. When I woke up, I was surprised that Fran would always still be sleeping, for I thought I was actually yelling. I was the only one that heard it, though.

Although I didn't have any major outbursts in my class or with any student, I knew that I was on the verge of losing it at school. I knew I needed help, and that the only place that could provide it was at the Brecksville VA hospital. Matt was busy in college, so I felt that he would no longer think he was responsible for me going back there. I decided to go back before I went completely nuts.

So, one day, I called in sick at work and drove myself to Brecksville. As I had done the first time, I didn't call ahead to make an appointment. I just showed up at my old ward and told them I needed some help. It was late '92, four years since my last visit. I talked to a therapist there named Gus, and told him the problems I was having. Gus wasn't there during my first stay. He told me that things were a lot different than when I had been there. He said that they knew more about PTSD, and how to treat it. He said that the new program focused more on what was happening to the patient now, instead of lingering on past traumas. They were more concerned with life skills, what we need to change, and how to cope with everyday life. He said he wanted to try something different with me. He suggested that I join a group that met one night a week. He also would arrange for me to have a personal therapist, who I also would meet with on a weekly basis. I told him I was willing to do anything. I just wanted to feel better.

Later that week, I had my first meeting with my group. There were about five or six guys in it, all Vietnam vets. They all had their own personal problems, but I felt comfortable with them right off the bat.

It wasn't until the first week in January that I met my new therapist. She was a really nice woman that I liked immediately. I felt I could really open up with her. After hearing me tell my story she said, "Charlie, you're a really easy case. You've got PTSD because you were shot." I was pretty surprised. I said, "Are you sure? They told me in 1988 that it couldn't be the reason." She said, "Well, we're beyond that now." She told me that the old program served a purpose, but that now it was outdated. I was glad to hear it

I went on to tell her how I usually felt energized at the beginning of the school year, but by Thanksgiving I was pretty wore down. I was miserable during the Christmas holiday, and by the beginning of January, I didn't want to go on. I said that I wished I could go to sleep on Thanksgiving and not wake up until February. After listening to me she asked me when I was shot. I told her January 9. She said, "Well, there's your answer." She explained that the anniversary of a traumatic event often triggered PTSD symptoms. She said that subconsciously January 9 had become the low point of my year. The holidays were not my problem. It was just that they fell too close to the anniversary date of me getting shot.

I was pretty amazed at all I had learned from just one session with this new therapist.

In addition to seeing my therapist once a week, I also had to see a psychiatrist once a month. It was the one part of the new PTSD program that I didn't care for. The psychiatrist was so busy that you only got a fifteen-minute session with him. He always seemed preoccupied, and didn't seem to listen to what you were saying. In the original program no medications were used. This guy had a pill for everything. During my first visit with him I told him that I was thinking that maybe I should retire from teaching. He said, "Oh no. I'll write you a prescription and you'll be fine. See you next month." I never liked any kind of drugs, but I thought I'd at least try it. Needless to say, they didn't help. Every month I'd go back and tell him that the drugs weren't working, and every month he'd write me a prescription for a different one. None of them helped. In fact, they usually made me worse. And to top it off, most of them had some physical side effects that went along with them. I had enough problems with my body without adding to them with worthless medications. Finally, I found one that didn't do any harm. I had him prescribe me the lowest dosage possible and I took them for a year just to appease him. I always felt that in the case of PTSD, drugs were not the answer. I felt that if you got to the point where you were really pissed off and about to go ballistic, there were no drugs that were going to stop you.

By the end of the 1993 school year, I didn't have anything left inside of me. I told the psychiatrist that I really think I should retire from teaching. He disagreed. He told me that I had made it through a very tough year, and I'd have the whole summer to relax and regroup. He thought it would be in my best interest to continue teaching. I wasn't convinced.

I had a pretty relaxing summer. I spent a lot of time out at our trailer on the lake, and I didn't do a whole lot. I just rested. I went back to Brecksville every other week, to meet with my therapist, and to let her know how things were going. Under the new PTSD program, you could arrange your sessions as you wished. As far as the VA was concerned, it was an ongoing therapy done at whatever pace the patient deemed necessary. I liked it, and I felt it really helped to see my therapist on a regular basis.

I started the school year rested, but still not feeling all that enthusiastic about teaching. I had a pretty nice class, a mixture of good, and not so good kids. Right away I knew that something wasn't right. My sweating attacks continued. I dreaded standing up in front of a class. I was just going through the motions. I wasn't fired up at all. I wasn't enjoying anything, including coaching tennis. I told Fran and Matt that I felt like I was getting to my wit's end, and that I was thinking of giving up teaching. They both tried to encourage me, telling me I was fine and not to worry about it. I told my psychiatrist about how I was feeling, but he just told me that I shouldn't worry about it, too. Nobody believed that I was very close to coming undone.

One day in class I very nearly proved them all wrong. I was at the front of the class and I had just started my lecture. All of a sudden, this girl, who was known to give me problems, crinkled up a piece of paper, got up from her desk, and walked right in front of me to deposit it in the waste basket. I was furious. As she walked back to her seat I grabbed an empty desk at the front of the room and started to pick it up. She looked at me and said, "Mr. Morris, are you going to throw that desk at me?" Fortunately, I caught myself. I said, "No. Now sit your ass back down." I thought to myself, "Charlie, you really are losing it."

I told my therapist about the incident. I told her I didn't think I could go on. I didn't want to hurt anybody. She was beginning to agree with me. She said that maybe I should begin to consider retiring from teaching. I went home and told Fran what she had said, but Fran wasn't buying it. I was just hoping my teaching career wasn't going to end in a disaster.

It wasn't long after that that I had another problem. Part of my class curriculum was making sure that the kids had basic math skills. This sometimes was a conflict, in that for the good students basic math was easy, but the poorer students had some difficulty with it. One day, we were going over a fairly easy math problem. I was getting pretty exasperated with some of the kids who seemed to lack even fundamental math skills. After going over this problem, one boy raised his hand and said that he still didn't understand it. I sighed and said, "Okay. I'm going to do it once more, on the blackboard, and we're all going to get it together." I began explaining the problem while writing on the blackboard, and I turned around to see the boy who said he didn't understand it faced towards the back of the classroom, talking to one of his buddies. I thought I was going to explode. I screamed, "Hey, asshole." All of a sudden, the class got deathly quiet. The boy was so embarrassed that he ran out of class. When I saw the looks on the kid's faces, I was embarrassed too. I was ashamed, and I immediately apologized to my class. But I knew that I had reached the end. If I kept on teaching someone was going to get hurt.

I went to my therapist and told her what had happened. I told her that I wanted to retire from teaching. She told me that there was a new psychologist on staff, and that she had been going over my case with her. She said that the new doctor wanted to interview me. After my experience with the pill-pushing psychiatrist, I was a little reluctant to deal with another potential quack, but to appease my therapist, I agreed.

The new psychologist turned out to be a wonderfully understanding woman. I felt very comfortable with her. After two sessions with her she said, "You're right. You shouldn't be teaching anymore. Bring me the paperwork and I'll do whatever I can to help you to retire." It was a great relief to have someone finally believe me.

I told Fran what I planned to do, but, for some reason, she didn't think I was serious. I called down to the teacher's union in Columbus and asked them what I had to do. I was trying to get a disability retirement. They said that in order to do that I would have to stop teaching as soon as my paperwork was approved. It was already March and I intended to complete the school year, but they told me I couldn't. I would have to end my teaching career immediately.

Part of the process for getting a disability retirement was that I would have to see the Teacher's Union psychiatrist for his assessment. I made an appointment, and, when I met with him, I found out that he also served in Vietnam. In fact, he was stationed at the same hospital where I had my initial brain surgery done. With him being a Vietnam vet, I really opened up. In fact I broke down. I told him that I didn't want to be another crazy Vietnam vet that ended up hurting somebody. It didn't take long for him to send his findings down to Columbus. My retirement was approved.

I went to my class for one last time. I told the kids that I was leaving. I explained to them that they were not the reason for me deciding to quit teaching. I told them about my problems with PTSD, and that the stress of teaching was becoming unbearable for me. I don't know whether they understood or not, but I felt that they had the right to know and to hear it from me. The school arranged for a teacher who had assisted me in class previously to become a permanent substitute for the remainder of the school year. I helped him get organized a little, but then, quickly, I was finished being a teacher.

Instead of feeling relief at ending a stressful job situation, I got depressed after quitting teaching. The person I was most proud of, Charlie the teacher, was no more. As far as I was concerned, I no longer had any worth. Even though, towards the end, I hated myself because I felt like I was failing as a teacher, at least I still felt like I was something. Now I was nothing. Fran wasn't happy about my retirement. Even though I tried to tell her that I was going through with it, when it finally happened she felt I went behind her back. My therapist at the VA was encouraging me to enter another inpatient program at Brecksville, but I didn't want to. And to top everything off, my father was getting sick.

23

I had time on my hands, but didn't really know what to do with it. During the summer I was able to cope by spending most of my time at the lake in our trailer. But when summer was over, and we returned home, I was like a man without a country. I took care of the housework, cooking and cleaning and laundry and such, but didn't find it very fulfilling. I still was working out everyday, but found myself putting on weight. By late fall I had put on almost 25 pounds. I was 47 years old, with nothing to do, and I felt that I was too young not to do anything. I tried working with the VA to find a new career, but didn't find any of their suggestions too appealing. I wasn't having much fun, that's for sure.

With the holidays approaching, I reached my lowest of lows. I thought I was going to end up killing myself. I even decided the way I was going to do it. I had a plan to drive my car off a cliff. I had the place where I was going to do it and everything. Every time I'd pass this spot, I would start to think about how fast I would have to be going to crash through the wooden guard rail. I was in bad shape, and I knew what I had to do. I needed to get back to another inpatient program at the Brecksville VA. And that's just what I did.

Just as I had been told, the program at Brecksville was totally different than when I had gone through it in 1988. About the only thing that was the same was that new guys were admitted each week, and some guys completed the program each week. The program still allowed for dealing with your individual trauma, but it was no longer the primary focus upon which all other things were based. The new program worked with the patient on making life goals, and on family living, along with anger management and stress reduction skills. As soon as I got in the program, I started to feel better. I knew that it was where I needed to be. Being in the program helped me to forget the sadness I had about leaving teaching and feeling totally worthless

One of the first group sessions I went to when I began the new program dealt with loss and mourning. I always thought that mourning was something you did when you lost a loved one. The therapist teaching this class said that mourning was an appropriate, and needed, reaction to all of our losses. I had never thought about mourning the loss of the right side of my body, but it made sense to me. I had replaced mourning with anger and frustration.

There came the time when I had to talk in a group about how I was feeling with the loss of my job. I vowed that I would remain unemotional, but as soon as I started talking I could feel the tears welling up in my eyes. I stopped until I felt I was in control again, and then I proceeded. After a few pauses the dam burst, and I was sobbing like a blathering idiot. I was so embarrassed. Here I was, in a group of grizzled Vietnam vets who had been to hell and back with their experiences in war, and I'm crying like a baby because I wasn't a teacher anymore. Some of the guys were kind of looking at me funny. I finally got a hold of myself and said, "Well, I hope that's it." The therapist looked at me and asked, "What's it?" I said, "I mourned."

The program made me feel better physically, too. I worked out every day in the hospital's weight room. I did a lot of running and walking on the hospital grounds. I also worked with a nutritionist to help me with my diet, and by the time the program was over I had lost over twenty pounds. The nutritionist was thrilled about my weight loss. She told me it was one of her rare success stories with Vietnam vets.

One of the new methods that the VA was employing was combining wards, so patients in all inpatient programs were grouped together. This meant that where before all of the PTSD patients roomed together, now you may have roommates from the drug or alcohol dependency programs. So it was in my case. I had two roommates, both of which were in the alcohol dependency program. To top it off, they were in the program because they were homeless. I was a little uncomfortable with that, but they were, after all, my brothers in arms, so I tried to make the best of it. One of my roommates never showered and never took his clothes off, even to go to bed. He carried a pretty strong odor with him, so I made sure that my bunk was as far away in the room that I could be from him. I tried to be understanding, because I knew that the Vietnam war had taken its toll on young men in a lot of different ways. Nonetheless, it was a unique experience for me to have lived for six weeks with a couple of homeless alcoholics.

During my inpatient stay at Brecksville I checked into the VA's Voc Rehab program to see if I could qualify again. My first idea was to get some sort of business degree. I thought that with some of the classes I took for my teaching degree that I might be able to get the business degree in a relatively short time. I was wrong. With the new requirements for the degree, it would be almost like starting from scratch, so I shelved that idea. Next on my list of grand schemes was to get a certificate to be a private counselor. I had looked into the program at Kent State and if I went full time for 11/2 years I could complete it. As a licensed private counselor I figured I could work with disabled people. The VA, however, wasn't too keen on that idea. They said I had enough problems of my own without taking on other people's, too. They highly recommended that I avoid any more potentially stressful job situations. To make their point perfectly clear, they told me that I was not eligible for any more assistance for college. They said I was too old and too stressed out to go back to school. They would have preferred that I just lay back and take it easy. But that wasn't going to work for me, so I went back to the drawing board to come up with a plan for the rest of my life.

After I completed my second PTSD program, I felt a lot better about my retirement from teaching. At least I was able to talk about it without breaking down. I used to run into former students all the time and they would always ask me what I was doing. I would tell them that I was retired, and then proceed to tell them all the nitty gritty details about why I retired, and my problems with PTSD, and so on. Fran, after hearing me tell my lengthy story to one of my former students, told me, "You don't have to be so thorough. Just saying 'I'm retired' would have been enough."

I was getting along with Matt okay, but his performance at college left a lot to be desired. He lived at home for his first year at Kent State and his grades were absolutely terrible. One of his buddies from high school was living in a dorm and had much better grades. Matt convinced us that allowing him to live in the dorm was the key to his educational success. I had my doubts, but he moved on-campus for his second year. Just like I thought, nothing improved. Matt treated being in college like being at a health club or a spa. His dorm was right next to the athletic complex and every time I would try to call him his roomate would say Matt was out playing hockey or Matt was playing volleyball or Matt was at the pool. I never heard that Matt was at the library studying. Whenever I would question him about his grades he'd give me the line, "It's so hard for me." That used to drive me nuts. I'd tell him, "I know it's hard, but I got through college with half a brain." It aggravated me to hear kids with all of their physical and mental capacities intact gripe and moan about how hard college was. It was hard, but you had to work at it and be committed to it, which is something I didn't see in a lot of kids, including my own. Aside from our differences about what college was really meant for, my relationship with Matt was getting better. As he got older, we became more like friends than father and son. He was very understanding about my retirement.

I wasn't getting too far with choosing a new career path, and I was getting restless being home all of the time. Financially we were fine, but I needed something to occupy my time and some sort of job seemed like a logical solution. I started scanning the classifieds in our local paper and one day I saw an ad for a golf course maintenance job. It didn't say where the golf course was or what the job actually entailed, but it sounded like something that might be right up my alley. I called and arranged for an interview. The golf course was a nearby country club and, when I went there, the maintenance foreman who I would be working for turned out to be a former Stow High School student who recognized me as a teacher from when he went to school there. The job sounded great. It involved taking care of the flower beds and the landscaping around the course. It was a part time job, which is exactly what I wanted. I'd work six or seven hours a day, two or three days a week. I was happy when they told me that I got the job.

They teamed me up with a retired auto worker, who was probably in his seventies. He was a World War II veteran and was pretty ornery. A lot of what we did involved the mulching of flower beds. We'd have to shovel mulch into a wheelbarrow and take it to the flower beds and rake it out. As you might imagine, a one armed shoveler and wheelbarrow operator is probably not the most efficient, but I did my best and, after a while, I got pretty good at it. But no matter how much mulch I moved, my partner was always making me work harder. I thought I was in pretty good physical shape, but I had a dickens of a time keeping up with this 70 year-old man. By the end of the day I was tired and sore, but he would never complain. After a few days of this I told him, "Man, I can't believe how you're busting my ass." I thought I saw a slight smile on his face. After that, once he knew that I was having trouble keeping up with him, he let up on me a little bit. I really loved that job. It was physical and it was outdoors and it was great therapy for me. They even let us play golf for free on Monday afternoons, but I was always too tired to play. I worked there until the course closed in October.

Like it happens to many other people whose parents start getting old, my parents began to require more attention and care. My dad was never the picture of health, going back to his heart attacks when he was in his early 40's. He never really took care of himself. He was overweight and still smoked despite all the warnings he received from his doctors. Eventually, he had a stroke and, although he recovered pretty well from it, it left him very weak. He always hated winter and his lifelong dream was to be able to move south. His physical condition made winter intolerable for him. So, despite my misgivings, after I was done working at the golf course in October, Fran and I took my parents down to Myrtle Beach, South Carolina to look for a place for them to stay. We ran into trouble almost as soon as we got there. My dad fell down and couldn't get himself back up. It took Fran and me all of our strength to get him back up and into a chair. He was just like dead weight. My mother looked on during this whole episode, and after things settled down she took me aside and told me, "I can't do this. We'll never be able to make it down here on our own." I agreed and I told my father that he was in no shape to be moving somewhere where his family wouldn't be able to help him. In order to appease him, I told him that if he went back to Ohio and worked real hard on getting more physically strong that maybe we could reconsider the move next year. He wasn't really happy about it, but he couldn't do much about it either. We brought them back to Ohio and I thought that was the end of it.

I was wrong. Near Thanksgiving I got a call from my sister. She said that my father had rented an apartment in Myrtle Beach and was moving there right away. I was pretty angry. I called my dad and told him that he was going against my wishes and not to expect me to come running down to South Carolina every time he had problems. Being as stubborn as I was, he said, "Fine" and with that my sister took them to their new home in Myrtle Beach. They ended up buying a trailer down there and, for the time being anyhow, seemed to be doing okay on their own. The next spring I went back to work at the golf course.

The spring and summer went by pretty uneventful. I enjoyed my job at the golf course and my mental state was pretty good, for once. I was still going to see my therapist at Brecksville on a regular basis just to make sure I stayed on the straight and narrow. In the fall, things started to come undone. My mom had a stroke and we had to go down to Myrtle Beach to help out. The stroke didn't do too much physical damage, but it left her confused a lot of the time. When it came time for her to leave the hospital and go to a rehab center, we decided it would be best if she came back to Ohio where we could help her out as needed. Heaven knows my father wasn't going to be able to do much insofar as helping her out. So, we drove my parents back to Ohio. We got my mom into a nursing home near where we lived, and my father moved in with my sister. He refused to live with me because I wouldn't allow him to smoke in the house.

My mom progressed nicely at the nursing home and it wasn't long before she was released and she came to live with us. She wasn't too much bother, although she still had bouts of confusion when she thought I was her brother instead of her son. My father, on the other hand, was becoming restless and irritable. One day he came over to visit her and he sternly told her, "You've got to snap out of this so we can get back to South Carolina." I was pretty surprised. I thought that he would've realized by then that he wasn't able to live on his own without his children nearby. But I wasn't going to argue with him anymore. I'd done enough of that already in my life. I just told him that if Mom got better that we would talk about them returning to Myrtle Beach. To be honest, I never thought my mom would ever get to the stage where they could consider moving back. But to my amazement, she did, and I took them back to South Carolina.

When I got back home life returned to normal and was going along pretty smoothly. I went back to the job I had at the Sheraton Suites in Cuyahoga Falls in their personnel department. It was a pretty good job and it gave me something to do over the winter. The normalcy didn't last too long, though. I got a call from my parent's neighbor in South Carolina. She said that my dad was back in the hospital with heart problems and that my mother was having a hard time with it. I told Fran that I was going to have to go down to Myrtle Beach for a while. I gave up my job and I went down.

My dad's heart problem wasn't too serious. He was only in the hospital for a few days before he was sent home. He was put on some medication and told to take it easy for a while. Of course my mother was in no condition to take care of him, so I decided to stay there for a couple of months to try to help out. It wasn't that much of a sacrifice for me. I never was much of a fan of the winter weather in Ohio. I always thought that a home down south for the winter would be nice. Although my parents trailer was hardly luxury accommodations, at least I was in sunshine and warmer temperatures. I was nearby a tennis club and I got to play there almost every day. That was pretty nice. Dealing with my ailing father was not too nice, though. He never wanted to be left alone. One time I took my mom to the store and left him at home. We were only gone an hour and returned to find the paramedics there. My dad got scared and thought he was having a heart attack and called 911. Not long after that episode my dad was back in the hospital. I could see that my parent's independent lifestyle was going to have to come to an end.

At the end of February I told my parents that I was going to bring them back to Ohio. I said that I needed to get back home, and that I couldn't be running back and forth to South Carolina every time they needed some help. I loaded them up and brought them back. My father was still not in good shape. My plan was to get him into a nursing home and to have my mother alternate living with me and my sisters. It wasn't easy finding a nursing home that had a smoking area, but eventually I did, and I have to say that he was pretty diligent with his rehab work. He even got to the point where he was able to leave the nursing home. Then I had to start looking for an apartment for my parents to live in. There was no way they were going back to South Carolina. I found an apartment and, in August, they moved in. My dad was happy to regain a little of his independence. Sadly, it was short lived. After only a week in the apartment, he was back in the hospital and after a week there, he was back in the nursing home. He died in early September.

I really felt terrible about my father's death. During his last months I was thrust into the role of parenting my parents, and I hated it. I felt bad that I had to yell at him so often for not doing what the doctors wanted him to do. I hated having to threaten to send him back to the nursing home if he didn't do what I told him. But most of all, I regretted that he died without me knowing what he thought of me. He died without me ever hearing, "I'm proud of you, son." I never knew how he felt about my joining the Navy, about my getting shot in Vietnam, about my rehabilitation, about my getting a college degree, about me becoming a teacher. I'm still not sure today how he felt about me. During his last years, after he had his stroke, I was always afraid that he resented me for getting over my disability. I used to cringe whenever his therapists would use me as an example for him to work hard at his rehab. "Look at how hard your son worked and how far he came back." I never knew for sure how much that bothered him, if at all. I wish we could have had some conversations that would have cleared that all up for me. But in the end, he went quickly, and there was no time to say the things that needed to be said.

Five months later, my mother died. Shortly after my dad passed away, my sister came home and found my mother passed out on the floor. They took her to the hospital where they discovered that she had had some sort of seizure. We hoped that it was due to the strain of my dad's death and that once her life settled down that the seizures would stop. For the time being, though, I got her into the same nursing home that my dad had been in. A while later, she had a violent seizure and she had to be taken back to the hospital. I met with a neurologist there who told me that they needed to induce a coma that would last about two or three days, and that when she came out of it things should be back to normal. I gave them my approval to do it. As part of the procedure, a feeding tube was installed. I was in the surgical waiting room while the operation was proceeding. All of a sudden the surgeon came in and told me that my mother's heart was racing out of limits, and they needed to know what I wanted them to do with her. He was pretty emphatic that he needed to know immediately. I was unsure of what to do, and, not having the time to consult anyone about it, I told the surgeon that if they could get her heart rate down that they should just continue with the procedure. He left, and finished inducing the coma.

When it came time to bring her out of the coma two days later, they found her unresponsive. It took two weeks before she finally came out of the coma, and when she did, her mind was completely gone. She didn't talk. She didn't recognize anyone. She didn't move. But because they had installed the feeding tubes before the coma, they could not take them out. Mercifully, after three weeks she caught a virus, and died. While I didn't feel responsible for her death, I felt responsible for her having to suffer for the last three weeks of her life. If I hadn't meddled, she would've died from the heart attack she was having when they were trying to induce the coma. It was another addition to my list of things that I felt guilty about.

I think that of all the people in my life it was my mother that understood me the best. Even when I was a child, she was the one I could go to and talk about any problems I was having. While my dad was the disciplinarian, my mother was the compassionate parent, especially with me. Even later in my adult life, I could always go to her and talk to her, just like I would my best friend. Just before her funeral I had a few minutes to spend alone with her as she lay in her casket. I took my hands, and put them over hers, and told her how sorry I was.

24

I put my plans for a new career on the back burner during the time I took to take care of my parents. I thought about it, but didn't take any action. I knew that the VA wasn't going to fund another college degree for me, so I tried to think of a job that I liked to do that might require a little technical training or something. When I worked at the golf course, I used to fool around with the golf carts every once and a while. I liked doing mechanical things and figuring out how things worked. I enjoyed working on the old Ford Torino that I had bought as a father-son restoration project. I thought that maybe I would like to be a golf cart mechanic. From my connection with the golf course I knew that these mechanics made up to $75 an hour for their expertise. Right about that time, though, golf carts started to change from the large American made carts to a more compact Japanese cart. I soon found out that these newer carts were much more difficult to work on than the old clunkers I fooled around with. They were not really compatible with a one-armed mechanic. I would have been okay if I had an assistant mechanic with me at all times, but that wasn't really feasible, so I gave up my notion of becoming a golf cart mechanic.

I kept in contact with my Voc Rehab counselor at the VA. Periodically, she would suggest something or I'd inquire about something, but we never could come up with a job that was accommodating to both of us. One day she asked me if I ever thought of doing anything with computers. At that time, I wasn't a big user and didn't really think of any potential career involving computers. Obviously, I wasn't a very fast typist, and I thought that would be a prerequisite for anything to do with computers. I mentioned to Fran what my counselor had asked, and she started telling me about this new computer driven embroidery machine she had seen demonstrated at a local fabric shop. She took me to see it, and I was pretty fascinated by it. It looked to me just like a sewing machine that was connected to a computer. But the things it could do all on its own were really amazing to me. I thought it would be a pretty neat small business, something that could be run right out of the spare bedroom in our house. I told the VA counselor about it and she thought it was a good idea too. We proceeded to work up a plan to put me in the embroidery business.

The first thing that she suggested was that I learn a little bit about computers. She got me signed up for a six-week class at a computer training school. I figured I would enjoy learning about computers as they were something new and exciting for me. In the class we learned both computer hardware and software. I learned about all the pieces/parts in a computer, and actually built one from the ground up in class. Then I learned about Windows and DOS, word processing, spreadsheets, and graphics. After the six-week course, I had a pretty good basic knowledge of computer operation.

The next step in getting my embroidery business going wasn't quite as enjoyable for me. It involved writing a business plan to present to the VA. The VA was getting to be a little more cautious about handing money out to veterans with grand business schemes. They found that too many of their funded business ventures were going belly up within a year after they started. For this reason, they now required a fairly extensive and concise business plan to be approved before money was handed out to start a new business. So, I was off to another class, this one to teach me how to write a business plan. This class was at another small technical training center. I was okay with gathering the information needed for the business plan, but getting it into the proper format for presentation was another story. Like I said, my typing skills left a lot to be desired. The teacher of the class showed a little pity on me, and told me that if I would give him all my information that he would put it into the proper format for me. I quickly accepted his offer, and turned over all of my information and notes to him. He said to give him a couple of weeks to put it together. That was fine with me because I was planning on going on a little vacation with Fran anyhow. I thought that by the time I got back, I would be ready to present my business plan to the VA.

We had a nice vacation, heading down the Atlantic coast and into Florida. We stopped along the way for a Seawolf reunion, and also to visit some of my old Navy buddies. By the time I got back I was anxious to get going with my new business venture. I waited a week to hear from the teacher, and when he didn't call, I called the school and got a message machine. I left a message and waited another week, but still didn't hear back from him. So, I took a ride over to the school and was very surprised to see a note on the door that said the school was permanently closed. There was a telephone number for the main office of the company that ran the school, so I called them up and told them my situation. I said that at the very least I wanted my paperwork for my business plan back. They told me that they would get back to me, but they never did. I called my VA counselor and she told me that the VA had cut all ties with the school and had stopped the program entirely. I was furious. I asked her why no one had bothered to tell me. She said that she was told not let out that information. I was pretty disgusted over the whole deal. I had spent a lot of my time and energy on this venture and, in the end, I was right back where I started from. I decided to shelve my career plans for a while.

Six months later, my Voc Rehab counselor called me. She asked me, "Are you still interested in going into a business?" I was still smarting from my last attempt, so I abruptly told her, "No. I'm tired of dealing with the VA bureaucracy." She said she understood. Then she asked, "Well, how about a hobby instead of a business?" At that time, the word "hobby" sounded a lot more appealing to me than the word "business", so after a moment of consideration, I blurted out, "Sure."

My counselor arranged for the VA to help me buy a small embroidery machine and enough equipment to get me started in my new hobby. It didn't take me long to figure out how to do things with the machine. I started out with little things. I embroidered the names of my friends I exercised with on small workout towels and gave them out. Soon I was making workout towels for everyone at the gym. I embroidered canvas book bags for my friends in the church choir. I made shirts for my car cruising buddies. Soon, people were always asking me to do this or that and my little machine was going constantly. I was working out of my home, but I was operating it as a hobby, not a business. Every little bit of money I made from the embroidery went back into buying more equipment and supplies. I enjoyed the work, and often I was up until 1 or 2 A.M. in order to keep up with the demand for embroidery. It wasn't long before I started thinking about getting into it on a larger scale. I thought that if I could get bigger equipment, I could do more work, and I could make a lot of money. With these visions of grandeur I decided to approach the VA again to see if I could get them to help me move from hobby to business.

Surprisingly, the VA was receptive to my idea and was willing to consider it if I turned in a business plan. They assigned a woman to help me write it. As much as I hated writing, I worked hard on it. But every time I would turn something in to this woman, she would find something wrong with it and tell me to redo it. After a few times of putting the business plan together and having it rejected, I grew frustrated. I decided to give it one last try and employed one of my old English teacher friends to help me with it. After a lot of late night sessions we got a final draft together and I turned it in to the woman. She read it and said, "If I tell you to redo this, you're probably going to give up on it, aren't you?" I said, "Probably." She said, "Well, then it's good enough."

Before I turned the business plan in to the VA, my Voc Rehab counselor wanted to come over to my house to see what I was doing with my present equipment. She knew I was asking for a lot of money, and wanted to know why I needed it, and what could be expected if I got it. When she came to my house I told her, "Let me show you what I can do with the equipment I have." I had a canvas book bag and I embroidered the Veterans Administration logo on it. I intended to give it to her as a present. She was pretty impressed. I told her that with a larger machine I could work much faster and more efficiently. She took my business plan and put it in that canvas bag and that's how she presented it to the Voc Rehab director. One week later, I got a call saying my plan had been approved for the full amount. I was ecstatic. Where else but in America could a one-armed Vietnam vet start his own embroidery business?

I did some research into available embroidery machines and decided to buy the one that was made in the United States. I thought that the VA would appreciate that since they were funding it. It turned out to be a good choice. The company arranged for me to take some training in Chicago on the operation and maintenance of the machine. I took Fran with me, partly because I wanted her to know how to operated the machine, too, but also because Fran took much more legible notes than I did. After that class, I went to a class that taught me how to digitize images. That was pretty complicated and computer oriented so I took Matt with me for that one. I got the new machine and, even though it was much larger than my previous one, I still was able to get it set up in the spare bedroom of our house. It was really an improvement over the smaller machine. I was able to get a lot more done, and for the first year we did a great business. I liked working at home. I still was able to go to the gym every morning and work out and still get all of my work done, even though sometimes my workday extended into the late evenings.

In addition to my new business venture, I started doing something else that was new and exciting for me: public speaking. First at the Brecksville VA, where I had been going for so long they finally decided to make use of all the therapy they had put me through and make me a guest speaker there. I talked about my experience in Vietnam and also my recovery and rehabilitation from my injury. Eventually my guest speaking extended to some local schools where I would talk to the kids. I really enjoyed standing in front of small groups and talking. It was like being a teacher again without all the headaches.

Then there was one day I was at a local car show trying to sell some of my embroidery work. A man in a wheelchair came up to my table and asked me who did my embroidery work. I told him that I did it myself. He asked me how I got disabled and I proceeded to tell him my story. He then asked if I had ever done any public speaking. I told him about my little talks with the VA and local schools. He said, "Well, I think you have a wonderful story." He handed me his card. It said he was from the Traumatic Brain Injury Center at Edwin Shaw Hospital. I took his card and put it in my pocket and forgot about it.

A few months later I got a call from that same man. He asked if I would be interested in speaking to one of their groups at the hospital the following week. I still wasn't comfortable speaking to groups of people that I didn't know, but I agreed to anyway. I figured it'd be good experience for me. The next week I spoke to a small group of people who had traumatic brain injuries, along with their families. Somehow, I felt the same sort of brotherhood with them as I did with my fellow Vietnam vets. I ended up not only speaking to them, but I also became a member of their group.

25

I really don't know how to end this story, mainly because it isn't over yet. My life has been like a roller coaster, with equal amounts of highs and lows. That trend continues as recently I've had some problems and some joys. Part of the problems are just me getting older. Aside from my head injury, I never had any serious illnesses in my adult life. I hardly ever even had a cold or the flu. But a few years ago, all of a sudden I started running a fever and had an upset stomach. I figured it was the flu. After a few days I still wasn't feeling better, so I went to the doctor and he gave me something to settle my stomach. After another week I still wasn't improving, so I went back to the doctor. He said I must have some sort of virile infection and he gave me some antibiotics. Another week went by and I started to really feel weak. I called the doctor and he assured me that the illness was just running its course, and that I should be patient. About that time, I got a delivery from UPS of a large box and I went outside to bring it in the garage. It was all I could do to drag it in, and when I finally did, I noticed that there was blood dripping down my shirt. My nose was bleeding, something that never had happened in my entire adult life. I got scared and called Fran. She came home from work and we called the doctor. I think that by this time he was getting a little tired of me complaining, so he said, "Just go to the emergency room, then." So we went to the hospital and, typically, waited for an hour to be seen by someone. They took some blood from me and then I waited another hour. Finally, a young doctor came to me and said, "I'm sorry for the delay, Mr. Morris, but when we tested your blood it was so far out of limits that we had to test it again." It seems I had a kidney and bladder infection. I was admitted and ended up staying in the hospital for a week while they cleaned out my insides. During this whole episode I had lost 30 pounds. I found out later that people with partial paralysis are prone to these types of problems later in life. I wish that someone at the VA would have told me what to expect as I got older so I could have been alert to some of the warning signs of these problems. I guess I should be happy that I made it through relatively unscathed.

It took me a long time to regain my strength. I was in pretty good physical shape before the infection, but the amount of time I wasn't able to do my regular workout caused some of my muscles to become atrophied. When I finally got back to my daily workouts it was like starting all over again from scratch. By the following winter I was just starting to get back into shape. I had regained most of the weight I had lost and was feeling pretty good. One winter morning I had an appointment scheduled with my therapist at Brecksville for 9:00 AM. I knew I didn't have time to fit in my regular workout, but I had finished a embroidery order for someone at the gym and I wanted to deliver it to them before I went to my appointment. The previous two days it had snowed quite a bit and it was hard to find a parking spot at the gym because of all the plowed snow. I had to park rather close to one of my buddy's brand new pickup truck, so I was careful opening my door and getting out of my van. What I didn't notice was that there was a patch of black ice between our vehicles, and when I stepped on it, I went down hard to the pavement. The minute I hit I knew I was hurt. I fell on my bad side and I never had felt the kind of pain I was in. I couldn't get up. Someone saw me and asked if I was okay. I said, "No." It was one of the few times in my life where I wasn't going to reject someone's offer to help. She ran inside to get someone. Some of my regular workout friends came out to see if there was anything they could do. After laying on the cold ground for several minutes I thought that maybe I had just bruised my hip and I should try to get up before I froze to death. But after a brief attempt I realized that there was no way I was going to stand up. My friends told me to lay still until the EMS got there. It took about twenty minutes before they showed up. They put me on a stretcher and loaded me into the ambulance. As I was getting in, I remembered my purpose in being there and I yelled to my friend that her embroidery order was laying on the ground near where I fell. Even in dire pain, I was always the astute businessman. On the ride to the hospital the EMS guys gave me some morphine, which put me in a much more pleasant frame of mind.

When I got to the hospital the first thing they did was take x-rays. While I was waiting for the results a nurse came by and said, "I'm not supposed to be telling you this, but your hip is broken." So there I was, in another great predicament. I didn't know what they were going to have to do to me. There were a bunch of resident orthopedic doctors who were looking me over. One of them said, "You know, there's probably the best hip surgeon in the area that's here today doing surgery. I'll go see if he can fit you in." A few minutes later a young looking doctor came up to me and introduced himself as an orthopedic surgeon. He told me I was very lucky. Usually you had to wait a week before he could fit you into his surgery schedule. But he said that he just had a cancellation and he could do the surgery right away. It was good because I didn't have any time to fret about it. Before I knew it, I was on a gurney being prepped for surgery. One of the last things I remember is the surgeon grabbing my leg and lifting it up. I thought I was going to go through the roof. He said, "How does that feel?" With tears in my eyes I yelled at him, "How do you think it feels?"

The surgery went fine. He installed a plate and a couple of screws in my hip. In a couple of days I was doing one of my favorite things: physical therapy. I did my rehab right there at the hospital, and after a short time, I was up and around. Since I am older, my healing has taken a little longer than when I was young. My hip is still not as strong as it once was. Sometimes I thought that this incident was just a piece of bad luck for me. But when I think about all that happened that day, I was very fortunate. All the right people were there when I needed them, from friends to surgeons. If they hadn't been, it could have been a lot worse than it was. It was just another little setback in my life that required a little effort on my part to get through. Oh, I forgot to mention the date that it happened: January 9.

Even though I preached to everyone never to give up, with all of my recent illnesses and injuries I began thinking that maybe it was time for me to die. Deep down, though, I still felt that I had more to do before I was finished. I became more involved with the Traumatic Brain Injury group, eventually becoming a member of the board of directors. I also took a course through the VA where I became a peer support counselor for PTSD veterans. I get a lot of satisfaction from both of these activities and my hope is to soon reduce my workload at my business and to become more involved with these groups.

But I did say that I had highs along with lows and, as through all of my life, the good times far outweigh the bad. Going back a bit, Matt finished college, although it took him a little longer than the standard four years. He eventually started his own business, selling trade show displays and promotional items. He even left me a little corner of his shop where I set up my embroidery business. So, just like the old days when I was his teacher at high school, I get to see my son most every day. I'll leave you to determine whether that's a high or a low.

As Matt approached his 30's, Fran and I were beginning to have our doubts as to whether there was someone in this world for Matt to settle down with. I wasn't asking for much, just someone that could get along with him. Then, another miracle occurred in my life. A romance blossomed between Matt and a girl that he had known for a long time from his activity in our church. She is beautiful and absolutely wonderful and I just love her. She's much more than I ever could have hoped for Matt. You know how some parents hope their children will marry doctors or lawyers so that they can get free professional services? Well, Matt's bride has the perfect occupation for me. She's a physical therapist. She's a perfect 10.

As thrilled as I was that Matt and Kara were getting married, I got even a bigger thrill once they started planning their wedding. I can't think of a greater honor a son could bestow on his father than to ask him to be his best man at his wedding. That's what Matt asked me to do. I was overwhelmed. Matt has lots of close friends, but he chose me to stand next to him at the most important occasion in his life. I just hoped I wouldn't disappoint him. One of the most important duties of a best man is the toast he gives to the bridal couple at the reception. In the time leading up to the wedding, I became increasingly anxious that my toast would be one befitting this great occasion. I was nervous about having to stand in front of a large crowd and make a speech, but I was more concerned that the content of my speech would be more than a few flippant remarks. I wanted it to portray how proud I was of my son, and how happy I was that Kara was my daughter in-law, but I also wanted to give them a bit of fatherly advice, too.

For months I labored over what I should say. Even the day before the wedding I still didn't have it down pat. I had a few ideas, but nothing really structured. In the end, I decided just to speak from my heart. At the beginning of the reception, I stood up to give my toast with my heart in my throat. To break the tension I started by telling a embarrassing story about Matt and one of his junk cars. I used it to explain that life with Matt wasn't always easy. I think I made my point. But then my heart came out of my throat and I told the story of how when Matt was a baby, and I would have to change his diapers, how we had a telepathic sort of communication between us. I was a new father struggling to change a baby's diaper with only one good arm. Somehow, Matt realized that I was having a difficult time and he tried to make it easier for me by lying completely still. Just by being quiet and still, Matt allowed me to get through a difficult task. I always appreciated that from Matt. I said that we all could learn something from that little baby. Sometimes, when we see that someone dear to us is having a difficult time, the best thing that we can do is just to be still, and allow them to find their way. With that, I raised my glass to the bride and groom.

At the beginning of this book I said that I never intended to be anyone's hero. I never considered myself as one, and I get very uneasy if anyone suggests that I am one. The names of 58,249 of my heroes are on a wall in Washington D.C. All I'm looking for is a place to fit in, and not stand out. After all of the years I spent sitting in church some of the sermons had to rub off on me. One of the things that stands out is when Jesus explained to his disciples that if any of them wanted to be the greatest that they should be a servant to all. I felt that what Jesus was saying was that instead of trying to be a big shot, that we should concentrate on trying to help those who need it. At some point in your life you realize that what you possess isn't so important. It's more important to be able to help somebody else. I like to think that I've mellowed a little bit through the years in the methods I use to help someone. I've come a long way since that time at the Great Lakes Naval Hospital, where I thought that a young paralyzed man wasn't trying hard enough to get out of a bath tub on his own, and I poured ice cold water on him until his lips turned blue. I've learned that sometimes, in order to help someone, you've got to balance encouragement with compassion. Not that I've become a complete softy. I still believe in the sign that I put at the front of my classroom my first day of teaching: Nobody knows what they can do until they try.

Another moniker I don't like applied to me is "survivor". It's not that I don't appreciate that I have survived some potentially disastrous things in my life. It's just that I think that there's a lot more to life than just surviving. I think that the greatest compliment that anyone ever gave me was from my friend Jack, who has been my workout partner for over twenty-five years. One day I was going into one of my tirades about how normal people don't understand disabled people. Jack looked at me and said, "Charlie, when I work out with you, I don't see you as disabled." Ever the smart aleck, I responded with, "Well thanks, Jack. When I work out with you, I don't feel disabled." But the point was that it's quite an accomplishment when we can get people to see past our faults and inadequacies. It takes a lot of work to do so.

There was a popular song out a few years ago titled "Superman" which had a line in it that is more familiar than the title. That line is "It's not easy to be me." I think that the reason that the song was so popular is that everyone could identify with it. In this day and age it's not easy to be anyone. To paraphrase another line in the song, we're all just out to find the better part of us. Sometimes we need a little help finding that better part. As much as I like to do things on my own without being dependent on anyone, I realize that I never would have made it as far as I did without the help of some very important people in my life. My wife Fran never allowed me to quit. Sometimes she was there with an encouraging word, and sometimes with a kick in the butt, but she was always there for me when I needed her. My son Matt was always supportive, even though there were many times I was less than an exemplary father. And I've been blessed with many friends who knew when to give me my space, but also stayed close enough to let me know that I was never alone.

One of the people I admire most is Helen Keller. She is obviously a shining star for all disabled people. My favorite quote from her is one of her most famous. "When one door of happiness closes, another opens; but often we look so long at the closed door that we do not see the one which had been opened for us."

Though not always successful, all through my adult life I've tried to focus on the doors that were open for me. And, so far, there always have been open doors for me to pursue. Just because I'm getting older doesn't mean there won't be any more open doors for me. I look forward to finding out where they may lead. It gives me added joy when I can help show others the doors that are open to them.

978-0-595-40453-
0-595-40453-7